Bloom's Modern Critical Views

African-American
  Poets: Wheatley–
  Tolson
African-American
  Poets: Hayden–Dove
Dante Alighieri
Isabel Allende
American Women
  Poets, 1650–1950
Hans Christian
  Andersen
Maya Angelou
Asian-American Writers
Margaret Atwood
Jane Austen
Paul Auster
James Baldwin
Honoré de Balzac
The Bible
William Blake
Ray Bradbury
The Brontës
Gwendolyn Brooks
Elizabeth Barrett
  Browning
Robert Browning
Albert Camus
Truman Capote
Miguel de Cervantes
Geoffrey Chaucer
G.K. Chesterton
Kate Chopin
Joseph Conrad
Contemporary Poets
Julio Cortázar
Stephen Crane
Don DeLillo
Charles Dickens
Emily Dickinson
John Donne and the
  17th-Century Poets

Fyodor Dostoevsky
W.E.B. DuBois
George Eliot
T.S. Eliot
Ralph Ellison
Ralph Waldo Emerson
William Faulkner
F. Scott Fitzgerald
Robert Frost
William Gaddis
Thomas Hardy
Nathaniel Hawthorne
Robert Hayden
Ernest Hemingway
Hermann Hesse
Hispanic-American
  Writers
Homer
Langston Hughes
Zora Neale Hurston
Aldous Huxley
John Irving
James Joyce
Franz Kafka
John Keats
Jamaica Kincaid
Stephen King
Milan Kundera
Tony Kushner
Doris Lessing
C.S. Lewis
Sinclair Lewis
Norman Mailer
David Mamet
Christopher Marlowe
Gabriel García
  Márquez
Carson McCullers
Herman Melville
Arthur Miller
John Milton

Toni Morrison
Joyce Carol Oates
Flannery O'Connor
George Orwell
Octavio Paz
Sylvia Plath
Edgar Allan Poe
Katherine Anne Porter
Marcel Proust
Thomas Pynchon
Philip Roth
Salman Rushdie
J.D. Salinger
José Saramago
Jean-Paul Sartre
William Shakespeare
Mary Wollstonecraft
  Shelley
John Steinbeck
Amy Tan
Alfred, Lord Tennyson
Henry David Thoreau
J.R.R. Tolkien
Leo Tolstoy
Ivan Turgenev
Mark Twain
Kurt Vonnegut
Derek Walcott
Alice Walker
H.G. Wells
Eudora Welty
Walt Whitman
Tennessee Williams
Tom Wolfe
William Wordsworth
Jay Wright
Richard Wright
William Butler Yeats
Émile Zola

Bloom's Modern Critical Views

STEPHEN CRANE
Updated Edition

Edited and with an introduction by
Harold Bloom
Sterling Professor of the Humanities
Yale University

BLOOM'S
LITERARY CRITICISM
An imprint of Infobase Publishing

Library of Congress Cataloging-in-Publication Data
Stephen Crane / [edited and with an introduction by] Harold Bloom. — Updated ed.
    p. cm. — (Bloom's modern critical views)
  Includes bibliographical references (p.   ) and index.
  ISBN-13: 978-0-7910-9429-7
  ISBN-10: 0-7910-9429-4
  1. Crane, Stephen, 1871–1900—Criticism and interpretation. I. Bloom, Harold.
II. Title. III. Series.
  PS1449.C85Z925 2007
  813'.4—dc22   2006101024

Bloom's Literary Criticism books are available at special discounts when purchased in bulk quantities for businesses, associations, institutions, or sales promotions. Please call our Special Sales Department in New York at (212) 967-8800 or (800) 322-8755.

You can find Bloom's Literary Criticism on the World Wide Web at
http://www.chelseahouse.com

Contributing Editor: Amy Sickels
Cover designed by Takeshi Takahashi
Cover photo: The Granger Collection, New York
Printed in the United States of America
Bang EJB 10 9 8 7 6 5 4 3 2 1

This book is printed on acid-free paper.

All links and web addresses were checked and verified to be correct at the time of publication. Because of the dynamic nature of the web, some addresses and links may have changed since publication and may no longer be valid.

Contents

Editor's Note   vii

Introduction   1
Harold Bloom

Crane's Art   7
John Berryman

Love and Death in the Slums   29
Eric Solomon

"The Blue Hotel": A Psychoanalytic Study   47
Daniel Weiss

This Booming Chaos: Crane's Search for Transcendence   57
Chester L. Wolford

The Spectacle of War in Crane's Revision of History   75
Amy Kaplan

Introduction to *The Double Life of Stephen Crane*   103
Christopher Benfey

Stephen Crane's Struggle with Romance in *The Third Violet*   111
Paul Sorrentino

The Drunkard's Progress   135
George Monteiro

Stephen Crane and the Transformation of the Bowery   149
    Robert M. Dowling

From Derision to Desire:
The "Greaser" in Stephen Crane's
Mexican Stories and D. W. Griffith's Early Westerns   167
    Juan Alonzo

Image and Emblem in *The Red Badge of Courage*   193
    Kevin J. Hayes

Chronology   201
Contributors   203
Bibliography   205
Acknowledgments   209
Index   211

Editor's Note

My Introduction links *The Red Badge of Courage* to Stephen Crane's three outstanding stories: "The Open Boat," "The Bride Comes to Yellow Sky," and "The Blue Hotel."

The poet John Berryman provided an overview of Crane's art, which he perhaps magnified, when he called Crane probably the greatest American story-writer. There are likelier candidates for that eminence: Hawthorne, Melville, Henry James, Hemingway, Scott Fitzgerald, among others.

Maggie is praised by Eric Solomon for its ironic sympathy, while Daniel Weiss attempts a psychoanalytic interpretation of the enigmatic story, "The Blue Hotel."

Crane emerged from an Evangelical Methodist family, and transcendence was for him both a necessity and an impossibility, as Chester Wolford demonstrates.

Amy Kaplan notes that war became a spectacle for Crane as for Hemingway and Mailer, after which Christopher Benfey traces the issue of why and how Crane lived out what he had so fully imagined.

The Third Violet, Crane's attempt to compose a popular romance, is seen as a subversion of the genre by Paul Sorrentino, while George Monteiro finds some value in Crane's novella, *George's Mother*, a temperance tract which I confess has defeated even my own obsessive quest as a reader.

Robert M. Dowling details Crane's intimate knowledge of life in the Bowery, the *materia poetica* of what became *Maggie*, after which Juan Alonzo brings together Crane's stories of Mexico and the primitive Westerns of D. W. Griffith.

In this volume's final essay, Kevin J. Hayes returns us to Stephen Crane's masterwork, *The Red Badge of Courage*, which he interprets as a drama in which Henry Fleming recreates himself as a star actor.

HAROLD BLOOM

Introduction

Stephen Crane's contribution to the canon of American literature is fairly slight in bulk: one classic short novel, three vivid stories, and two or three ironic lyrics. *The Red Badge of Courage*; "The Open Boat," "The Blue Hotel," and "The Bride Comes to Yellow Sky"; "War is Kind" and "A Man Adrift on a Slim Spar"—a single small volume can hold them all. Crane was dead at twenty-eight, after a frantic life, but a longer existence probably would not have enhanced his achievement. He was an exemplary American writer, flaring in the forehead of the morning sky and vanishing in the high noon of our evening land. An original, if not quite a Great Original, he prophesied Hemingway and our other journalist-novelists and still seems a forerunner of much to come.

I

Rereading *The Red Badge of Courage*, it is difficult to believe that it was written by a young man not yet twenty-four, who had never seen battle. Dead of tuberculosis at twenty-eight, Stephen Crane nevertheless had written a canonical novel, three remarkable stories, and a handful of permanent poems. He was a singular phenomenon: his father, grandfather, and great-uncle all were Evangelical Methodists, intensely puritanical.

Crane, precocious both as man-of-letters and as journalist, kept living out what Freud called "rescue of fantasies," frequently with prostitutes. His common-law marriage, which sustained him until his early death, was with Cora Taylor, whom he first met when she was madame of a Florida bordello. Incongruously, Crane—who was *persona non-grata* to the New York City police—lived a brief, exalted final phase in England, where he became close to the great novelists Joseph Conrad and Henry James, both of whom greatly admired Crane's writing.

Had Crane lived, he doubtless would have continued his epic impressions of war, and confirmed his status as a crucial forerunner of Ernest Hemingway. And yet his actual observations of battle, of Americans against Spaniards in Cuba, and of Greeks against Turks, led to war-writing greatly inferior to his imaginings in *The Red Badge of Courage*. Perhaps Crane would have developed in other directions, had he survived. It is difficult to envision Crane improving upon *The Red Badge of Courage*, which is better battle-writing than Hemingway and Norman Mailer could accomplish. The great visionaries of warfare— Homer, Virgil, Shakespeare, Tolstoy—necessarily are beyond Crane's art, but in American literature he is surpassed in this mode only by the Cormac McCarthy of *Blood Meridian*. McCarthy writes in the baroque, high rhetorical manner of Melville and Faulkner. Crane, a very original impressionist, was a Conradian before he read Conrad. I sometimes hear Kipling's prose style in Crane, but the echoes are indistinct and fleeting, almost as though the battlefield visionary had just read *The Jungle Book*. Kipling, though also a great journalist, could not provide Crane with a paradigm to assist in the recreation of the bloody battle of Chancellorsville (May 2–4, 1863). Harold Beaver suggests that Stendhal and Tolstoy did that labor for Crane, which is highly feasible, and Beaver is also interesting in suggesting that Crane invented a kind of expressionism in his hallucinatory, camera-eye visions, as here in chapter 7 of the *Red Badge*:

> Once he found himself almost into a swamp. He was obliged to walk upon bog tufts and watch his feet to keep from the oily mire. Pausing at one time to look about him he saw, out at some black water, a small animal pounce in and emerge directly with a gleaming fish.
>
> The youth went again into the deep thickets. The brushed branches made a noise that drowned the sound of cannon. He walked on, going from obscurity into promises of a greater obscurity.
>
> At length he reached a place where the high, arching boughs made a chapel. He softly pushed the green doors aside and

entered. Pine needles were a gentle brown carpet. There was a religious half light.

Near the threshold he stopped, horror-stricken at the sight of a thing.

He was being looked at by a dead man who was seated with his back against a columnlike tree. The corpse was dressed in a uniform that once had been blue, but was now faded to a melancholy shade of green. The eyes, staring at the youth, had changed to the dull hue to be seen on the side of a dead fish. The mouth was open. Its red had changed to an appalling yellow. Over the gray skin of the face ran little ants. One was trundling some sort of a bundle along the upper lip.

This is a kind of pure, visual irony, nihilistic and parodistic, beyond meaning, or with meanings beyond control. On a grander scale, here is the famous account of the color sergeant's death in chapter 19:

Over the field went the scurrying mass. It was a handful of men splattered into the faces of the enemy. Toward it instantly sprang the yellow tongues. A vast quantity of blue smoke hung before them. A mighty banging made ears valueless.

The youth ran like a madman to reach the woods before a bullet could discover him. He ducked his head low, like a football player. In his haste his eyes almost closed, and the scene was a wild blur. Pulsating saliva stood at the corners of his mouth.

Within him, as he hurled himself forward, was born a love, a despairing fondness for this flag which was near him. It was a creation of beauty and invulnerability. It was a goddess, radiant, that bended its form with an imperious gesture to him. It was a woman, red and white, hating and loving, that called him with the voice of his hopes. Because no harm could come to it he endowed it with power. He kept near, as if it could be a saver of lives, and an imploring cry went from his mind.

In the mad scramble he was aware that the color sergeant flinched suddenly, as if struck by a bludgeon. He faltered, and then became motionless, save for his quivery knees.

He made a spring and a clutch at the pole. At the same instant his friend grabbed it from the other side. They jerked at it, stout and furious, but the color sergeant was dead, and the corpse would not relinquish its trust. For a moment there was a grim encounter. The dead man, swinging with bended back, seemed to be obstinately tugging, in ludicrous and awful ways, for the possession of the flag.

It was past in an instant of time. They wrenched the flag furiously from the dead man, and, as they turned again, the corpse swayed forward with bowed head. One arm swung high, and the curved hand fell with heavy protest on the friend's unheeding shoulder.

The flag and the color sergeant's corpse become assimilated to one another, and the phantasmagoria of the flag-as-woman is highly ambivalent, being both an object of desire, and potentially destructive: "hating and loving." Crane's vision again is nihilistic, and reminds us that even his title is an irony, since the ultimate red badge of courage would be a death-wound.

II

As in his masterpiece, *The Red Badge of Courage* (1895), Stephen Crane relies upon pure imagination in composing his first narrative fiction, *Maggie: A Girl of the Streets* (1893). Crane had never seen a battle when he wrote *The Red Badge of Courage*, and he scarcely had encountered the low life of the Bowery before he produced *Maggie*. Ironically, he was to have all too much of slum life after *Maggie* was printed, and to see more than enough bloodshed as a war correspondent, after *The Red Badge of Courage* had made him famous.

Maggie is a curious book to reread, partly because of its corrosive irony, but also it hurts to encounter again the over-determined ruin of poor Maggie. Her ghastly family, dreadful lover, and incessant poverty all drive her into prostitution and the ambiguous death by drowning, which may be suicide or victimage by murder.

The minimal but authentic aesthetic dignity of *Maggie* results from the strangeness so frequently characteristic of nineteenth-century realism and naturalism. Zola, whose influence seems strong in *Maggie*, actually created a visionary naturalism, more phantasmagoric than realistic. Crane, impressionist and ironist, goes even further in *Maggie*, a laconic experiment in word-painting. Crane's imagery is Hogarthian yet modified by an original perspectivism, irrealistic and verging upon surrealism. Maggie herself is an uncanny prophecy of what was to be the central relationship of Crane's brief life, his affair with Cora Taylor, who ran a bordello in Jacksonville, Florida. She accompanied him to England, where their friends included Joseph Conrad and Henry James, and she sustained him through the agony of his early death.

III

Stephen Crane's primary contribution to American literature remains his Civil War novel, *The Red Badge of Courage*. Yet his talents were diverse: a handful of his experimental poems continue to be vibrant, and his three finest stories are perpetually rewarding for lovers of that genre.

A war correspondent by enthusiastic profession, Stephen Crane was the Hemingway of his era, always in pursuit of material for his narrative art. "The Open Boat" is directly founded upon Crane's own experience, while "The Blue Hotel" and "The Bride Comes to Yellow Sky" reflect his travels in the American West. Crane's death, from tuberculosis at age twenty-eight, was an extraordinary loss for American letters, and his three great stories examined in this brief volume can be regarded as the most promising of his works.

"The Open Boat" intended, as Crane said, to be "after the fact," but is very different from "Stephen Crane's Own Story," his journalistic account of surviving the sinking of the *Commodore*, a cargo ship bearing arms for the Cuban rebels against Spain in January 1897. Much admired by Joseph Conrad, "The Open Boat" so handles reality as to render it phantasmagoric. The four survivors of the *Commodore* find themselves floating off a coast that absurdly declines to observe them. Even when people on shore waved to them, it is without recognition of the survivors' predicament. Compelled to make an unaided run to land, the boat is swamped in the icy water, and Crane swims ashore with the greatest difficulty. "The Open Boat" concludes with a sentence that memorializes the complex nature of the ordeal:

> When it came night, the white waves paced to and fro in the moonlight, and the wind brought the sound of the great sea's voice to the men on shore, and they felt that they could then be interpreters.

One thinks of Melville and Conrad as interpreters of the mirror of the sea; if Stephen Crane is of their visionary company, it can only be in an outsider's sense. What Crane conveys is the incomprehensibility of the sea when seen from a land-perspective. When I think of "The Open Boat," what I recall first is the frustrated helplessness of the survivors in the boat, who cannot communicate to those on shore the precariousness and desperation of shipwreck. Crane, neither a moralist like Conrad nor a Gnostic rebel like Melville, cannot quite reveal his interpretation to us.

"The Bride Comes to Yellow Sky" is a genial comedy, yet it also turns upon the absurdity of non-recognition. Scratchy Wilson, the story's insane and alcoholic gunman, cannot take in the enormous change that Jack

Potter, town marshal of Yellow Sky, stands before him not only unarmed but accompanied by his new bride:

> "Well," said Wilson at last, slowly, "I s'pose it's all off now."
>
> "It's all off if you say so, Scratchy. You know I didn't make the trouble." Potter lifted his valise.
>
> "Well, I 'low it's off, Jack," said Wilson. He was looking at the ground. "Married!" He was not a student of chivalry; it was merely that in the presence of this foreign condition he was a simple child of the earlier plains. He picked up his starboard revolver, and placing both weapons in their holsters, he went away. His feet made funnel-shaped tracks in the heavy sand.

As in "The Open Boat," Crane relies upon a total clash of incongruities. Sea and land are as far apart as marriage and Scratchy Wilson, who knows only that part of his world has ended forever. Crane acts as interpreter, and yet keeps his distance from the absurd gap that is very nearly beyond interpretation.

Crane worked very hard writing "The Blue Hotel," his masterpiece of narrative. The Swede is a kind of culmination for Crane: an authentically unpleasant character, whose reality is so persuasive as to become oppressive. Lured by the myth of the West, the Swede attempts to incarnate its code, but individuates himself instead as a bully and an interloper. His fight with young Scully is a false victory, isolating him totally, until he provokes the gambler into murdering him. The rest is irony:

> The corpse of the Swede, alone in the saloon, had its eyes fixed upon a dreadful legend that dwelt a-top of the cash machine: "This registers the amount of the purchase."

Yet has the Swede purchased death or been tricked into it? Crane's final irony is to reveal that young Scully *has* been cheating at cards, thus rightly provoking the Swede to combat. Is the Easterner correct when he ends the story by asserting that five men, himself included, pragmatically murdered the Swede? I think that the reader decides differently. The Swede, and the myth of the West, are the only culprits.

JOHN BERRYMAN

Crane's Art

I

Since Dr. Johnson observed that a century was the term commonly fixed as the test of literary merit, authors have crowded each other out of sight more and more rapidly. The term cannot be now so long. An English critic says the present point is to write a book that will last just ten years; but a decade must be too short—fashion can catch up older trash than that. For Johnson, remember, the "effects of favour" must have ended. Under our industry of literary scholarship, having to be kept supplied with subjects, "survival" is a more ambiguous condition than it used to be: one may stand to gain by overvaluing his author however meager, or his author's toe. Other conditions make a term difficult to fix. But Crane has been dead half a century, academic interest has avoided him as both peculiar and undocumented, and some of his work is still decidedly alive. This is long enough. We are not dealing with absolutes: the questions of interest with regard to an author remembered at all are how, and what part, and why, and whether justly. Perhaps a question more general arises too in connection with Crane. American genius has not been literary. The executive idealism of a few men like Washington represents our spirit at a higher level, probably, than can any of our literary masters. It may be merely our failure so far to have produced a national author that creates this impression, though we have to reckon also with a kind of national

From *Stephen Crane*, pp. 263–293. © 1950 by William Sloane Associates.

commitment as different as possible from, say, French cultural commitment. At any rate the fact is certain: we have had little genius in literature. The question is this: whether we have not in Stephen Crane a genius very formidable indeed, an artist of absolute and high vision—the sort of writer before whom most of our imposing earlier authors utterly shrivel away—a national glory, if the nation cared.

Let us lay aside at the outset matters of influence. Enough has been mentioned in passing, of influences felt by Crane (Tolstoy, Mark Twain, Goethe, Emerson, Whitman, Olive Schreiner, others), to rescue him from the status of a "sport." He concentrates tendencies and powers already tentatively in play. At the same time these influences certainly tell us very little about him; Crane was perhaps as original as an author can be, and be valuable. We shall have to study him by himself. More interesting by a good deal is the influence he exerted, great and distinct upon Conrad, Willa Cather, Ernest Hemingway, very decided upon others of his contemporaries and then upon Theodore Dreiser, Sherwood Anderson, Carl Sandburg, even Sinclair Lewis, as well as T. E. Lawrence, F. Scott Fitzgerald, more recent figures. Strong and lasting despite interruptions in his fame and availability, this influence is part of his importance. "The stones he put in the wall"—as Anderson said it—"are still there...." But critics have read him so little that the source of this whole aspect of recent English and American literary art has gone mainly unrecognized and must remain matter for special study. Crane's influence will be found no simple affair, traced through these authors: it affected vision, technique, material. Whether, however, it has ever been commensurate with the degree of revolution Crane effected is doubtful. I think it has not, and look for an explanation to the fact that his work of characteristic power has not yet been isolated from his inferior, ugly, and trivial work.

I ought to say where this power is. It is in "The Open Boat" above all, and "The Blue Hotel"; in the single long work *The Red Badge of Courage* and short war-studies from "A Mystery of Heroism" through "Death and the Child," "The Price of the Harness," "Virtue in War," to "The Clan of No Name," "An Episode of War," "The End of the Battle," "The Upturned Face"; in the early and late companion studies of society's ferocity, *Maggie* and *The Monster*; in two singular visions of happiness, "The Pace of Youth" and "The Bride Comes to Yellow Sky"; in other prose constructions delicate, dreadful and humorous, from "A Dark Brown Dog," "The Reluctant Voyagers," "An Experiment in Misery," through "The Veteran" to "Shame" and "An Illusion in Red and White"; in two dozen poems from "Once I Saw Mountains Angry" through the title-poem of *War Is Kind* to the posthumous marvelous "A Man Adrift on a Slim Spar." The list by no means exhausts Crane's excellence—very little behind some of this work come a number of other stories, such as

"The Little Regiment" and "Three Miraculous Soldiers," the three Mexican stories, chapters even in *George's Mother* and "War Memories," passages scattered everywhere. But at any rate not much less than this list will do in instance of where this author remains vivid, living.

You need very little to live. With *Wuthering Heights* and some verses one woman is with us always. But my display of Crane's work will certainly surprise both in bulk and variety most readers and critics. The truth is that Crane sprang into fame amid a storm of excited bewilderment and has passed into permanence in almost perfect silence. The occasional critic or historian who looks at him is just puzzled. A few are not comfortable yet about his being here at all, and among the majority who accept him there is no agreement about what kind of author he is. The most considerable attempts to account for him are still those by two of his English friends: first the very able ten pages written by H. G. Wells for the *North American Review* just after Crane's death in 1900. Wells spoke of his "persistent selection of the elements of an impression," of his ruthless exclusion of mere information, of the direct vigor with which the selected points are made; distinguished calmly the perfect restraint of "The Open Boat" from overinsistence in "Death and the Child" (then the critical favorite in England among Crane's stories); and concluded with a prophecy brilliantly fortunate: "It seems to me that, when at last the true proportions can be seen, Crane will be found to occupy a position singularly cardinal.... In style, in method and in all that is distinctively *not* found in his books, he is sharply defined, the expression in literary art of certain enormous repudiations.... It is as if the racial thought had been razed from his mind and its site ploughed and salted. He is more than himself in this; he is the first expression of the opening mind of a new period, or, at least, the early emphatic phase of a new initiative—beginning, as a growing mind must needs begin, with the record of impressions, a record of a vigour and intensity beyond all precedent." Crane's position sank for a generation nearly to zero, and for forty years Wells's essay was never reprinted. Meanwhile Edward Garnett, whose "Appreciation" in *The Academy* (December 17, 1898) was the most acute view taken during Crane's lifetime, added some remarkable sentences when he extended it in 1921 for *Friday Nights*. Two qualities in especial, he said, combined to form what is unique in Crane, "viz., his wonderful insight into and mastery of the primary passions, and his irony deriding the swelling emotions of the self. It is his irony that checks the emotional intensity of his delineation, and suddenly reveals passion at high tension in the clutch of the implacable tides of life. It is the perfect fusion of these two forces of passion and irony that creates Crane's spiritual background, and raises his work, at its finest, into the higher zone of man's tragic conflict with the universe." I do not feel sure of the meaning of the impressive middle sentence here, but the other two show that Garnett understood Crane better than everyone since taken together and would form a happy point of critical departure for us if we had not some elementary difficulties to encounter.

There is first the question, baffling to most of his friends, his critics, and his age, of whether Stephen Crane did not write almost entirely from *inspiration*. His work seemed to come from nowhere, prose and poetry alike. The word "dream" is recurrent in comment on him—even Hemingway, vouching for the authority of *The Red Badge*, uses it when he calls that book "a boy's long dream of war." When Crane told an interviewer that it was a product of labor, the man was not less but more astonished, that Crane should have "kept this story in hand for nearly a year, polishing and bettering it. Perhaps this is the most amazing thing about a thoroughly amazing book. If he had said he wrote it in three days (as he wrote the 'Black Riders') one might understand such a *tour de force*." Crane's rejection of the notion of "inspiration" is irrelevant. Of course he *did* write from inspiration, and of course he wrote also from close long observation, inquiry, study, and then he rewrote. He was like other men of genius, in short, often inspired and immensely deliberate. Yet this double explanation does not really account for the impression his work has always given, which might be put as follows: one is surprised that it exists at all—and one's surprise, if it diminishes, does not disappear with familiarity. Hamlin Garland tells us indeed that Crane just "tapped" his brain for his poems. He certainly went through no apprenticeship in poetry; he just began—began, we shall see, at a very high level—and if *The Black Riders* was not, evidently, written in three days, it was written abruptly and with effortless rapidity. As for prose, we have discovered an early development there, but so early and masterly that the prodigy remains. All this is thoroughly exceptional.

At the same time, Crane looks like a polar type of modern self-consciousness. He copied into his notebook—whether as program or as confirmation is unknown—a sentence from Emerson which comprehensively defines one effect of this art which lighted the 'nineties: "Congratulate yourselves if you have done something strange and extravagant and have broken the monotony of a decorous age." Literary ambition unusually deliberate and powerful is manifest all through his early life. "I began the war with no talent but an ardent admiration and desire. I had to build up." Readers and critics have recognized an effort in his work, and it forms a large basis for critical objection. They see affectation, strain. A word applied nearly as frequently as "dream" is its converse: "trick." Just before his death, a feminine critic put the objection as established: "Men of intelligence yawn. The trick is too easily seen through."

Impressions more contradictory are hard to imagine, and a third must be mentioned. Crane's work ever since it appeared has struck readers as "barbaric." His poems were "crazy," and they still—in standard anthologies—look very weird. The ferocity of his prose, whether intended or casual, seems primitive. His animism is like nothing else in civilized literature. Mountains, trees, dogs, men, horses, and boats flash in and out of each other's identities. The sun "had its hat over one eye" and one man's voice makes another man "wish that he was a horse, so that he could spring upon the bed and trample him to death." This is characteristic and frequent. A disappointed boatman has a "face like a floor." If Crane lulls you into safety for a minute, wait only. He is examining the electric chair in Sing Sing: "the comfortable and shining chair ... waits and waits and waits" for "its next stained and sallow prince ... an odor of oiled wood, a keeper's tranquil, unemotional voice, a broom stood in a corner near the door, a blue sky and a bit of moving green tree at a window so small that it might have been made by a canister shot." The sentence concludes like an electrocution, and when the keeper is quoted he might be a friendly aesthetician describing Crane's effect on the reader: "We calculate that the whole business takes about a minute from the time we go after him." These images come all from early, negligible, unreprinted newspaper stories; assaults in his important work may be more violent still. Crane's humor, finally, and his irony are felt as weird or incomprehensible. When he began a book of poems with the line,

Do not weep, maiden, for war is kind,

the reviewers treated him, reasonably, as an *idiot*.

A dream, a trick, a savage or imbecile attack: any account of his work which hopes for assent will have to try to reconcile these views with each other, and with still other views. All we need agree yet is that it seems to display an essential, *obvious* coherence, originality, and authority, such as will justify any care we may take to appreciate it.

2

Let us begin with his poetry. The poetry and the prose show difference as well as unity, but an understanding of the poetry, if we can arrive at one, will help us with the prose. Since Crane is the important American poet between Walt Whitman and Emily Dickinson on one side, and his tardy-developing contemporaries Edwin Arlington Robinson and Robert Frost with Ezra Pound on the other, it has interest that he perhaps drew on both of his predecessors. He does not sound much like them.

I saw a man pursuing the horizon;
Round and round they sped.
I was disturbed at this;
I accosted the man.
"It is futile," I said,
"You can never—"

"You lie," he cried,
And ran on.

This does not sound much like a poem either. Here is another one:

On the horizon the peaks assembled;
And as I looked,
The march of the mountains began.
As they marched, they sang,
"Ay! we come! we come!"

A conflict here between the sense of terror communicated and a suggestion of desire ("Ay!" answers as it were a question or entreaty) produces more appearance of a poem. But both look rather like *impressions of fatal relation* than poems. They are a world away from Whitman, an includer, an accumulator; these pieces would plainly do with even less if they could, though less is inconceivable. They differ too from Emily Dickinson, who as R. P. Blackmur has shown *tried* always to write regular verse, in that there is obviously no attempt to write regular verse, or even, perhaps, verse at all. On the other hand, no immaturity can be heard in them. Whatever it is they try to do they do; they are perfectly self-possessed. Very odd is the fact that in the first piece, despite its smallness, the rhymes are almost inaudible. There they are: sped-said-cried, horizon-man-on. Quite a set of rhymes for eight lines; yet even after you know they are there, you can scarcely hear them. It opens indeed with a regular heroic, but this effect is destroyed so rapidly that it scarcely affects the ear as regular. Now it does not appear to be deliberately destroyed, just as it does not appear to have been deliberately arrived at. So with the rhymes: the writer does not appear to fight their effect but seems to have come into the rhymes themselves by accident, and simultaneously, by instinct, arranged for their muting. The famous color and style of Crane's prose are absent, blankly absent.

All this is peculiar. Let us try a technical approach to two other pieces, which stand at opposite limits of Crane's poetry. The first is tiny:

A man feared that he might find an assassin;
Another that he might find a victim.
One was more wise than the other.

The other is one of the major lyrics of the century in America and I must quote it all.

Do not weep, maiden, for war is kind.
Because your lover threw wild hands toward the sky
And the affrighted steed ran on alone,
Do not weep.
War is kind.

    Hoarse, booming drums of the regiment,
    Little souls who thirst for fight,
    These men were born to drill and die.
    The unexplained glory flies above them,
    Great is the battle-god, great, and his kingdom—
    A field where a thousand corpses lie.

Do not weep, babe, for war is kind.
Because your father tumbled in the yellow trenches,
Raged at his breast, gulped and died,
Do not weep.
War is kind.

    Swift blazing flag of the regiment,
    Eagle with crest of red and gold,
    These men were born to drill and die.
    Point for them the virtue of slaughter,
    Make plain to them the excellence of killing
    And a field where a thousand corpses lie.

Mother whose heart hung humble as a button
On the bright splendid shroud of your son,
Do not weep.
War is kind.

There is nothing to approach in the first piece, though, technically. For a moment you don't hear it, then you do, with a little fear, as if a man had put his face suddenly near your face; and that's all. The indifference to craft, to *how* the thing is said, is lunar.

The second poem is based on the letter *i* in the word "kind." There are rhymes "die" and "lie" in the set-in stanzas; wild, sky, affrighted, flies, bright; just these, and they ought to make a high lament. But of course they do nothing of the sort. The author is standing *close* to one, not off on some platform, and the poem takes place in the successful war of the *prose* ("unexplained," "gulped," and so on) *against* the poetic appearance of lament. It takes some readers a while to hear this poem. Once heard, it is passionately moving; and it is moving then exactly in the lines where ordinarily a poet would not be moving,—not at all in the "bright splendid shroud" line, but in the beautiful and *i*-less line before it. A domestic, terrible poem, what it whispers is: "I would console you, how I would console you! *If I honestly could.*" In all its color and splendor, this is really not much more like an ordinary poem than the other three; its method is theirs. The four pieces have in common also cruelty and pity, their nakedness, a kind of awful bluntness; and contemptuous indifference to everything that makes up "poetry" for other people. What shall we do with them?

The poems have an enigmatic air and yet they are desperately personal. The absence of the panoply of the Poet is striking. We remember that their author did not like to be called a poet nor did he call them poetry himself. How unusual this is, my readers will recognize: most writers of verse are merely dying to be called poets, tremblingly hopeful that what they write is real "poetry." There was no pose here in Crane. His reluctance was an inarticulate recognition of something strange in the pieces. They are not like literary compositions. They are like things just seen and said, *said for use.* The handwriting of doctors is not beautiful; the point of their prescriptions is just to be made out. (It is very remarkable, I have noticed since the present chapter was written, that Crane used the peculiar word "pills" for his poems. He had often a mysterious and even dreadful exactness of terminology. "Some of the pills," he said in New York when *The Black Riders* was under attack, "are pretty darned dumb, anyhow. But I meant what I said." He had in mind no doubt their lack of sugar-coating.) Robert Graves, one of the shrewdest, craziest, and most neglected students of poetry living, laid out a theory of the origin of poetry once. A savage dreams, is frightened by the dream, and goes to the medicine man to have it explained. The medicine man can make up anything, anything will reassure the savage, so long as the manner of its delivery is impressive; so he chants, perhaps he stamps his foot, people like rhythm, what he says becomes rhythmical, people like to hear things *again*, and what he says begins to rhyme. Poetry begins—as a practical matter, for *use*. It reassures the savage. Perhaps he only hears back again, chanted, the dream he just told the medicine man, but he is reassured; it is like a spell. And medicine men are shrewd: interpretation enters the chanting, symbols are developed and connected, the gods are invoked, poetry booms. Now Crane's poetry is like a series of primitive anti-spells. Sometimes he chants, but for the most part on principle he refuses to (no coating). He has truths to tell. Everybody else in the 'nineties is chanting and reassuring and invoking the gods. So Crane just says, like a medicine man *before* chanting or poetry began. And what he says is savage: unprotected, forestlike. Man's vanity and cruelty, hypocrisy and cowardice, stupidity and pretension, hopelessness and fear, glitter through the early poems. God may exist; if so, He rolls down and crushes you. Part of the irony in Crane's poetry results from the imposition of his complex modern doubt upon a much stronger primeval set of his mind.

> A man saw a ball of gold in the sky;
> He climbed for it,
> And eventually he achieved it—
> It was clay.
>
> Now this is the strange part:
> When the man went to the earth
> And looked again,
> Lo, there was the ball of gold.
> Now this is the strange part:
> It was a ball of gold.
> Ay, by the heavens, it was a ball of gold.

The first four lines were written by a minister's son and intellectual of the 'nineties, the rest by a bushman.

Now I wish to be more serious and explode some errors. Crane has a textbook fame for his "experimentation" and for his "anticipation" of the free-verse movement. The notion of writing irregularly Crane probably got from Whitman; possibly the notion of very short short-line poems came to him after hearing Howells read Emily Dickinson; W. E. Henley's free verse may have affected him, the English Bible certainly did. There is no evidence in the poetry or outside it that he ever experimented in verse. Instinct told him to throw over metrical form, visions were in his head, and he wrote them down. Some of the poems were no doubt more consciously composed than others, and he revised some of them; their parable and proverbial form they owe in part to the Bible and to Olive Schreiner's *Dreams*; but "experiment" is not the word. As for "anticipation": some of the later people probably learned from him (Pound mentioned him early, and it was Sandburg who introduced

Sherwood Anderson to his verse), and more would have if his books had been more available; but his work is quite different from theirs. A comparison of any of the short poems of Pound or H. D. with the piece of Crane last quoted will make this clear. The later poets are deeply interested in manner; Crane is deeply uninterested in manner. In order to appreciate Crane's poetry, you must understand that it differs in intention and mode from the poetry both of his period and of ours. It is primitive; not designedly so, but naturally primitive.

Some assistance for this view, which may perhaps need it, turned up recently. T. S. Eliot in his paper on Poe and Valéry distinguishes three stages in the development of poetry: a middle stage in which the auditor or reader is interested in both the subject and the way it is handled (the style), an earlier stage in which attention is directed entirely upon the subject, and our stage, in which the subject has become "simply a necessary means for the realization of the poem. At this stage [Mr. Eliot goes on] the reader or listener may become as nearly indifferent to the subject matter as the primitive listener was to the style." This account is less incompatible with Mr. Graves's than it may appear, for the savage is not aware that he is worked upon by the chanting: he thinks he is attending wholly to the matter. So Crane's phrasing and pausation affect us insensibly, and the subject appears naked. One conclusive aspect of this whole analysis will be considered fully when we come to the prose, but the curious ground of Crane's personal preference of *The Black Riders* to *The Red Badge* (expressed in a letter to Hilliard) must have a word. Though absolutely opposed to "preaching" in literature, he nevertheless preferred his poetry as "the more ambitious effort," attempting "to give my ideas of life as a whole, so far as I know it," while the novel was "a mere episode."

Crane as a poet, in fine—a poet is the only thing we can call him—I take to represent an unexampled reversion. I take the steady drift of our period toward greater and greater self-consciousness, an increasing absorption in style, to be what has obscured the nature of his work and delayed its appreciation. How far its point of view really is from ours can be seen as well in a comparatively conventional, gentle piece as in the others:

Ay, workman, make me a dream,
A dream for my love.
Cunningly weave sunlight,
Breezes, and flowers.
Let it be of the cloth of meadows.
And—good workman—
And let there be a man walking thereon.

He writes as if this presence of the man were inconceivable. "War is kind" is perhaps his finest poem. The phrase is so repeated and with such pity that in the face of reason one cannot learn to believe he does not mean it; the poem may be compared to Webster's great dirge in *The White Devil*, actually a nightmare of horror behind the consolation, and contrasted with Hart Crane's *Voyages (II)*, a serious beautiful desperate poem less mature than these others. But a considerable number of Stephen Crane's poems, once their range is found, will be remembered. They do not wear out and there is nothing else like them. It is said by Thomas Beer and others that Crane lost his poetic faculty several years before his death; but not all the poems have been collected, and the dating is very uncertain. Fewer, certainly, of the more personal poems in the second book (1899) are valuable. One first printed long after his death, and presumably late, is one of his best, "A man adrift on a slim spar"—

> ... A pale hand sliding from a polished spar.
> God is cold.

> The puff of a coat imprisoning air:
> A face kissing the water-death,
> A weary slow sway of a lost hand
> And the sea, the moving sea, the sea.
> God is cold.

The poetry, then, *has* the character of a "dream," something seen naively, in a new relation. It *is* barbaric, and so primitively blunt that one sees without difficulty how it can be thought a trick. But tricks are not this simple. And tricks can be learned; whereas none of his innumerable parodists could simulate either the gleam or the weight of his true work—they hang out at the edges of Crane's tone. Neither

> The sea was blue meadow,
> Alive with little froth-people
> Singing

nor

> A horse,
> Blowing, staggering, bloody thing
> Forgotten at foot of castle wall

would ever be seen again. Crane was not only a man with truths to tell, but an interested listener to this man. His poetry has the inimitable sincerity of a frightened savage anxious to learn what his dream means.

3

Moving from Crane's poetry to his prose, we recognize the same sincerity, the same bluntness, the same hallucinatory effect, the same enigmatic character, the same barbarity. There is a formal difference, however; and before taking it up, I want to say something of an aspect of his art Garnett correctly thought fundamental, namely, his irony.

This word has spread and weakened until it scarcely means anything, or it means whatever we like in the general direction of difference-from-appearance. Accepting it seriously so, as *abdita vis quaedam* or "a certain hidden force"—the phrase quoted by Saintsbury from Montaigne who quoted it from Lucretius—Crane's work is a riot of irony of nearly every kind. A baby, consumed with grief for the killing of his dog (Crane does not say so), is so small that he can go downstairs toward its body only very slowly, backwards. Henry Fleming hands back the packet to his shamefaced friend (who has *not* run away the day before) with sentiments equally generous and self-congratulatory. A Swede, crazy with fear of Western aggression, gets drunk and stirs it to life. Examples plunge for citation and classification. But Crane is strong enough, as will appear, to bear any weight; we want the force of a concept.

Suppose we take two modern impressions of irony: as a comment downward, the expression, that is, of a superior man, antisocial; and as a refuge of a weak man. Both are trivial, but the first is more debased than the second. A refuge is a serious matter, and no human is very strong. The careful student J. A. K. Thomson observes that, tracing the Ironical Man to his beginnings, we "find him, not the remote and fastidious Intellectual, but someone far more elemental, simple, grotesque, and pitiful." This habit of mind—which one possesses by nature or not at all; it cannot be learned—is a form of *lying low* before the Divine Jealousy. Thomson associates it with man's development away from animism. Under the gradual growth of the recognition that Nature is inanimate, man learns to distrust the universe and pretends that he is nothing so as not to be an object of destruction. So long as trees and brooks were like him, he could understand them; once he cannot, the way is open to general fear: he had better hide. Thrusting back through this recognition, as Wordsworth had to and Crane, the exceptional modern man—animistic—is opened to both the primitive and the ironic.

Specifically, early Greek comedy presented a contest between the *Alazon* (Impostor) and the *Eiron* or Ironical Man: after vauntings and pretensions, the *Alazon* is routed by the man who affects to be a fool. The Impostor pretends to be more than he is, the Ironist pretends to be less. Now in most of the criticism of Stephen Crane that displays any sensitivity, whether outraged or not, one nearly makes out a nervous understanding that this author is simultaneously *at war with* the people he creates and *on their side*—and displays each of these attitudes so forcibly that the reader feels he is himself being made a fool of; so that Crane's position is still disproportionate with his achievement, and people after his death were so eager to forget him that it took a World War, and later another World War, to recall him generally to attention. I wonder whether explanation will ease this feeling; for the truth is that, in a special and definite sense, the reader *is* being made a fool of. Who are the creations Crane is most at war with? His complex ones, his "heroes"? or his simplest ones, his babies, horses, dogs, and brooks? With the first class his art is a Greek comedy, a contest with the impostor. Not even Maggie escapes this: "At times Maggie told Pete long confidential tales of her former home life, dwelling upon the escapades of the other members of the family and the difficulties she had had to combat in order to obtain a degree of comfort." God knows these distresses are real enough; one feels them, and at the same time one is made to feel even more strongly that the character has to run a gauntlet to the author's sympathy. So far as his creations of the first class are striving to become members of the second class, they become candidates for pathos or tragedy; so far as they fail, they remain figures of (this deadly-in-earnest) comedy. Crane never rests. He is always fighting the thing out with himself, for he contains both *Alazon* and *Eiron*; and so, of course, does the reader; and only dull readers escape. As comedy, his work is a continual examination of pretension—an attempt to cast overboard, as it were, impediments to our salvation. With creations of the second class, his work is much more simply an irony of talisman, a prayer to Heaven for pity; and it *technically* resembles Greek tragedy, in which the theme is the Jealousy of Heaven.

There is regularly an element of pathos, therefore, in his ironic (oppositional) inspection, and an element of irony regularly in his pathos. A Crane creation, or character, normally is *pretentious* and *scared*—the human condition; fitted by the second for pathos, by the first for irony. If the second feeling can save the first, as in Henry Fleming, the first can doom the second, as in the Swede. This pattern in his work seems hardly to have been perceived at all and is worth some insistence. The received account of Crane depends heavily upon the Gratuitous. He was bored by "plots," he drew "maps of accident," he emphasizes and ends in the "senseless," or he just brutalizes both his characters and the reader. The gratuitous is certainly very prominent, *outside* the central fate by which either one is lost or one is saved. Everything else—but only everything else—spins in irrelation; why pretend otherwise? in effect he says. And when he pretended himself, as he did sometimes, he was craftless as a sore thumb.

Let us look at this "fate" a little. It is against it that Crane's irony is most complex and energetic, and yet there is always one standpoint from which the product of this irony is not ironic at all. The Gordian example in his work would be the dreadful legend upon which the Swede's dead eyes rest, over the cash-machine: "This registers the amount of your purchase." But this death does. The Swede begged for it, *bought* it with his excess of fear and then his pretentiousness and even his over-protest against a boy's cheating in a game where no money was at stake. There is nothing accidental in the murder of this Swede except that it was the gambler who committed it and he gets a light sentence. Collins, in "A Mystery of Heroism," pretentiously gets himself into the position of taking an extreme risk to get a drink of water; he takes it, and finds out that this is what heroism is—not so much; but then the water is spilt. But that the water is spilt is the point, one way. He pretended that he could be a hero, he found that he could, and he found that it got him nothing, that nothing was changed; or, that everything was changed. The elimination of the water sends our eyes straight to the mysterious fate. In "The Open Boat" the community of the four men is insisted on, and Higgins is given special attention throughout, so that he is specially fit to be the price the others pay for their rescue: a sacrifice. Nothing of Crane's seems more gratuitous than the chapters devoted to the self-pity of her persecutors after Maggie's death. But besides serving as ironical distribution of the remorse that society ought to feel, this self-pity *is* suffering. Pete suffers agonies of drunken self-abasement and is fleeced. The mother's final scream is one of "pain"—she invents it, as we know, revels in it, but then she actually suffers it. If the author's tacit contempt here is intense, so is a (carefully guarded from pretentiousness) passion for retribution.

Carefully guarded—and the pattern of justice in his art has to manifest itself as best it can under the dreadful recognitions of honesty. Life is what it is. The consequences of these recognitions, bitterness and horror, disguise themselves in his grotesquerie of concept and style, his velocity, his displacements of rage. Open, they would be insupportable; and this will bring us in a moment to the difference between Crane's prose and his poetry. But I am afraid his use of grotesquerie will not be clear without illustration. I take two of its great strokes, one verging towards this author's wonderful humor, the other towards horror. "Many a man ought to have a bathtub larger than the boat which here rode upon the sea." This dry, gay, senseless remark enables him to contrast like lightning, with the sinister wilderness of water, isolation, and danger where the men toil, the most domestic, sheltered, comfortable home-situation imaginable: with the painfully moving, the stationary; with the effort for salvation, the pleasant duty of washing oneself. Note the mock-heroic outset—"Many a man ..."—at once abandoned. Many a man is to *own* a bathtub—these men own nothing but, precariously, their lives. Instead, the boat is alive, it "rides," running the risks of a rider. And then the point of a bathtub is to have water in it, water rising in it—and with this ominous flash of the tiny dinghy shipping water, the little sentence has done its work and is superseded by: "These waves were most wrongfully and barbarously abrupt and tall...." Clearly, an artist able to give such compact expression to such complexly bitter alternative reflection, with an air of perfect good nature, will not easily be found at the mercy of bitterness. My other illustration is the famous ninth chapter of *The Red Badge*, where the death of the tall soldier occurs in a prolonged uncanny ecstasy. Several million readers have been appalled by this and perhaps no reader has ever explained to himself what Crane was doing, as perhaps Crane never to himself named it: the Dance of Death.

Between the verse and the prose of an author who has written both successfully we expect to find a relation of a certain kind. Poetry, as the more highly organized form of communication, requires and evinces more art. The interminable verse of various Nineteenth Century novelists (Dickens, Thackeray, George Eliot) is indeed artless but this is not successful verse. The relation I am speaking of appears clearly in Keats, in Gray, even in Swift, even in Shakespeare. The greater nervousness of Meredith in his prose, for instance, is not the nervousness of art but the nervousness of temperament; his poetry is more artful. Hardy is a better craftsman in prose than critics allow. When young Jude is described as walking carefully over plowed fields lest he tread on earthworms and not liking to see trees lopped from a fancy that it hurt them: "This weakness of character, as it may be called, suggests that he was the sort of man who was born to ache a good deal before the fall of the curtain upon his unnecessary life should signify that all was well with him again." The Shakespearian stress upon this "well" is a product of style; the sentence stays in the mind. But the art of his poetry has been usually slighted also, and is much greater. Crane, so far as I am aware, is singular in this regard. Crane's poetry is characteristically and recognizably by the author of his prose; it shows the style of a master—as the soldier "raging at his breast," the horse a "Blowing, staggering, bloody thing"—and this is almost his prose-style. But it shows *less* style, less of devoted *art*. The prose looks often crafty, the poetry scarcely ever. We shall come back to this.

Crane I daresay is one of the great stylists of the language. These words "master" and "great" will trouble some readers, as they trouble me. But they seem unavoidable. The trouble we feel arises from several causes, which are worth examination. Crane's works that matter are all short. We don't see how works so little can be with any decency called great. Greatness of prose-style, however, does not require length for display. We hear Dryden in his *Essay of Dramatic Poesy*, Johnson in the letter to Chesterfield, fully. Another trouble is that Crane was writing greatly, if he ever did, in his early twenties. We are told that prose-writers mature slowly; scarcely anyone writes prose worth reading under thirty. There are exceptions. Congreve is a large one, Miss Austen is, there are others; and Crane anyway, as I have been trying and shall try more exactly to show, is in several respects a case unique. We wish if we can to avoid preconceptions. A third trouble is just that he is comparatively recent; this matters less. Then there are the words themselves, grandiose. We have no objection to calling the boy Keats a master, Rimbaud a master, but the word "great" sticks a little. It looks like a catchword. Our major troubles, though, I think are two, both of them proceeding from the nature of his work and of its historical situation. There is first the relation of his style to prose style in English and American before him, and second the relation of his general art-form, the story, to Western fiction before him. (The term Western is unsatisfactory because it must include Russian fiction, but no other seems better.) Though these troubles are closely related, we must take them separately.

Nothing very like Crane's prose style is to be found earlier; so much will probably be granted at once by an experienced reader. Here I must observe that Crane wrote several styles. He had even an epistolary style—extended, slow, uninflected, during most of his life, curter and jotty towards the end— but we are interested in his narrative styles. He began with the somber-jocular, sable, fantastic prose of the "Sullivan County Sketches" and the jagged, colored, awkward, brilliant *Maggie*. *Maggie* he probably revised much barbarousness out of before anyone except brothers and friends saw it, and he abandoned deliberately the method of the sketches—though fantasy, and fantasy in the quality of the prose, remained intermittently an element in his work to the end. A movement towards fluidity increases in *The Red Badge* and the "Baby Sketches" he was writing at the same time and produces a Crane norm: flexible, swift, abrupt, and nervous—swift, but with an unexampled capacity for stasis also. Color is high, but we observe the blank absence of the orotund, the moulded, which is Crane's most powerful response to the prose tradition he declined to inherit. In the fusion of the impassive and the intense peculiar to this author, he kept on drawing the rein. "Horses—One Dash" and "The Five White Mice" lead to the supple majesty of "The Open Boat," a second norm. *The Monster*, much more closed, circumstantial, "normal" in feeling and syntax, is a third. Then he opened his style again back towards the second norm in the great Western stories, "The Bride Comes to Yellow Sky" and "The Blue Hotel," and thereafter (for his two years) he used the second and the third styles at will, sometimes in combination, and the third usually relaxed as his health failed but peculiarly tense and astonishing in "The Kicking Twelfth." In certain late work also, notably in "The Clan of No Name," a development toward complexity of structure is evident, which death broke off. Nevertheless we may speak of "Crane's style" so long as we have these variations in mind, and my point is that it differs *radically* both from the tradition of English prose and from its modifications in American prose. Shakespeare, Dryden, Defoe, Johnson, Dickens, Arnold, Kipling, as these develop into Edwards, Jefferson, Hawthorne, Melville, James—Crane writes on the whole, a definite and absolute *stylist*, as if none of these people had ever existed. His animation is not Kipling's, his deadpan flatness is not Mark Twain's. He is more like Tacitus, or Stendhal in his autobiography, say, than like any of the few writers of narrative English who actually affected his development. He was a rhetorician who refused to be one. In Crane for the first time the resources of American spareness, exaggeration, volcanic impatience, American humor, came into the hands of a narrative author serious and thoughtful as an artist as Hawthorne or James, and *more* serious than any others of the New England–New York hegemony. Thus he made possible—whether by way of particular influence or as a symbolic feat in the development of the language—one whole side of Twentieth Century prose. It is hard to decide that a boy, that anyone, did this, and so we feel uncomfortable about the word that characterizes the achievement with great justice.

The second difficulty with "great" is the newness of his form. I am not referring to the immense burst of talented story-writing in England and America during the 'nineties, though this is relevant; the short story had scarcely any status in English earlier, and we are less eager, naturally, to concede greatness to its artist than to crown a novelist. Poe is an exception, absolutely genuine, very seldom good, more limited than Crane, superbly overvalued. Any sort of standard has hardly been in force for a generation. As late as 1923, in a survey not exceptionally stupid (Pattee's *Development of the American Short Story*), Crane existed merely at the head of thirteen nonentities (all save O. Henry and Harold Frederic) of whom Jack London was the one perhaps "most sure of literary permanence." The intensive literary criticism of the last twenty years has devoted itself largely to poetry and literary criticism, less to the novel, less still to the short story and the nearly extinct drama. If we are in a more enlightened state than Pattee was, we still owe it mostly to Mencken's generation. But I was referring to an operation that Crane performed. As he stripped down and galvanized prose, so he gutted the story of practically everything that had made it a story. "One fact is certain," Hardy decided in 1888: "in fiction there can be no intrinsically new thing at this stage of the world's history." This was one of the major blunders of all time, as James was then demonstrating, Crane would in a moment, and Joyce would presently. Hardy's novels can now be seen as really traditional and conservative when they are compared with something revolutionary, when *Tess* for instance is compared with *The Ambassadors*. Kipling, a story-writer neglected just now except by several of the best critics on both sides of the Atlantic, is less conservative and profounder than Hardy. But both Englishmen keep to the range. By setting a sentence characteristic of Crane against the sentence by Hardy quoted some pages ago, one learns. It is the two Americans who make formal war. James warred in the direction: elaboration of sensibility, consistency of point of view, qualification of style. The campaign cost him, progressively in his work, narrative in the old sense, even though he goes to every *length*. But his stories are still recognizably stories. Idiosyncratic and extended though they are, they are essentially far more like Kipling's[1] than the stories of either are like Stephen Crane's.

Crane's stories are as unlike earlier stories as his poems are unlike poems. He threw away, thoughtfully, plot; outlawed juggling and arrangement of material (Poe, Bierce, O. Henry); excluded the whole usual mechanism of society; banished equally sex (Maupassant) and romantic love (Chekhov—unknown to him); decided not to develop his characters; decided not to have any conflicts between them as characters; resolved not to have any characters at all in the usual sense; simplified everything that remained, and, watching intently, tenderly, and hopelessly, blew Fate through it—saying with inconceivable rapidity and an air of immense deliberation what he saw. What he saw, "apparently." The result is a series of extremely formidable, *new*, compact, finished, and distressing works of art. Mencken dated modern American literature from *The Red Badge of Courage*. The new *Literary History of the United States*, coming to hand as I write, dates it from the reissue of *Maggie* in 1896. It must come from about there, apparently.

Of course Crane did nothing such as I have just described. He was interested, only, in certain things, and kept the rest out. It is the ability to keep the rest out that is astounding. But the character of the deliberate in his prose too is conspicuous. We saw that this was absent from his poetry, and it is time to come to the difference. The difference is that between presentation (in the poetry) and apparent presentation (in the prose); in the figure of the savage's dream that we were employing, between *rehearsal* and *investigation*. The poem can simply say what the dream (nightmare) was; at once it gets rid of the dream, and is solaced in hearing it said. An effect of style is undesirable. To *study* the dream, to embody it, as in a story—this is another matter. One needs a suit, a style, of chain armor to protect the subject from everything that would like to get into the story with it: the other impressions of life, one's private prejudices, a florid and hypocritical society, existing literature. The style of the prose aims at the same thing as the unstyle of the poetry, namely, naked presentment, but its method is ironic. Other authors are saying what things "are," with supreme falsity. Crane therefore will only say what they *seem* to be. "The youth turned, with sudden, livid rage, toward the battlefield. He shook his fist. He seemed about to deliver a philippic.

"'Hell—'

"The red sun was pasted in the sky like a wafer."

Half of Crane's celebrated "coldness" is an effect of this *refusal to guarantee*. "He seemed about to deliver a philippic." It sounds as if he weren't going to; but he is; but he isn't; but—one does not know exactly where one is. The style is merely honest, but it disturbs one, it is even menacing. If this extremely intelligent writer will not go further than that insistent "seemed," says the reader nervously to himself, should *I*? The style has the effect of obliterating with silent contempt half of what one thinks one knows. And then: a policeman begins "frenziedly to seize bridles and beat the soft noses of the responsible horses." In the next sentence the noses are forgotten. But to tell us about the horses if the author is not going to commiserate with them seems brutal. It makes the reader do the feeling if he wants to; Crane, who cared more for horses than any reader, is on his way. Again the reader is as it were rebuked, for of course he *doesn't* feel very strongly about horses—he would never have put in that "soft" himself, much less clubbed it in with "responsible." Or: "A saloon stood with a voracious air on a corner." This is either funny, a little, or an affront: it might be after the reader. One is not enough guided. Just: there it is, hungry, very hungry.

This is supposed, by the way, to be Realism or Naturalism. Frank Norris, who was a romantic moralist, with a style like a great wet dog, and Stephen Crane, an impressionist and a superlative stylist, are Naturalists. These terms are very boring, but let us agree at least to mean by them *method* (as Howells did) rather than *material* (as Norris, who called his serious works "Romance," did). "Tell your yarn and let your style go to the devil," Norris wrote to somebody. The Naturalists, if there are any, all *accumulate*, laborious, insistent, endless; Dreiser might be one. Crane selected and was gone. "He knew when to shut up," as Norris put it. "He *is the only* impressionist," said Conrad in italics to Garnett, "and *only* an impressionist." This is not quite right either: Crane's method shows realistic and also fantastic elements. But it would be better, as a label for what has after all got to be understood anyway in itself, than the categorical whim established now in the literary histories. Crane was an impressionist.

His color tells us so at once. This famous color of his plays a part in his work that has been exaggerated, but it is important. Gifted plainly with a powerful and probably very odd sense of color, fortified then by Goethe, he did not refuse to use it; sometimes he abused it, and he increasingly abandoned it. Most authors use color. "The sun emerges from behind the gray clouds that covered the sky and suddenly lights up with its bright red glow the purple clouds, the greenish sea ... the white buildings." So Tolstoy at the end of *Sevastopol*, and it bears no relation whatever to Crane's use of color. "At this time Hollanden wore an unmistakable air of having a desire to turn up his coat collar." This is more like one of Crane's colors than Tolstoy's actual colors are. Color is imposed, from an angle, like this apparently physical and actually psychological detail. Crane was interested in what Goethe called the "moral-sensual effect of color." He owes nothing whatever, apparently, to painting.[2] The blue hotel "screaming and howling"—"some red years"—"fell with a yellow crash." The color is primitive. So with adverbs, metaphors. A man leans on a bar listening to others "terribly discuss a question that was not plain." "There was a general movement in the compact column. The long animal-like thing moved slightly. Its four hundred eyes were turned upon the figure of Collins." Here there is none of Crane's frequent, vivid condensation; and yet the eyes are not human eyes. It is primitive, an impression. A psychologist lately called red the most panicky and explosive of colors, the most primitive, as well as the most ambivalent, related equally to rage and love, battle and fire, joy and destruction. Everywhere then, in style, a mind at stretch.

We may reach toward the subject of all this remorseless animation through his characters. They are very odd. To call them types is a major critical error, long exposed, ever-recurrent. The new *Literary History* describes the hero of *The Red Badge* as "impersonal and typical," for which read: intensely personal and individual. George Wyndham (and Wells after him) fifty years ago showed the boy an idealist and dreamer brought to the test. Pete in *Maggie* is not a bartender, but Pete. Billy Higgins in "The Open Boat" is not an oiler, but the oiler. Crane scarcely made a type in all his work. At the same time, he scarcely made any characters. His people, *in* their stories, stay in your mind; but they have no existence outside. No life is strongly imaginable for them save what he lets you see. This seems to me to be singular, to want explanation. I think he is interested in them individually, but only as a crisis reaches them. The "shaky and quick-eyed" Swede of "The Blue Hotel" is certainly an *individual* mad with fear, one of Crane's most memorable people, but it is as an individual *mad with fear* that he grimly matters. "Stanley pawed gently at the moss, and then thrust his head forward to see what the ants did under the circumstance." When this delightful thing happens, a love-scene is taking place two feet away, one of the most inhibited and perfunctory ever written. It is only or chiefly in animals that Crane can be interested when a *fate* is not in question. Once it is, he is acutely and utterly present with the sufferer, attending however to the fate.

"Apparently" the state of the soul in crisis: this is his subject. The society against the person will do; he uses the term "environment" in regard to *Maggie*, and this is more generally dramatized in *The Monster*, more particularly dramatized in "The Bride Comes to Yellow Sky." But one has less feeling in these works, and in a number of others like them, that the men are themselves against each other, than that they have been set simply facing each other—not by Crane—by a fate. War is the social situation that does this most naturally and continually, so he possesses himself of it; in imagination first, again and again, and then in fact. "The Open Boat" is his most perfect story partly because here for once the fate is in the open: one is *fully justified* in being afraid, one can feel with confidence that one is absolutely tested. The antagonist will not fail one, as another man might, as even society might. The extraordinary mind that *had* to feel this we shall look at in the next chapter; here we are concerned with the art. Now these states of crisis, by their nature, cannot persist; so Crane succeeded only in short work. *The Red Badge of Courage*, as most critics have noticed, is not really a novel at all, but a story, and it is a little too long, as Crane thought it was. His imagination was resolute in presenting him with conditions for fear; so that he works with equal brilliance from invention and from fact. To take "The Open Boat," however, as a *report* is to misunderstand the nature of his work: it is an action of his art upon the remembered possibility of death. The death is so close that the story is warm. A coldness of which I was speaking earlier in Crane is absent here. Half of this I attributed to the stylistic refusal to guarantee. The other half is an effect from far in the mind that made the art, where there was a passion for life half-strangled by a need for death and made cold. Life thaws under the need when the death nears. In the eggshell boat, the correspondent knew even at the time, under dreadful hardship, that this was "the best experience of his life"—the comradeship, he says this is, but it was really something else: "There was a terrible grace in the move of the waves, and they came in silence, save for the snarling of the crests...."

The immense power of the tacit, felt in Crane's accounts of Maggie's brother's nihilism, her mother's self-pity, Henry Fleming's self-pride, George's dreams, gives his work kinship rather with Chekhov and Maupassant than Poe. "I like my art"—said Crane—"straight"; and misquoted Emerson, "There should be a long logic beneath the story, but it should be carefully kept out of sight." How far Crane's effect of inevitability depends upon this *silence* it would be hard to say. Nowhere in "The Open Boat" is it mentioned that the situation of the men is symbolic, clear and awful though it is that this story opens into the universe. Poe in several great stories opens man's soul downwards, but his work has no relation with the natural and American world at all. If Crane's has, and is irreplaceable on this score, it is for an ironic inward and tragic vision outward that we value it most, when we can bear it. At the end of the story a word occurs that will do for Crane. "When it came night, the white waves paced to and fro in the moonlight, and the wind brought the sound of the great sea's voice to the men on the shore, and they felt that they could then be interpreters." Crane does really stand between us and something that we could not otherwise understand. It is not human; it is not either the waves and mountains who are among his major characters, but it acts in them, it acts in children and sometimes even in men, upon animals, upon boys above all, and men. Crane does not understand it fully. But he has been driven and has dragged himself nearer by much to it than we have, and he interprets for us.

For this reason, as well as for his technical revolution, he is indispensable. By a margin he is probably the greatest American story-writer, he stands as an artist not far below Hawthorne and James, he is one of our few poets, and one of the few manifest geniuses the country has produced. For a large sane art we will not go to Crane of course, nor to any other American so far. We do not go to Dostoievsky either. For a *normal* art you have to go to artists much greater still: Shakespeare, Mozart, Tolstoy; and not alone to their greatest works, where the range of experience dealt with is utterly beyond any range yet dealt with by an American, but to their small works also, like "Master and Man." Whether Tolstoy's is a *better* story than Crane fantastic *The Blue Hotel* it is less easy to decide. *The Red Badge of Courage* is much better than *Sevastopol*.

NOTES

1. It has interest that James was repeatedly prostrated by Kipling, as his letters show, and, though very generous, looked hard for holes; the persistent exaggeration of his letters everywhere does not conceal his eagerness, his particular eagerness, about "the infant monster," "the absolutely uncanny talent," the talent "diabolically great."

2. This is an opinion. Wells disagreed, relying on very late passages like this in "War Memories": "I bring this to you merely as ... something done in thought similar to that which the French impressionists do in color ..." But all such allusions are metaphorical in Crane, who does not use color in the least like a painter. He knew, by the way, few real painters—Linson, Jerome Myers, later Ryder; mostly illustrators.

ERIC SOLOMON

Love and Death in the Slums

With eye and with gesture
You say you are holy.
I say you lie;
For I did see you
Draw away your coats
From the sin upon the hands
Of a little child.
Liar!
    —Crane, *The Black Riders*, LVII

... one makes room in Heaven for all sorts of souls (notably an occasional street girl) who are not confidently expected to be there by many excellent people.
    —Crane to Hamlin Garland, March? 1893[1]

In a little-known story published in *Town Topics* in 1896 Stephen Crane set forth, indirectly but in more detail than was his custom, some of his critical credos. The story—"In the Tenderloin"—is one of Crane's best. It displays near-perfect control and selectivity, remarkably fresh dialogue, and psychological insight. Subtitled "A Duel Between an Alarm Clock and a Suicidal Purpose," the tale shows a thin slice of underworld life: a young

From *Stephen Crane: From Parody to Realism*, pp. 19–44. © 1966 by the President and Fellows of Harvard College.

man—probably a pimp—named Swift Doyer is represented brutally attacking his girl for having lied to him. After he strikes her with an alarm clock, she says quietly, "I've taken morphine, Swift,"[2] and the rest of the plot concerns his rough but successful attempts to save her. The story ends as the two fall asleep.

"In the Tenderloin" attacks the conventions of contemporary popular fiction in three ways: in the lack of formal plot, in social attitude, and in the absence of melodrama. We never discover who the characters really are, how they live, or what the girl lied about—if, indeed, she did. We only know that these two people, of marginal social position at best, have a stormy love–hate relationship. And we know that they are living in a tiny flat in the Tenderloin, that area of bars and restaurants, theaters and opium dens, vice and prostitution, that Crane had studied closely in the fall of 1896.[3]

The social implications of Crane's sketch are clear; he adopts neither the reformer's pity and anger nor the naturalist's acceptance and defeat. His couple are simply human beings having a difficult passage, and they manage to survive. Neither a supporter nor an attacker of the Tenderloin way of life—seeking neither to display local color nor to arouse indignation—Crane accepts man's nature as anguished and fallible. An ironic opening differentiates Crane's narrative from traditional slum reportage. "Everybody knows all about the Tenderloin district of New York.... It is wonderful—this amount of truth which the world's clergy and police forces have collected concerning the Tenderloin. My friends from the stars obtain all this information, if possible, and then go into the wilderness and apply it" (p. 200). Here, as in most of his fiction of social comment, Crane eschews direct protest. Unlike other writers, he does not express outrage; he simply exhibits how human beings live under certain conditions. That their lives are impoverished and violent, marked by illicit sex, whiskey, beatings, and suicide attempts, is far less important than that they are struggling people, doing the best they can. "When broad day came they were both asleep, and the girl's fingers had gone across the table until they had found the locks on the man's forehead. They were asleep, and this after all is a human action, which may safely be done by characters in the fiction of our time" (p. 203).

Stephen Crane uses the whole tale as a commentary on contemporary modes of fiction and as an argument for his kind of honesty and objectivity. Despite his allusion to the "indifferent people whose windows opened on the air-shaft," Crane shows that a whore need not be drawn as totally different from the rest of mankind. He remarks ironically on her "woe that seemed almost as real as the woe of good people," and comments that Swift Doyer knows "as well as the rest of mankind that these girls have no hearts to be broken" (p. 201). But Crane proves that a Tenderloin whore can kill herself for love—just as William Faulkner in *The Bear* shows that a Negro has the capacity for suicide. Swift's methods of saving the girl are ugly: he forces whiskey down her throat, hits her furiously—out of a love and despair that "our decorous philosophy" cannot understand. When Swift carries her to the kitchen for coffee, the narrator takes the opportunity to make a comment on the art of fiction. "He was as wild, haggard, gibbering, as a man of midnight murders, and it is only because he was not engaged in the respectable and literary assassination of a royal duke that almost any sensible writer would be ashamed of this story" (p. 201). Romanticism, then, is ruled out.

And melodrama. In the story's finest passage, the girl does not, as might be expected from the narrative's heady diction, whirl her soul into the abyss. "The girl saw a fly alight on a picture. 'Oh,' she said, 'there's a little fly.' She arose and thrust out her finger. 'Hello, little fly!' she said, and touched the fly." Full of remorse because her touch fells the fly, she finds it and tries to bring it back to life by warming it at the gas jet. " 'Poor little fly,' she said, 'I didn't mean to hurt you. I wouldn't hurt you for anything ...' " (p. 202).[4] The realism of the scene and of the dialogue is in itself a commentary on the ordinary modes of describing a recovery from near death, but the author moves into Swift Doyer's mind in order to hammer home the point that "this scene was defying his preconceptions," and the preconceptions of much nineteenth-century fiction. "His instruction had been that people when dying behaved in a certain manner. Why did this girl occupy herself with an accursed fly? Why in the names of the gods of the drama did she not refer to her past? [So much for stage melodrama.] Why, by the shelves of the saints of literature, did she not clutch her brow and say: 'Ah, once I was an innocent girl'? [the fallen woman of Victorian literature]" (p. 202). Crane scoffs at the protagonist's "scandalized" sense of propriety, and, while parodying the traditional, he also uses the scene to prove to the hero that the girl could not die, for the "form was not correct."

In *The Red Badge of Courage* Crane employs real war to shatter the hero's romantic dreams of battle, and in so doing creates a new and finer form of war fiction; in "The Open Boat" his correspondent comments on the way matters *should* be, and in the process of the narration Crane rejects the familiar conception of the confrontation of man against nature on the sea and also writes a marvelous sea adventure. Similarly in the novels *Maggie* and *George's Mother* he parodies the accepted forms of slum fiction and, with the same materials, makes fresh and powerful slum novels. The critical and creative method exemplified in "In the Tenderloin" is operative throughout his fiction.

In *Maggie*, his earliest novel (1893), Crane reacts sharply to some familiar modes of popular fiction. *Maggie* is about novels, as well as being a novel, and, as Frank Kermode has said about another writer's book, this technique is simply part of the work's "perfectly serious way of life."[5]

Maggie involves a complete reversal of the sentimental themes of the nineteenth-century best sellers that dealt with the life of a young girl. These novels, from such active pens as those of Susan Warner, Maria Cummins, E. D. E. N. Southworth, and E. P. Roe, displayed a manifest religious bias; Maggie is scorned by a clergyman and Jimmie finds organized religion abhorrent. The conventional novels treated romantic love and the salvation of female honor; Crane's heroine is sexually betrayed and falls to the lower depths. A key scene in the sentimental novel was the slow, beautiful death of the heroine's mother; here Maggie herself dies, off stage, and her drunken, blaspheming mother survives. The villain in the sentimental novel was generally regenerated by the heroine's good influence; Crane's Pete the bartender becomes increasingly degraded and ends in a drunken stupor, mocked by thieving streetwalkers. The essential lesson of the sentimental novel was that happiness (and wealth) came from submission to suffering; suffer Maggie does, but the result of her pangs is only further misery, poverty, and death.[6]

The sentimentalist's approach extended into the slum novel itself. In Walter F. Taylor's words, "In 1890 appeared the key-book of the entire anti-slum movement, Jacob Riis's *How the Other Half Lives*.... Thence-forward—and especially for the next five years—the slum was in effect a fresh literary field ... and both writers and readers appear to have explored the new area with an intense curiosity in which were mingled compassion, morbid fascination, and something akin to horror."[7] While there were many writers who saw life in the big city as full of charm and adventure—Richard Harding Davis, Bayard Taylor, and H. C. Bunner, for example—others with more active social consciences, like Howells or H. H. Boyesen, were aware of the city's dangers but treated the slum dwellers only in passing. The life of the poor, according to Bunner, writing in 1896, was enjoyable because of the "pitiful petty schemes for the gaining of daily bread that make up for them ["Bohemians"] the game and comedy of life." Bunner could view casually "the daily march of the mob of drunks, detectives, butcher's boys, washerwomen, priests, drunken women ..."[8] because he never probed beneath the surface of these lives. And for the writers of melodrama the slum girl was a creature of romance, sure to rise above her situation, as did the dime novel heroines of *Orphan Nell, the Orange Girl; or the Lost Heir* (1880) and *The Detective's Ward; or The Fortunes of a Bowery Girl* (1871). Whatever stresses life might present to the slum heroine, she was proof against temptation: "I am but a poor shop-girl; my present life is a struggle for a scanty existence; my future a life of toil; but over my present life of suffering there extends a rainbow of hope ... Life is short, eternity endless—the grave is but the entrance to eternity. And you, villain, ask me to change my present peace for a life of horror with you. No, monster, rather may I die at once!"[9]

The same combinations of humor, melodrama, and sentiment marked the novels of Edward Townsend, who invented Chimmie Fadden, one of the early vernacular heroes. In his *A Daughter of the Tenements* (1895) the life of the poor was shown in some detail—more than exists in Crane's *Maggie*, just as De Forest included more combat reality than Crane did in his war novel—and there was liberal irony directed toward people of other classes who could not understand that the poor might have feelings. But the heroine rises from her slum background of sweatshops and fruitstands to become a ballet dancer, the hero becomes a newspaper illustrator, and they live happily ever after—on Long Island. Only a minor character is permitted to be ruined by drink and opium, and even he manages to perform a shining good deed before he dies. Crane's remark is worth noting: "My good friend Edward Townsend—have you read his 'Daughter of the Tenements'?—has another opinion of the Bowery, and it is certain to be better than mine."[10] The slums in these novels were grim and dangerous, but hard work finally conquered them, and the basic passage was from rags to riches. For those trapped there, the authors sustained a tone of pity and humor that reminds one of a famous *Life* cartoon of the period that showed two ragged tots staring at the sky and remarking that the stars were as thick as bedbugs. From these studies of the depths of the city came the work of O. Henry and Damon Runyon, not of Theodore Dreiser, James Farrell, and Nelson Algren.

Perhaps closest to *Maggie* in theme and texture was Edgar Fawcett's tale of a poor girl's betrayal and destruction, *The Evil That Men Do* (1889). The miseries of the working girl, the loathsomeness of drunken, fighting parents, the assumption that innocence is only temporary, get the novel off to a serious start. But the confrontations of the heroine and her would-be seducers are hysterical, and the sufferings of the working girl at the hands of the rich are overdone.[11] Fawcett created a world of corruption, venality, and weakness, true; and his heroine is not saved at the end—rather she declines from housemaid to kept woman to drunken whore and dies in an alley at the hands of her equally degraded working-class lover. But two hundred sixty-two pages of bombast must pass before she finally gives in to her seducer, and much of the novel is given over to the depiction of wealthy cardboard villains.[12]

I believe that Stephen Crane's *Maggie* is in part a reaction to these "realistic" city novels that were as sentimental and melodramatic, finally, as was the other traditional popular fiction of Crane's time.[13] Critics have tried to show the influence on Crane of Riis's slum studies, Zola's *L'Assommoir*, various tracts and sermons; but Crane did not write *Maggie* either to bring about reforms or, as the city novel often does, to offer "an interpretation and a judgment of the city."[14] Unlike Upton Sinclair, Stephen Crane did not call for social action. He was of course aware—even in 1893, before he wrote his severe reports of city poverty—that, as an earlier reporter had said, "a little more than half the population of New York are living under conditions which murder the children, degrade and ruin the young, corrupt every aspiration and stifle every hope."[15] Yet Crane wrote only as an observer. To be sure, his inscriptions in presentation copies of *Maggie* often call attention to the novel's social viewpoint (" 'And the wealth of the few shall be built on the patience of the poor'—Prophesy not made B.C. 1090"),[16] but Crane always dodged the kind of direct attack that marked Sinclair's reform novels or would characterize the proletarian novels of the thirties.[17] He was unwilling to editorialize in his fiction.[18] In his nonfiction, the well-known "Experiment in Misery," or the less famous "Experiment in Luxury," Crane's criticism of society is manifest. In the latter piece, written for the New York *Press* a year after *Maggie* first appeared, Crane tells how "the eternal mystery of social condition exasperated him at this time. He wondered if incomprehensible justice were the sister of open wrong." Here Crane is willing openly to attack organized religion, at which his fiction includes only a passing glance. "When a wail of despair or rage had come from the night of the slums they [theologians] had stuffed this epigram ["The rich are made miserable by their wealth"] down the throat of he who cried out and told him that he was a lucky fellow. They did this because they feared.[19] Indeed, the very absence of any sense of class warfare or economic motivation on Crane's part may be emphasized by a certain vagueness of setting. Crane does not state that Rum Alley is in the Bowery any more than he indicates that *The Red Badge of Courage* treats Chancellorsville. The lack of joy and release in Crane's slum characters comes not from any political position on the author's part but from a sense of reportorial honesty, fidelity to the real emotions of his characters, and understanding of the nightmare of the city.[20]

Stephen Crane cut a few passages in revising for the 1896 edition of *Maggie*, in addition to toning down some of the language. It has been persuasively argued that these cuts were made to avoid any "false and melodramatic" tones.[21] The entire production of *Maggie* seems to me to be an emendation, a cutting, as it were, of traditional slum fiction. Crane sliced away the false humor, the sentiment, the melodrama, and the social editorializing. What is left makes the stereotypes seem flatulent in comparison to the harsh, controlled, bare fiction of *Maggie*.

That Crane would not directly preach does not mean that his novel is amoral. In 1896 he published in the *Bookman* a fable—a parody of a fable, actually—that explains his attitude toward the "message" of his fiction:

A beggar crept wailing through the streets of a city. A certain man came to him there and gave him bread, saying: "I give you this loaf, because of God's word." Another came to the beggar and gave him bread, saying: "Take this loaf; I give it because you are hungry."

Now there was a continual rivalry among the citizens of this town as to who should appear to be the most pious man, and the event of the gifts to the beggar made discussion. People gathered in knots and argued furiously to no particular purpose. They appealed to the beggar, but he bowed humbly to the ground, as befitted one of his condition, and answered: "It is a singular circumstance that the loaves were of one size and of the same quality. How, then, can I decide which of these men gave bread more piously?"

The people heard of a philosopher who travelled through their country, and one said: "Behold, we who give not bread to beggars are not capable of judging those who have given bread to beggars. Let us, then, consult this wise man."

"But," said some, "mayhap this philosopher, according to your rule that one must have given bread before judging they who give bread, will not be capable."

"That is an indifferent matter to all truly great philosophers." So they made search for the wise man, and in time they came upon him, strolling along at his ease in the manner of philosophers.

"Oh, most illustrious sage," they cried.

"Yes," said the philosopher promptly.

"Oh, most illustrious sage, there are two men in our city, and one gave bread to a beggar, saying: 'Because of God's word.' And the other gave bread to the beggar, saying: 'Because you are hungry.' Now, which of these, oh, most illustrious sage, is the more pious man?"

"Eh?" said the philosopher.

"Which of these, oh, most illustrious sage, is the more pious man?"

"My friends," said the philosopher suavely addressing the concourse, "I see that you mistake me for an illustrious sage. I am not he whom you seek. However, I saw a man answering my description pass here some time ago. With speed you may overtake him. Adieu."[22]

The philosopher wrote *Maggie*, but, refusing the role of illustrious sage, he left it to the citizens to derive the novel's meaning.

It is true that Stephen Crane includes more indirect, unstated social comment in *Maggie* than in any of his other works except, possibly, *The Monster*. The story that traces the fall of the beautiful girl who "blossomed in a mud puddle" (X, 156), the chronicle that has the subtitle "A Girl of the Streets," tries, in Crane's words, "to show that environment is a tremendous thing in the world and frequently shapes life regardless."[23] The streets, the mud puddle, the brutal environment, suggest excessive editorial comment, despite Crane's desire to present without preaching. In this early work Crane is not yet in control of his gift for hinting and foreshortening. For example, the concept that life in the slums is a war—an obvious naturalistic idea—is hammered into the reader's consciousness by heavy repetition of metaphor and situation. In the opening scene Maggie's brother is doing battle with the urchins of Devil's Row, and the chapter resounds with battle imagery— "valiant roar," "the fury of battle," "small warriors," "one who aimed to be some vague kind of soldier, or a man of blood" (pp. 137–41). The novel is a collection of battle scenes. Chapter I shows Jimmie at war with other children; chapter II recounts the violent beating administered to Maggie by her mother; III provides a kind of climax to the domestic warfare in a savage, chair-splintering fight between the Johnson parents. Actually, one of the flashes of humor in this early section comes from an old neighbor's comment on the fighting: "Eh, child, what is it dis time? Is yer fader beatin' yer mudder, or yer mudder beatin' ye fader?" (p. 146). Chapter IV is given over to Jimmie's battles, as a truck driver, against the street-dwellers. "He was continually storming at them from his throne" (p. 154). Pete wins Maggie's admiration by his accounts of his prowess in bar brawls: "Dey knows I kin wipe up d' street wid any t'ree of dem" (p. 159). Chapter IX centers on a fist fight between Jimmie and his mother: "The mother and the son began to sway and struggle like gladiators" (p. 175). Chapter XI provides a climax of battle in the long, detailed report of the fight between Pete and Jimmie and his friend, when Pete's bar is wrecked by Jimmie's attempts to avenge his sister's seduction. Maggie, the reader notes, takes no part in this warfare. She is passive, a victim—her role in the novel. Yet Crane's satiric point is far too obvious. The amount of mock warfare is much greater than is necessary to indicate that Maggie is the loser in a battle with the slum.

Other aspects of social commentary, though indirect, are also blunt. Crane disapproves of the hypocrisy of the double standard that allows a man to philander but turns a woman's sexual involvement into utter corruption. In order to indict the society that insists upon such hypocritical standards, Crane counterpoints the sexual athleticism of Maggie's brother Jimmie to her one affair with Pete—an affair that is forced upon her by the callous brutality of Jimmie and his mother. Again and again, Crane reminds us that two women are seeking Jimmie's support for their children whom he fathered; just before Jimmie and his mother exchange shocked views of Maggie's behavior, his ex-mistress begs him for help, and he roughly evades her. "Jimmie thought he had a great idea of woman's frailty, but he could not understand why any of his kin should be victims." And, in case we haven't grasped Crane's ideas, "Again he wondered vaguely if some of the women of his acquaintance had brothers." To leave not a trace of doubt, Crane ends, "Nevertheless his mind did not for an instant confuse himself with those brothers nor his sister with theirs" (p. 193).

Some of the author's interpretation is more restrained. The antireligious bias is limited to a few carefully assimilated vignettes: the profane old lady who can don an expression of virtue when begging and can modulate her collection of "God bless yeh's" in assorted keys; a beautifully rendered scene of the mission church where the preacher composes his sermons of "you's," and the listeners only want soup tickets; the mother's alternations of curses and prayers directed at Maggie. When Crane brings the fallen Maggie, in her moment of greatest need, into contact with "a stout gentleman in a silk hat and a chaste black coat, whose decorous row of buttons reached from his chin to his knees," and the man preserves his respectability by sidestepping her, we are not completely sure that he is a clergyman. Maggie "had heard of the grace of God," Crane remarks, but the man still may be only a well-dressed business man (p. 207). Crane makes no judgments about the sources of the slum mud puddle. Indeed, economic determinism is absent from *Maggie* since in it, unlike most slum novels, poverty per se is not a salient issue, and even when Maggie takes to the streets it is because of her rejection by Pete and her family rather than her need for money. Surely the best indication of Crane's method of oblique comment is his treatment of Maggie's job in a sweatshop. Working conditions, grimly described, were clichés of contemporary slum fiction, as in the pathetic descriptions of *A Daughter of the Tenements* (or *Sister Carrie*); here Crane simply hints at Maggie's work in an establishment where they make collars and cuffs. "She received a stool and a machine in a room where sat twenty girls of various shades of yellow discontent. She perched on the stool and treadled at her machine all day, turning out collars with a name which might have been noted for its irrelevancy to anything connected with collars" (p. 156). Later Crane shows Maggie at work, afraid that she will shrivel in "the hot, stuffy room." The author glances at the traditional "heavy" of this scene, the fat foreigner who owns the shop: "He was a detestable creature. He wore white socks with low shoes. He sat all day delivering orations in the depths of a cushioned chair. His pocket book deprived them of the power of retort. 'What do you sink I pay fife dolla a week for? Play? No, py tamn!'" (p. 169). And this is all. The reference to the socks and shoes casts doubt on Maggie's authority for criticizing her boss, and Crane's view of the conditions in the shop is deliberately ambiguous—a far cry from, say, Sinclair's *Jungle*.

Stephen Crane's social view in *Maggie* might be summed up in the phrase that echoes throughout the novel and appears on the lips of every major character except the heroine. "What d' Hell!" At once a cry of profanity, despair, disengagement, and unreason, the phrase may exculpate society from direct blame. Unlike the usual run of slum novels, *Maggie* finds no cause—not religion, nor class stratification, nor poverty, nor even those naturalistic staples, coincidence and dark natural forces. Maggie's destruction is as obscure as her creation and her survival. Her little brother Tommie dies; Maggie lives, for a while. "Ah, what d' Hell."

Many aspects of *Maggie* reflect generic traditions of the city novel. As Jean Cocteau once said about two works, they are alike save in everything. As in most slum novels, Crane uses dialect to an excess to characterize his slum dwellers and to indicate the paucity of their linguistic, intellectual, and emotional resources. The author's prose, on the other hand, is rich in metaphor and wit when he speaks in his own voice. The novel is packed with evocations of the streets, jammed with wagons and trolleys, the crumbling, crowded tenements, the barrooms and music halls, dime museums, menageries.[24] Crane's penchant for rapid successions of sharply outlined pictures is given full release in *Maggie*. The city itself takes on a personality, as in Dreiser's pages, threatening, uncaring, jostling, fast-moving. Nevertheless, despite the novel's realistic details, the special quality of *Maggie* comes from its parodic nature, which finally controls the novel's characterizations and structure.

In chapter VIII Crane presents an extremely full parody of traditional melodrama, of everything that *Maggie* is not. Pete often takes Maggie to plays "in which the dazzling heroine was rescued from the palatial home of her treacherous guardian by the hero with the beautiful sentiments." We recall that Maggie first thought of Pete as a knight who would rescue her from her cruel mother. The play shows the hero "out at soak in pale-green snow-storms, busy with a nickel-plated revolver rescuing aged strangers from villains." Maggie and the audience—and, Crane would indicate, the reading public of 1893—accept all this, with sympathy, as "transcendental realism"; the gallery cheer on the struggling hero and jeer the villain, "hooting and calling attention to his whiskers." But Crane's fiction does not lead *his* readers to hiss vice and applaud virtue. His villains are not bearded, his heroes not exposed in snowstorms. Nor do Crane's heroes "march from poverty in the first act to wealth and triumph in the final one," as happens in the play and in the contemporary fiction that *Maggie* parodies. Crane's novel remains faithful to the conventions of the genre lampooned in his play—a poor heroine, a grim environment—but he breaks down the formal assumptions within the body of his novel. Maggie "rejoiced at the way in which the poor and virtuous eventually overcame the wealthy and wicked" (pp. 171f). This description of the play should provide us with the key to Crane's strategy in his first novel. The characters and events of the novel counter the traditional elements of slum melodrama; they also transcend this disintegration of an accepted prototype and rise to a renewal and revitalization of the form. The comic melts into the serious. The parody of itself that is contained within the novel heightens the sense, of reality that surrounds the parodic passages, reality that constitutes the bulk of the novel. This mock melodrama is reflexive, not referential; the counterpointing of "literature" and life makes Maggie's real role more convincing, for the conventions parodied are not only parts of slum fiction in general, but are also at work as life expectations in the consciousnesses of Crane's characters.

The structure of the novel itself is that of a three-act drama with an appended conclusion; the technique is that of ironic counterpoint. A further parodic element appears in the characterization of the heroine, who is barely sketched and has only the faintest of emotions, in contrast to the stock heroine's catalogue of fading charms and hysterical passages. To be sure, Crane's controlling idea enforces this method. Maggie is a victim, bearing the brunt of others' lusts and hypocrisies. Everyone else seems to swirl around her. They are always in motion, while she is passively dragged in their currents until, at the end, she floats along the gutters of the city streets, impelled by the force of others' vigor—and then slips quietly into the waters of the East River, her stillness at last become permanent obscurity.

The first act encompasses three chapters and establishes the detail and color of slum life. Street urchins war against a stolid background: "From the window of an apartment house that uprose from amid squat ignorant stables ... labourers, unloading a scow at a dock at the river ... The engineer of a passive tugboat ... Over on the island a worm of yellow convicts came from the shadow of a grey ominous building and crawled slowly along the river's bank" (p. 138). Here are all the strands of the novel—the river, the indifferent observers, the street battles, the squalor of a great city. All the important characters are introduced in these first pages, the brawling Jimmie, the swaggering sixteen-year-old Pete (already muttering "Ah, what d' Hell"), the sullen, brutal, drunken father, and the savage, hysterical, massive mother. Maggie, "the heroine," is barely present. She is a product of the others' emotions, a tiny recipient of their blows, "a small pursued tigress" (p. 145). Her attempts to care for her infant brother, to soothe the mauled Jimmie, to help her intoxicated mother, all meet with the curses and cuffs of the hostile world that will eventually destroy her. The stereotypes of parental or brotherly love are ruthlessly reversed; emotions are as crude as the environment. "Long streamers of garments fluttered from fire-escapes. In all unhandy places there were buckets, brooms, rags and bottles.... A thousand odours of cooking food came forth to the street. The building quivered and creaked from the weight of humanity stamping about in its bowels" (p. 141f). Crane carries the ugliness of his scene to naturalistic limits. The various fights are overdone, as is the passage where Jimmie, sent out for a can of beer by the mendacious old lady beggar who serves as a Hardyesque choral figure, is set upon by his father, robbed of the beer, and then hit on the head with the empty can. Yet the first act ends on a note of peace, Maggie quivering with fear, watching the prostrate, heaving body of her drunken mother. "Out at the window a florid moon was peering over dark roofs, and in the distance the waters of a river glimmered pallidly" (p. 1–50).

Act II starts with a chapter completely given over to a careful and fairly interesting character study of Jimmie, who is analyzed much more acutely than Maggie. Crane explains the brother's cynical temperament, his motivation, and indicates that, despite his sins, he is not totally depraved. "Nevertheless, he had, on a certain star-lit evening, said wonderingly and quite reverently, 'Deh moon looks like hell, don't it?'" (p. 156). All we learn of Maggie appears in a short paragraph saying that by some rare chance of alchemy, she grew up to be a pretty girl. Crane seems to be more interested in describing the mother's rise to fame in the police courts. The relationship between Maggie and Pete, the slum flower and the uncouth bartender, is ironic, too heavily so. Here Crane's parody gets out of hand. After Pete describes his brawls in filthy language, "Maggie perceived that here was the ideal man. Her dim thoughts were often searching for faraway lands where the little hills sing together in the morning. Under the trees of her dream-gardens there had always walked a lover" (p. 159). The counterpoint is thunderous, as in the next line where Pete responds to the girl: "Say, Mag, I'm stuck on yer shape. It's outa sight." To Maggie, "He was a knight" (p. 161). The only motivation for Maggie's perverse romanticizing of this oaf, quixotically converting him from a brute into a knight, is the ugliness of her dark, dusty home that clouds her vision. Pete represents a way of escape to a world of finer quality, at least in her estimation, and when he does take her out, it is from a home once more crumbled by her mother. "The curtain at the window had been pulled by a heavy hand and hung by one tack, dangling to and fro in the draught through the cracks at the sash.... The remnants of a meal, ghastly, lay in a corner. Maggie's mother, stretched on the floor, blasphemed, and gave her daughter a bad name" (p. 163).

Pete takes Maggie to a dance hall that seems to her, in contrast to her home, to be the height of elegance. Crane lovingly describes this Bowery institution, the first of three to which Pete will take Maggie. This establishment is bourgeois, numbers only a very few tipsy men among the customers, and presents fairly wholesome entertainment. While Crane views the crowd with some irony, particularly during their warm response to an anti-British song, his description is mixed with affection. And from this respectable place Maggie emerges a respectable girl, refusing to kiss Pete. The second act of Maggie's little drama ends with an emphasis on her honesty and goodness. She seems impervious to her lover's temptations, even that of a life filled with visits to theaters and museums.

The final act commences immediately after the melodramatic play discussed earlier. In contrast to the events of the play, Maggie's descent into sin is casual. There is no villain and no heroine. Driven out of her home by a vilely intoxicated mother, accused of sin while still virginal, forced, as it were, into Pete's arms, Maggie goes—"falls." " 'Git th' devil outa here.' Maggie went" (p. 177). Her "ruin," of course, must be handled obliquely, and Crane treats this problem of Victorian reticence with great skill. The old beggarwoman with relish tells Jimmie of Maggie's tears and pleas for the assurances of Pete's love, as if these were uproariously funny. " 'Oh, gee, yes,' she called after him. She laughed a laugh that was like a prophetic croak" (p. 178). Crane's comedy is effective here; so much so that the pathos inherent in this traditional situation catches the reader unawares. The reader familiar with sentimental fiction must be amused at Jimmie's commonplace responses to the hackneyed situation of the fall from grace of the innocent daughter and sister—but with laughter comes also a measure of real pity for Maggie. This pathetic parody, this travesty of the mother and the son—far more sinful themselves than Maggie—lamenting over her damnation, calls to mind a similar mockery of parental affection in John Gay's *The Beggar's Opera*. The parody of bourgeois standards is superb. " 'May she be cursed for ever!' she shrieked. 'May she eat nothin' but stones and deh dirt in deh street. May she sleep in deh gutter an' never see the sun shine again. D' bloomin'—' " (p. 179). Their mutual hypocrisy and self-congratulation is as harrowing as it is comic, so that the scene that starts in parody ends in seriousness. This response, Crane says, is the blindness and hypocrisy of society—and he underlines the terrible lack of insight on the part of Maggie's relatives by calling forth the same rapid, unjust condemnation of the girl's character from the other slum dwellers who

accuse Maggie of years of licentious behavior. The reader not only feels a
sense of pity for Maggie, who, as usual, is not on the scene, but also attains
a genuine sense of the absurdity of moral pretension. That these reprobates
should judge Maggie on the basis of their loss of "respectability" because of
her love affair is a cruel commentary on the ways of the social animal. Later
Jimmie will be embarrassed because Maggie's new role "queers" him and his
mother. As for the mother, she rapidly learns how to use her daughter's fall
to excuse her own drinking habits. Yet the words of a cynical police judge
help to sustain the needed antisentimental tone: "Mary, the records of this
and other courts show that you are the mother of forty-two daughters who
have been ruined" (pp. 193f). Jimmie, finally, is not as bad as his mother. He
does have a brief flash of insight, as he did on the night when he noticed the
moon's beauty. He is able to understand, for a moment, that Maggie might
have been better had she known how. "However, he felt that he could not
hold such a view. He threw it hastily aside" (p. 194).

A second dance-hall scene establishes the distance Maggie has fallen,
although this device seems rather strained. Now the singer wears a scarlet
gown and does a strip tease; more drinking takes place; Maggie is totally
submissive and the object of stares, as if she were not a person, but a thing.
"Grey-headed men, wonderfully pathetic in their dissipation, stared at her
through clouds. Smooth-cheeked boys, some of them with faces of stone
and mouths of sin, not nearly so pathetic as the grey heads, tried to find
the girl's eyes in the smoke wreaths. Maggie considered she was not what
they thought her" (p. 190). She is not, for she is merely a cipher, a victim;
Maggie is not now, and she never has been, an identity. In a passage at the
end of this section she shrinks from two painted women, harbingers of her
future in which she must become what people—parents, brothers, lovers,
society—make of her. The most delicate aspect of Crane's achievement in
the novel is this facelessness of his heroine that at once makes his point about
her victimization and allows him to crush her pitilessly without falling into
sentiment or bathos. The ironic mode prevails.

The third dance-hall scene transpires three weeks after Maggie has left
home. It is a wild scene, a Walpurgisnacht of noise, alcohol, savage music.
Maggie loses Pete to Nellie, an old flame, a more sophisticated woman of the
(under) world. Pete goes off with Nellie as if Maggie does not exist. Nellie's
date, "a mere boy," discusses this unfair action as if Maggie does not exist. He
even condescends to offer to sleep with her: "You look bad longsider her, but
by y'self ain't so bad. Have to do anyhow. Nell gone. O'ny you left" (p. 200)—
as if Maggie does not exist.[25] And she *does* not exist. There are no persons
or places available for her to use as a mirror for her identity. Her attempt to
return home is thwarted by her mother's cruel and indignant rebuff, "Look ut

her! Ain' she a dandy? An' she was so good as to come home teh her mudder, she was!" Jimmie echoes the mother's jeers. "Radiant virtue sat upon his brow, and his repelling hands expressed horror of contamination." The neighbors who rescue their children from Maggie's path echo again the taunts. Only the old beggar realizes that Maggie, if not a human, is at least a thing: "Well, come in an' stay wid me t'-night. I ain' got no moral standin'" (pp. 203f).

Since her family and her lover have failed to recognize her identity, Maggie must assume the only role available, the traditional role of fallen woman in which they have cast her. The third act ends with one of the finest passages of sustained power and restraint in all of Crane's writing, the chapter (XVII) that indirectly treats Maggie's death. Crane showed his realization of the importance of this chapter by paying more attention to it than to any other section of the novel when he revised his privately printed 1893 version for commercial publication in 1896. He describes a wet evening several months later; the Tenderloin aglow with lights and people as the theaters empty; an atmosphere of pleasure and prosperity, of misery and horror. Then: "A girl of the painted cohorts of the city went along the street." She has no name, no identity, for, as we have seen, whatever individuality she had possessed was denied her by those who should have cared. Now the uncaring men whom she meets, in the cleverly foreshortened series of encounters that represents the complete pattern of her decline and fall, merely repeat the rejections by Maggie's clan. Down the chain of being she goes. A handsome young man in evening dress scorns her because she is neither new, Parisian, nor theatrical. A stout gentleman, a businessman, a city tough in a derby hat, a laboring man, a nervous boy—down the path of whoredom Maggie hurries. A drunk without cash, a man with blotched features (who, in a cut passage, says that he has another date), complete her attempts at assignations. (In the earlier version she meets one more, a revolting, obese pig of a man who follows her, chuckling. Crane probably removed this character because, no matter how disgusting, he at least *sees* Maggie, in order to follow her, and for Crane's purposes she is, metaphorically, invisible.) The section ends, and Maggie's life ends, as was inevitable from the beginning, and Crane returns to the water images of the novel's start. "At the feet of the tall buildings appeared the deathly black hue of the river. Some hidden factory sent up a yellow glare, that lit for a moment the waters lapping oilily against timbers. The varied sound of life, made joyous by distance and seeming unapproachableness, came faintly and died away to a silence" (p. 211).[26]

The novel does not end yet, even though Maggie's life is played out. Since she has never been a subject, only an object, the final section of the book rightfully concentrates on the responses to her death. Chapter XVIII is a long treatment of Pete's degradation. He is slobbering, incoherent, maudlin. He mumbles about his pure motives while a gang of whores, led by Nellie, hover about, only waiting for him to pass out so they can roll him. Too much like a wood-cut of "The Corrupter Corrupted," the barroom scene is anticlimactic. The final section is also pictorial—"a woman sat at a table eating like a fat monk in a picture" (p. 216)—but wretchedly effective. To Jimmie's remark, "Mag's dead," her mother responds, " 'Deh blazes she is!' ... She continued her meal." Fitting as this sentence is as an obituary for Maggie, Crane must end the novel on the parodic note that has informed most of the work. The faked sentimentality of the mother's subsequent hysterical sobbing and her maudlin emphasis on the memory of Maggie's wearing worsted boots is an obscene—if pitiful—parody of mother love, of the familiar excesses of the fiction of domestic sentiment. With vocabulary "derived from mission churches" the mourners join the mother's laments. For all the satire, Crane's wake is effective in its own right. When the mother begs Jimmie to go and get Maggie so they can put the little boots on her feet, the narration transcends parody—without turning away from the form—and touches upon genuine anguish. And the book closes to the choir of old ladies begging the mother to forgive Maggie her sins. The final words highlight the novel's terms, as the mother weeps and screams in real pain. The parody remains operative; this version of mourning is grotesque. The ironic tone is still present—she should be begging Maggie's forgiveness. Somehow, through Stephen Crane's art, the scene attains a fine fictional effect: the Maggie who never existed as a person in her own self, when alive, is passively made into a figure to justify the society that has ignored her. "Oh, yes, I'll fergive her! I'll fergive her!" (p. 218). As he rejects the society's cheap lies, Crane's sympathy, controlled by his irony, becomes ours.

NOTES

1. Stephen Crane: *Letters*, ed. R. W. Stallman and Lillian Gilkes (New York: New York University Press, 1960), p. 14.

2. Stephen Crane, "In the Tenderloin," reprinted in *Stephen Crane: Uncollected Writings*, ed. Olov W. Fryckstedt (Uppsala, 1963), p. 200. Page references for subsequent quotations from this story are given in the text.

3. See Olov W. Fryckstedt, "Stephen Crane in the Tenderloin," *Studia Neophilologica*, 34 (1962), 135–63, for a fine study of Crane's experiences in the slums, particularly his relationship with the prostitute Dora Clark, whom he attempted to protect from the police. The girl in Crane's story seems to have elements of Dora's nature.

4. The fly passage brings to mind a similar incident in Dostoevsky's *The Idiot*, which Crane almost certainly had not read.

5. Frank Kermode, "The Prime of Miss Muriel Spark," *New Statesman*, 66 (1963), 397.

6. I have drawn on Alexander Cowie's excellent discussion of sentimental fiction in his *The Rise of the American Novel* (New York, 1948), pp. 412ff.

7. Walter F. Taylor, *The Economic Novel in America* (Chapel Hill, 1942), pp. 79–80.

8. "The Bowery and Bohemia," *The Stories of H. C. Bunner* (New York, 1916), pp. 370, 336.

9. Quoted in Mark Sullivan, *Our Times* (New York, 1926), I, 218–19.

10. Crane, letter to Catherine Harris, Nov. 12? 1896, *Letters*, p. 133.

11. The novel fits into the category called by Friedrich Engels the "old, old story of the proletarian girl seduced by a man of the middle class." Letter to Margaret Harkness, April 1888, quoted in *Documents of Modern Literary Realism*, ed. George F. Becker (Princeton, 1963), p. 483. Crane avoids, as Fawcett did not, the trap that Engels noticed in such fiction: "a mediocre writer would have attempted to disguise the trite character of the plot under a heap of artificial details and embellishment."

12. It is interesting to note that in this novel there is a character named Maggie who goes bad; Townsend's *A Daughter of the Tenements* also has a fallen Maggie.

13. "In plot, Crane's book is the most faithful of all to the stereotype ... [and involves] travesties." Leslie Fiedler, *Love and Death in the American Novel* (Cleveland, 1960), pp. 238–39.

14. Blanche Gelfant, *The American City Novel* (Norman, 1954), p. 6.

15. Helen Campbell, *The Problems of the Poor* (New York, 1882), p. 114.

16. *Stephen Crane: An Exhibition*, ed. Joan H. Baum (New York, 1956), p. 15.

17. As Crane inscribed in one presentation copy of *Maggie*, "It is indeed a brave new binding and I wish the inside were braver." To De Witt Miller, July 3, 1896, *The Modern Library in First Editions* (New York, 1938), p. 53.

18. Stephen Crane, "Fears Realists Must Wait" (1894), *Uncollected Writings*, p. 79.

19. "An Experiment in Luxury" (1894), in *Stephen Crane: Uncollected Writings*, ed. Olov W. Fryckstedt (Uppsala, 1963), pp. 47, 51. Also in 1894 Crane wrote bitterly of the contrast between the "resort of wealth and leisure" (Asbury Park) and the plodding, tired laboring men who paraded there. ("On the Jersey Coast," *ibid.*, p. 19). Although he avoids direct comment in his savage vignette of a tramp's treatment at the hands of railroad brakemen who kick him, pour icy water on him, and hurl him off a train, Crane's sympathies break through his ironies. "Billie boarded trains and got thrown off on his head, on his left shoulder, on his right shoulder, on his hands and knees. He struck the ground slanting, straight from above and full sideways.... His skin was tattooed with bloody lines, crosses, triangles" ("Billie Atkins Went to Omaha," *ibid.*, pp. 56–57).

20. See Arthur Bartlett Maurice, *The New York of the Novelists* (New York, 1916), p. 107. "'Where are Rum Alley and Devil's Row?' the present scribe asked him many years ago.... But Crane did not know. He had seen them. They were somewhere in the city. They had haunted him and still haunted him.... Stephen Crane explained that he could not have written the tale otherwise than he did. He had never been able to find in his types sunshine and sentiment and humour."

21. See William M. Gibson, "Textual and Bibliographical Note," *Stephen Crane: The Red Badge of Courage and Selected Prose and Poetry* (New York, 1956), p. xvii.

22. "The Judgment of the Sage," *Uncollected Writings*, p. 177.

23. Stephen Crane, inscription in copy of *Maggie* presented to Dr. Lucius L. Button, March 1893? *Letters*, p. 14.

24. One of Crane's earliest newspaper articles, "Travels in New York: The Broken Down Van" (1892), provides a version of the streets which Maggie walks and young Jimmie travels through on his way for beer and later traverses as a van driver: "... a girl, ten years old, went in front of the van horses with two pails of beer ... a sixteen-year-old girl without any hat and with a roll of half-finished vests under her arm crossed the front platform of the green car." *Uncollected Writings*, p. 12.

25. Crane often remarks on the difficult position of the woman who is loyal, whom the more brutal male often deserts. In "The 'Tenderloin' As It Really Is" (1896), he depicts a girl gallantly helping her man in a barroom brawl; in "Yen-Nock Bill and His Sweetheart" (1896), the faithful girl helps an opium-wrecked, pneumonia-wracked wretch back to health, and he later bullies, abuses, and rages at her.

26. See Crane's bitter little "Legends," ii, *Bookman* (New York), 3 (1896), 206: "When the suicide arrived at the sky, the people there asked him, 'Why?' He replied: 'Because no one admired me.'" The water image often stands for Crane's idea of city death. In "A Street Scene in New York" (1894) a body on the pavement is like "a bit of debris sunk in this human ocean," a "human bit of wreckage at the bottom of the sea of men" (XI, 191–92).

DANIEL WEISS

"The Blue Hotel": A Psychoanalytic Study

The Blue Hotel," as an intensive study of fear, is perhaps the finest thing Crane has done, if it is not the finest thing any American writer has produced on this subject. Behind it lie the images of terror and violence which make *The Red Badge of Courage* a masterpiece of intuition. Behind it lies the uneasy sense of invulnerability that drove Crane to test his own courage, to advance from his literary dream of "broken-bladed glory" to become in his own right the foolhardy war-correspondent who, during the Cuban war, "let himself quietly over the redoubt, lighted a cigarette, stood for a few moments with his arms at his sides, while the bullets hissed past him into the mud, then as quietly climbed back over the redoubt and strolled away."[1]

A psychoanalytic study of "The Blue Hotel" is best made within the context of Crane's other works, principally *The Red Badge of Courage*, but including subsequent war and adventure fiction. The principle of selection involves Crane's treatment of the protagonist. It is the introspective and analytic mind of Henry Fleming, or Nolan, or the New York Kid which may provide us with the keys to the beautifully articulated but hermetically sealed imagination of the Swede.

If we approach *The Red Badge of Courage* as the reconstruction on Crane's part of an emotional rather than an historical event, we emerge with an inventory of regressive aims and fantasies whose main fixtures are a variety

From *Stephen Crane: A Collection of Critical Essays*, edited by Maurice Bassan, pp. 154–164. © 1967 by Prentice-Hall, Inc.

of defenses against anxiety, and a displacement, on to the army, of parental and sibling identifications. Henry Fleming's career is a series of strategies by which he denies the existence of personal danger; these are describable in terms of counterphobic defenses, regressive magical formulae, a recourse to those mental processes which either ignore reality, or finally substitute a system of delusions linked to reality only as magical formulae are linked to the phenomena they presume to control.

To defeat anxiety one must persuade oneself that there is no cause for it. In the beginning Fleming denies danger by projecting it into the past or seeing it as a game—a "Greeklike struggle," or a "blue demonstration." Next, he denies his own fears by projecting them on to others, his mess-mate Wilson, for example, when he fortifies himself by the disparagement of others. Again, he may seek his security in the passive dependence on institutionalized parent-figures who stand omnipotently on guard over him. Fleming takes refuge within the collective maternal figure of the regiment itself, enclosing whole pods of siblings in a "moving box," the "battle brotherhood," or in the paternal shadow of the authoritarian officer on his great black horse.[2]

The movement of the novel involves in great part the failure of these illusionary defenses to sustain him against what is essentially an intra-psychic problem. The maternal regiment confuses death with self-forgetfulness; the paternal officer awakens the self-reproaches of a hostile superego, and one's fellow siblings compete for the favors of authority if they do not actually threaten one's own safety.

In the main, Henry Fleming's counterphobic techniques may be described as alternating "flights" to activity and passivity. The flight to activity involves the primitive logic of becoming the thing or person one fears and then proceeding to intimidate others. Reassurance is bound up with the obsessive display of fierceness; seeming *is* being, pretensions are genuine. At such moments tensions clamoring for discharge convert fear into anger, hatred and aggression. In *The Red Badge of Courage* the flight to activity manifests its primitive nature by the blind and objectless rage Fleming manifests on the firing line. Of the two flights it is the more truly motivated by anxiety and anxiety alone.

The flight to passivity is describable in terms of Henry Fleming's readiness to accept protection, to yield rather than to advance, to depend on the "cheery man" who leads him back to his bivouac, and to engage finally in a *fraternal* competition for the love, protection and esteem of *both* parent-symbols. His role is qualified by its being exclusively filial and submissive. His flight to passivity acquires an ethical dimension. This does not at first seem apparent until we measure his new-found valor against his new-found protectress, the flag, in terms of his inner satisfaction.

After resolving to die in the sight of the angry officer, the novel ends with Fleming's choice of role as flag-bearer, a role which is thenceforth that of the spectator among scenes of violence. It is of interest to note that when Crane finally got to see *his* war, it was not as a combatant but as a war-correspondent, a *spectator*. His behavior under fire was, as his biographer points out, "somnambulistic," passive, made up of useless gestures. The essential nature of his description of war changed but little. Thus the equation evolves: Henry Fleming, color-sergeant = Stephen Crane, war-correspondent. Having beaten his pen into a sword in *The Red Badge of Courage*, he subsequently beats it back into a pen. Yet, in his fiction, the same bronze father-images stand guard, and the same passive neophyte (behind whom now stands the war-correspondent) remains the ironist of his ordeal.

Subsequent works of fiction attest to the permanence of Crane's initial insights. "The Price of the Harness," written out of the Spanish-American War, contains familiar elements: "The whole scene would have spoken to the private soldiers of ambushes, sudden flank attacks, terrible disasters if it were not for those cool gentlemen with shoulder straps and swords, who, the private soldiers knew, were of another world and omnipotent for the business." The hero of the story, Nolan, combines in his character and the effect of his death on his comrades qualities inherent in both Jim Conklin and Henry Fleming. He is at once the passive spectator and the good soldier. Crane describes him as if, having overlaid his original fantasy with fact, he could not for the sake of integrity obscure either. Nolan, actively engaged in the charge which costs him his life, thinks:

> He had loved the regiment, the army, because the regiment, the army, was his life. He had no other outlook; and now these men, his comrades, *were performing his dream-scenes for him. They were doing as he had ordained in his visions.* It is curious that in this charge he considered himself as rather unworthy.... His part, to his mind, was merely that of a man who was going along with the crowd. [My italics.]

"The Five White Mice" illustrates with more intimate directness the relationship between fraternal competition and parental omnipotence than their institutionalized equivalents in *The Red Badge of Courage*. The New York Kid, whose companion, the drunken 'Frisco Kid, has jostled a proud Mexican, is challenged to fight. He has just bluffed his way out of losing a bet on a throw of the dice, and now his bluff is being challenged in an invitation to mortal combat. Again, as in *The Red Badge of Courage*, the same massive inhibitions against self-assertion and aggression turn the Kid's gun into an

"impotent stick." The gun he draws feels "unwieldy as a sewing machine...
Some of the eels of despair lay wet and cold against his back." At the same
moment he thinks of his father:

> He witnessed the uprising of his mother and sister, and the
> invincible calm of his hard-mouthed old father, who would
> probably shut himself in his library and smoke alone. Then his
> father would come, and they would bring him here, and say: "This
> is the place." ... He pitied his old financing father, unyielding and
> millioned, a man who commonly spoke twenty-two words a year
> to his beloved son. The Kid understood it at this time. If his fate
> was not impregnable, he might have turned out to be a man and
> have been liked by his father.

Behind the passage is Henry Fleming, who has decided to die, a "salt
reproach" to the colonel, exchanging a plausibly heroic death for a speculative
manhood. With this flashback in his mind the New York Kid draws his pistol,
convinced that he will be killed. The Mexican and his friends step back in
fear, and the Kid realizes that the "tall," "stout" Mexican, "a fine and terrible
figure," is vulnerable:

> He had never dreamed that he did not have a complete monopoly
> of all possible trepidations.... Thus the Kid was able to understand
> swiftly that they were all human beings.... He was bursting with
> rage because these men had not previously confided to him that
> they were vulnerable.... He had been seduced into respectful
> alarm by the concave attitude of the grandee. And after all there
> had been an equality of emotion—an equality!

"Had he not resembled my father as he slept," says Lady Macbeth
(her dagger as "unwieldy as a sewing machine"), "I had done't." We can,
with Crane's heroes, postulate a closed season on fathers. The Kid's flight to
activity (so out of character with the gambling man Crane has described) is
inhibited by his recognizing in the "Spanish grandee" the authoritarian figure
of his "unyielding and millioned" father. The inhibition is released when he
realizes that he has only to deal with a vulnerable sibling like himself. Here,
rage is the equivalent of laughter, a violent release from tension.

In considering "The Blue Hotel" in its psychological affinities with
Crane's other fiction of war and physical danger, we face first of all an
archeological problem. Excavating for the characterological sources of Henry
Fleming's or Nolan's or the New York Kid's actions, we have run across a

structure that is obliquely but intrinsically a part of the counterphobic techniques examined in those works. Digging on the battlefield of Homeric Troy we have found a city below the war-torn site.

The Red Badge of Courage presented a reasonably normal youth making a tolerable adjustment to an unreasonably tough situation. His anxieties were finally and convincingly assuaged when certain psychic imperatives found satisfaction under the shelter of the flag. Certain shadowy relationships, parental and sibling, resolved themselves in the process with nothing more untoward in their nature than would be compatible with the ambivalences of adolescence—identifications and projections and flights, all in the service of an urgent adjustment to danger. In "The Blue Hotel" the firm ligature of counterphobic defense techniques unites the story with the others that have been considered, but now they are in the service, not of a real danger situation, but of a paranoid delusional system and all that such a system implies. *The Red Badge of Courage* can be called a strategic fantasy of fear overcome. "The Blue Hotel" is a nightmare.

The rational framework of "The Blue Hotel" is trivial, perhaps a weakness. The widespread, half-comic assumption on the part of Easterners and Europeans in the nineties that the western United States were inhabited solely by cowpokes, Indians, and bandits, is used by Crane as a foundation for the Swede's immediate suspicion of everyone. But the Swede, like Bartleby the Scrivener, is too austere an "isolato," the very mask of fear, to be measured by ordinary standards. He ennobles the trumpery plot.

The Swede, with some other travelers, arrives at the Palace Hotel, Nebraska, convinced from the start that he will be robbed and murdered by the proprietor, Pat Scully, his son Johnnie, or one of the cowboy transients about the place. At first he is timidly apprehensive, then hysterically frightened. Scully calms him down and invites him to play a friendly game of cards with the group. The Swede now undergoes a complete change of personality. He plays cards with manic verve, "board-whacking" as he takes his tricks. The card game is upset when he accuses the proprietor's son, Johnnie, of cheating, and then beats him in a fist fight. Flushed with this triumph he extends his circle to the local saloon where, trying to browbeat the local gambler into drinking with him, he meets the death he has long feared. The Easterner speaks the epilogue. Johnnie, he says to the cowboy, *was* cheating. "And you—you were simply puffing around the place and wanting to fight. And then old Scully himself! We are all in it.... Every sin is the result of a collaboration. We, five of us, have collaborated in the murder of this Swede."

In discussing *The Red Badge of Courage*, I touched upon Henry Fleming's attempts, first and last, to still his excitement by seeing the war first as a "blue demonstration" and finally as a "matched game." As a defense against a danger situation, either one's own rebellious impulses or an environmental threat, the game satisfies the compulsion to repeat in a mitigated, controlled form an experience which was originally terrifying. Children's games often play out deaths, murders, mutilations, with the child playing the active role in a drama which originally cast him as its passive, frightened victim. Such games, as we all know, are played with a frantic joy that comes close to being pain. It is, in fact, a joy that celebrates a release from painful anxieties.

There is, in the stories we have considered, a sort of "game syndrome" that operates in this way. We have seen it in the imagery of the "matched game" of *The Red Badge of Courage*. It shows itself briefly in "The Price of the Harness" in Nolan's relegating the charge he is engaged in to a level of "dream-scenes." In "The Five White Mice" the game is more ambitiously employed: it is an analogous foreshadowing of the main action. The New York Kid in a friendly dice game in the Mexican bar puts fifty dollars, sight unseen, on a die. There are no takers; the die is a low number; he would have lost. The same bluff and backing-down takes place in the street, in what the Kid thinks of as the "unreal real." This time it is the Kid himself who is the losing die, and the Spanish grandee is the timid bettor who will not call the Kid's bluff. The full psychological function of the game as a release from anxiety is subordinated to its value as a symbolic statement of self-evaluation. The Kid says, in effect, "I am not what I seem to be, but only my father will call my bluff."

In "The Blue Hotel" the play's the thing, and Crane apparently knew it, the same way he knew something about the Swede's mind, somewhere between a conscious and an intuitive level of insight. As a man the Swede is past redemption; the game of cards is not his undoing. It merely serves as the last scrap of reality on which he can found his delusions of persecution.

When the Swede enters the hotel, Scully's son Johnnie and an old farmer are playing cards for fun. Serious money-gambling is too close to reality for mock-hostility to function as it does in child's play. Playing for fun, Johnnie and the old man are engaged in serious quarrels over their game. Following each such outburst the Swede laughs nervously, and makes some remark about the dangers of Western life, incomprehensible to the others. When he is first invited into the game, he plays nervously and quietly, while the cowboy is the "board-whacker." "A game with a board-whacker in it is sure to become intense," and for the Swede the intensity, because all occasions inform against him, becomes unendurable, and he voices his fears: "I suppose I am going to be killed before I can leave this house!"

Old Scully, with a fine sense of the problem, exhibits the domesticity of his life to the Swede, pictures of his wife and dead daughter, an account of his sons and the life of the town. He draws the Swede into the circle of fraternal fellowship to which his son, the cowboy, and the transients of the Palace Hotel belong. The Swede, finally induced to take a drink (which he first rejects, as Scully says, because he "thought I was tryin' to poison 'im"), discharges all the energy that was a part of his anxiety in an outburst of false relief. He becomes a part of the family with a vengeance, presiding over the supper table with a joyless, feverish joy: "The Swede domineered the whole feast, and he gave it the appearance of a cruel bacchanal. He seemed to have grown suddenly taller; he gazed, brutally disdainful, into every face. His voice rang through the room."

When he plays cards again with the group he becomes the "board-whacker" while the cowboy is reduced to a sad silence. It is the discovery of Johnnie's cheating which precipitates the catastrophic sequel. The Swede is mad; he "fizzed like a fire-wheel"; but the game of cards is a benign way for him to work off his aggressions harmlessly, his hostilities intelligently displaced to the card table. Ironically, however, the game is denied its therapeutic value. The scrap of reality that will revive the Swede's original delusion, which he has not relinquished, merely mastered, is provided by the fact that Johnnie is *really* cheating. *Real* cheating in a game for fun violates the make-believe, like acid in a water-pistol. For the Swede the cheating restores the game to the world of outlaws, professional gamblers, and gunmen. It then follows, with maniacal logic and poetic justice both, that the next and last victim of the Swede's attentions should be the town's professional gambler, whom the Swede unwittingly but unerringly singles out. He is the institutionalized reality of which Johnnie was merely the precursor.

I have reviewed here the elements which relate most apparently to Henry Fleming's actions in *The Red Badge of Courage*. The Swede exhibits, albeit madly, alternate flights to passivity and activity. Wary apprehension succeeds to panic and a passive acceptance of annihilation, to be succeeded by a triumph of mastery, an identification with the aggressor, the pursuer and no longer the pursued. And above all, there is the framework of the game, danger passing off in play, only to return again as danger.

There are other resemblances, however, obscured, not by their existing in "The Blue Hotel" as traces, but because in "The Blue Hotel" these elements are more intense. They have the vividness of mania.

The inference in connection with paranoid delusions of persecution is that the subject is defending himself against his own homosexuality. In his relations with other men he denies his love by substituting an equally dynamic attraction—that of hate. He then denies the hate itself, since it lacks any foundation in reality, and puts upon him, moreover, the guilty burden of aggression, and projects his hatred upon the object of his original desire.

The ego in such cases regresses from its ability to test reality to the archaic delusional systems, the animistic world of childhood, in which all nature is equally sensate. Thus the wish to be the passive victim of some homosexual violation may express itself in the fear of such violation—which displaces itself to other bodily openings. The fears arise in connection with being poisoned, invaded by dangerous rays, brainwashed, etc. What may also result is that the paranoid may identify *with* his persecutor in order actively to do *to* him what he might otherwise have suffered himself. The transformation of the repressed erotic attraction in favor of an overt sadistic aversion finds its literary expression in such relationships as Prince Hal's and Harry Hotspur's, "I will embrace him with a soldier's arm," or Claggart's persecution of Billy Budd in Melville's novel.

The Swede's emotional swing from apprehensive depression to manic elation reflects, internalized, the same battlefield as that on which Henry Fleming fought his fears. The problems of self-esteem, alienation, and reunion with the omnipotent superior present themselves, along with the techniques of mastery involved. We can only add, tentatively, in view of the Swede's paranoid delusions, that the Swede's anxieties involve the mastery of his own homosexual aggressions rather than a threat from the external world.

Anyone arriving in a strange town will experience that sense of narcissistic starvation that comes with the feeling that one is a social cypher in the life of the community. The Swede, psychotic to begin with, arrives, already prejudiced, in the small Western town, bringing with him a massive and insatiable need for reassurance against his own unfathomed wishes.

"We'll git swallowed," says a soldier meekly, just before a charge in *The Red Badge of Courage*. It is perfectly descriptive of the oral level of fixation that prevails in a raging battle. Eat or be eaten. The Swede's repressed oral fixations involve "swallowing" the world in order to be reunited with omnipotence, the way a hungry child cleaves savagely to the breast that comforts it. But the obverse side of the coin is his manifest fear that the world will just as savagely attack him.

In this spirit he refuses the first drink Scully offers him as if Scully's teeth were at his throat. But Scully's kindness and the drink itself, once he has swallowed it and found it harmless—experiences which would, with a rational man, effect a pleasant reunion with society—return the Swede's impulse to its original, uninhibited form. Scully behaves like a father toward the Swede. What is more he offers him the oral satisfaction of a drink. "'Drink,' said the old man affectionately.... The Swede laughed wildly. He grabbed the bottle, put it to his mouth; and as his lips curled absurdly around the opening and his throat worked, he kept his glance, *burning with hatred*, upon the old man's face" [my italics]. The image is the image of a fierce baby, its feeding time long overdue, glaring over the nipple at the source of its relief.

The combined gestures are the symbolic fulfillment of a deeply repressed fantasy. Scully has, in effect, "adopted" the Swede, whose exaggerated need for assurance and oral sadistic drives will extend themselves to the absorption of everything and everyone in sight. His foster father, Scully, he swallows at one gulp. A few minutes after he has drunk he is contradicting Scully "in a bullying voice," or has "stalked with the air of an owner off into the executive parts of the hotel." He must enter into this cannibalistic relationship with everyone at once. In the card game he takes all the tricks. At supper he almost impales the Easterner's hand as they reach for the same biscuits. His fight with Johnnie is a still more intimate encounter, a sibling struggle for the attention of the same father, the translation into sadistic (and therefore socially plausible) activity of the Swede's repressed homoerotic drives. There is no clear line here between the various components which move the Swede to action. His mind is a graveyard of decaying realities, baseless fears, disguised desires, and futile strategies.

Manic elation is the literal rendering of the ancient "Whom the gods destroy they first make mad." Its shrill laughter and high spirits and sense of unlimited power are a celebration of the release of the ego from the bonds of a self-derogatory conscience. Now the ego has become the lord of its own misrule and embarks on defiant pursuit of forbidden pleasures, which here involve the aggressive humiliation of other men. The Swede discharges his new, liberated energies in cards, drinking, and fighting. He has achieved his reunion with omnipotence at the expense of his intellect. He had begun in self-effacing humility by fearing for his life; he ends, bloated with his triumph over his imagined persecutors. He *is* the group. His commanding the gambler to drink with him, the sadistic counterpart to Scully's earlier, kinder command, is his moment of *hubris*. He has become the manic travesty of the father. The gambler knifes him, the knife itself a translation (and therefore socially acceptable, more so, at least, than its phallic equivalent) of the Swede's repressed wish for sexual violation; and like an enchantment dispelled, the Swede reverts to his former role of the passive, helpless victim of another man. "The Blue Hotel" has, incidentally, been compared with Hemingway's "The Killers." And this is interesting, because psychologically, they are diametrical opposites meeting only at the antipodes, in fear itself. Ole Andreson, in "The Killers," exemplifies in almost pathological terms the flight to passivity, the "strategic abandonment of hope," in his fatalistic resignation to death. The Swede is the other side of the coin, a pathological flight to activity.

The Easterner's self-accusatory indictment of all of them as murderers—
"Every sin is the result of a collaboration"—is too oriental, too transcendental
a statement to be confined within a blue hotel or a platitude of social
consciousness. It has karmic ramifications, whose psychological equivalents
are consistent with that omniscient "Indefinite Cause" which threatens to
seal Henry Fleming's doom, that fascinated dread and disbelief with which
Crane's characters enter on to the stage as spectators and actors both. In
summing up "The Five White Mice" John Berryman writes, "The Kid's
faith, in substance—Crane's new faith—is in Circumstance as *not* making
impossible the individual's determination of his destiny."[3] It is, we may say,
Crane's vision of normality, a mind turned outward upon the world, away
from its crippling presentiments. The Easterner's epilogue, as it gestures
inward towards an infinity of secret causes, is Crane's cry of resignation.

NOTES

1. John Berryman, *Stephen Crane* (New York, 1950), p. 222.
2. Relevant discussions of anxiety, defense mechanisms, and the psychology of
combat are to be found in the following works: Otto Fenichel, *The Psychoanalytic Theory
of Neurosis* (New York, 1945), pp. 122, 126; H. W. Frink, *Morbid Fears and Compulsions*
(London, 1925); A. Kardiner and H. Spiegel, *War Stress and Neurotic Illness* (New York,
1947); "Real Warfare," in *The American Soldier, Combat and Its Aftermath* (Princeton, 1949),
Vol. II; and Gregory Zilboorg, "Fear of Death," *Psychoanalytic Quarterly*, XII (October
1943).
3. Berryman, p. 110.

CHESTER L. WOLFORD

This Booming Chaos:
Crane's Search for Transcendence

The Old World has had the poems of myths, fictions, feudalism, conquest, caste, dynastic wars, and splendid exceptional characters and affairs, which have been great; but the New World needs the poems of realities.

WHITMAN
"A Backward Glance o'er Travel'd Roads"

And not to have is the beginning of desire.
You must become an ignorant man again
And see the sun again with an ignorant eye
And see it clearly in the idea of it.

STEVENS
"Notes toward a Supreme Fiction"

TRAVELING INWARD

Stephen Crane was nearly a writer of epic. Certainly he wrote the great American epic into *The Red Badge*, but then he wrote it out again, mocking accepted notions of heroism central to Western consciousness. Crane depicted archetypes of unconsciousness very early in his career, particularly in the Sullivan County, New York City, and Asbury Park sketches, where he approached transcendence only occasionally, as in "Killing His Bear."

From *The Anger of Stephen Crane: Fiction and the Epic Tradition*, pp. 127–148. © 1983 by the University of Nebraska Press.

Transcendence, when it appears, tends to exist in the stories separate from and unperceived by the protagonists, as in "The Reluctant Voyagers." Later, in *Maggie*, Crane scoffed at the idea that any world existed except the material, and his scoffing was aided by his use of a classical hierarchy of gods and goddesses of heaven (Sol and Phaethon) and hell (Dis and Proserpina) to mock ideas about transcendence to either higher or lower planes of existence—one of the reasons, as Gullason explains, that *Maggie* fails as a tragedy.[1] After writing *The Red Badge* Crane traveled west for Bacheller's Syndicate in 1895 and saw for himself what Frederick Jackson Turner was showing: the frontier was closed. Possessed like any other American by the myth of manifest destiny, Crane nevertheless knew that the myth had been invalidated. Consequently, his western stories portray the demise of an almost heroic, nearly Homeric society. Into the garden of Crane's idea of the West had come the machine: a society of Pullmans, electric streetcars, businessmen, and progress. If the former was naive, bombastic, and childishly honest, the latter was insidious, conspiratorial, and corrupt.

The West encompassed an irony interesting to Crane: the early western society was old to the world but new to white America; the society that replaced it was relatively new to the world but old to the United States. By blending these histories with classical allusions and genres Crane revitalized and universalized his theme and its ironies. The American West was simply the latest example of the recurring death of an ageless dream of possibility, of starting anew in a new land, a dream possessed by most epic heroes. To take the epic to task on its own terms is a requirement for writers of epic, but then to attempt systematically to destroy the epic's claim to veracity is perhaps unprecedented. To the degree that he succeeded, Crane may have called in question beliefs about myth, history, religion, government, and perhaps many of mankind's other cultural foundations.

During 1897 and 1898, when most of his great short stories were written, Crane's interest in exposing cultural aspects of epic to ridicule begins to diminish and in some works his obvious use of traditional epic lessens. Certainly, those devices of epic which stood him in good stead in *The Red Badge* do not disappear entirely; still, one of the less cultural elements of epic always more or less present in his work begins to accrue comparatively more importance: the requirement that the protagonist face death squarely and by doing so overcome it. Transcendence seems to result more from the protagonist's individual strengths than from his cultural strengths. "The Open Boat," written shortly after Crane was shipwrecked in January of 1897, and "Death and the Child," published not long after Crane first saw battle in the Greco-Turkish War of 1897, illustrate this shift in Crane's interests from cultural to individual (or psychological) aspects of epic. Manifest destiny takes a turn in Crane and begins to look for a way to conquer the "other" by mastering the self.

To be sure, "The Open Boat" repudiates traditional epic, and the repudiation begins, as is common for Crane's stories, with the first paragraph:

> None of them knew the color of the sky. Their eyes glanced level, and were fastened upon the waves that swept toward them. These waves were of the hue of slate, save for the tops, which were of foaming white, and all of the men knew the color of the sea. The horizon narrowed and widened, and dipped and rose, and at all times the edge was jagged with waves that seemed to thrust up in points like rocks. [5:68]

The main thrust of the paragraph is that these four men are utterly absorbed by the sea, or, in terms of the epic of consciousness, that they are battling an archetype of unconsciousness. The first sentence is pointedly after-the-fact and contributes both to the notion of the men's absorption and to the idea that they are bereft, permanently or temporarily, of those qualities symbolized by the sky: light, knowledge, consciousness. While the first is Crane's most often quoted sentence, its complement is seldom mentioned, even though it is at least as important as the first: "all of the men knew the color of the sea." There may be, as well, in the simile of the waves as rocks a deliberate allusion to the famous Wandering, or Clashing, Rocks of Homer's *Odyssey* and Apollonius's *Argonautica*.

On one level a perfectly accurate and impressionistic description, on another level the paragraph's last sentence serves as a literary allusion supporting shifting reference points on and above the water. Occasionally in Greek epics heroes lose their frame of reference. Odysseus, for example, temporarily loses sight of his goal while a captive in Calypso's cave. More specifically, he and, earlier, the Argonauts of Apollonius's epyllion temporarily lose sight of the sky while they pass through the tented waves of the Wandering Rocks. Crane could have chosen this allusion for many reasons, but one of the most important may have been that it depicts a moment during a sea journey when, even in classical epics, what appears to be true is not. The difference between these Greek works and Crane's is that in the former the condition is temporary, while the language of "The Open Boat" suggests that man may be permanently benighted. The *Odyssey*, the *Argonautica*, and "The Open Boat" concern a quest for "home," but only in "The Open Boat" does the quest seem to be futile. Odysseus knows he will reach home. Most of the Argonauts, informed by various oracles or by such signs from the sky as birds, stars, and thunderings, know they will return. Some know they will not. Even ancient audiences knew who would and who would not survive. The men in the dingey have no such assurance. And the reader is assured only of the survival of one to tell the story.

"The Open Boat" is extremely inclusive, for it seems that not only classical epics, but Christian ones as well, specifically Dante's *Inferno*, are targets for Crane's irony, as Kenneth Reed has shown. The point of allusions and parallels to classical and Christian epic in "The Open Boat" may be to invert the epics' original intentions. This would be consistent with Crane's earlier uses of epic allusions. "The Open Boat" may provide, as Reed says, "a dramatic illustration of the naturalist's rejection of the fundamental principle that human experience may lead to moral certainty."[2]

This view, described by Gerstenberger as "epistemological existentialism," makes "The Open Boat" a story about "man's inability to know anything about the complex whole of existence."[3] The story may be explained epically in exactly the same terms as *The Red Badge*. Having sloughed off cultural beliefs in the first two-thirds of the story—there are "no bricks and no temples"—the correspondent comes finally to a confrontation with death, and the narrator relates it in the present tense as a purely existential reflection: "Perhaps an individual must consider his own death to be the final phenomenon of nature" (5:91). At this point in the story the correspondent faces death and perhaps achieves a kind of transcendence. Unceremoniously dumped into the sea, that grand archetype of the unconscious, and yet utterly conscious at the same time, the correspondent is momentarily caught in an undertow and considers his own death. His achieving this conscious unconsciousness, during which his mind revolves like a man in a maelstrom around the question of his own death, would seem to be much like Henry Fleming's discovery of heroism in *The Red Badge*: man has transcended nature by transcending himself. Moreover, if the ending of the story is as ironical as it is lyrical—and some have pointed out that lyricism in Crane signals irony—then the correspondent, like Henry, also forgets what he has learned; the idea that they can then "be interpreters" is absurd: "When it came night, the white waves paced to and fro in the moonlight, and the wind brought the sound of the great sea's voice to the men on shore, and they felt that they could then be interpreters" (5:92).

But "The Open Boat" is, as Conrad said, "a symbolic tale." It is also so finely shaped that it tends to act as a prism for almost any well-polished and intelligent interpretation to penetrate and yield a finely ordered array of colors. This quality alone would make the story, for Aristotle, Crane's best; it is so inclusive as to support an opposite interpretation from that discussed here. One which concludes that the men do learn and which further illuminates Crane's use of epic is that summarized by J. C. Levenson, who discusses the story in terms of "the fiction of consciousness": "'The Open Boat' is ... a movement toward understanding. Technically, the fiction of consciousness simply makes dramatically immediate the way things felt.... Formally ... there are cumulative changes whereby men, though they cannot control what happens, can at least come to a rational perception of their fate" (5:lxvi–lxvii).

The last paragraph can be looked at differently under this light. The paragraph is lyrical because true: the interpretation of the men lies in the content of nature: white waves, moonlight, the "great sea's voice," *and* the imaginative construct of the paragraph, which creates beauty and order and value in a meaningless universe. Here, then, the transcendence is permanent, or at least has the capability of being permanent.[4] As Levenson puts it:

> The expansion of consciousness leads at last to the encounter with that absolute finality, the extinction of consciousness. The progress from self-engrossment to clear vision, from fanciful outrage to puzzled acceptance, is a growth of moral intelligence which does not simply come from within. The encounter with reality has made a crucial difference. From it the men *learn*.... Self-mastery and self-knowledge come only with the capacity to interpret the world outside oneself. [5:lxviii]

Levenson has described not only "The Open Boat" here, but also a prerequisite for epic transcendence. The only addition to be made is that Levenson's last sentence is reversible for epic: the capacity to interpret the world outside oneself comes only with self-mastery and self-knowledge. Drained of all physical strength, immersed in the unconscious energy of the sea, the correspondent reflects unconsciousness through his repetitions, his chants of "Can it be possible? Can it be possible?" An extraordinary consciousness is conveyed by his reflecting upon his death as nature's "final phenomenon."

Crane throws bricks at cultural temples in "The Open Boat," but soon discovering that "there are no bricks and no temples," he spends more time than ever before facing the prerequisite for transcendence: death. He also advances from the clear denunciation of a lasting epic transcendence in *The Red Badge* to the deliberate ambivalence of "The Open Boat." The question is: Is the last paragraph ironic?

Separated from the rest of the canon, "The Open Boat" remains beautifully ambivalent. And since everything to come before that story clearly repudiates lasting epic transcendence, it would be nice to accept Levenson's reading that the "men do learn," and learn permanently. There are two problems with this interpretation, sound as it may be. First, as

Griffith shows, all of Crane's lyrical endings earlier than "The Open Boat" are patently ironic:[5] *Maggie*, *The Red Badge*, and "The Veteran" to cite only three. Second, "Death and the Child," a story which follows "The Open Boat" chronologically as one of his greatest and which also follows the pattern of the epic of consciousness, provides an ending more devastatingly ironic in terms of epic and nihilistic in terms of life than any of Crane's other works: Peza is Crane's Kurtz, albeit a pale copy, for Peza has only imagined the horror. If transcendence occurred in "Death and the Child," there would be grounds for accepting a "transcendent" interpretation of "The Open Boat" as *the* interpretation. But since there are none, it is difficult to exclude the possibility that the ending of "The Open Boat" is ironic.

If Crane is finally able to deal at length with the existential heart of epic—facing death—in "The Open Boat" in part because he had come so close to death, he is able perhaps to pursue the subject again in "Death and the Child" because of what he saw in Greece only four months after his experience off Daytona Beach. Greece was another disillusionment for Crane, much like his trip west, but even more so. Holton suggests that Crane first retreated from staring at reality as a result of his Greek experiences, having discovered there that "war is only an instinctive killing, conducted and then marveled at by a gawking crowd. For the sensitive man ... like Crane ... there is only one possible response. From this intolerable reality he can only turn away."[6]

It is possible that Crane also turned away even further from his classical sources because of this experience. "I'd a great idea of Greece," he said after returning to England from reporting what was then popularly known as the Thirty Days' War but is now called the Greco-Turkish War of 1897: "Say, when I planted those hoofs of mine on Greek soil, I felt like the hull of Greek literature."[7] If the past tense is significant in contrasting his feelings before with those after his first war experience, then it would be safe to say that the "great idea of Greece" had been shattered. Certainly the Greek nation was, because from about mid-April through mid-May of 1897 Greek forces were routed on all fronts, largely, if not exclusively, through the apparent incompetence and inexperience of the Greek rulers. Retreat after seemingly needless retreat was ordered, often from nearly impregnable positions and occasionally long before Turkish forces arrived at the scene. Only one of many examples, "Crane at Velestino" (9:19–23) provides a barely controlled description of Crane's own private disappointment at Greece's national disgrace:

I hoped the Greeks on the plain would hurry and drive the Turks
from their position. They did this gallantly in a short, ferocious

infantry fight in the woods. The bit of woods seemed to be on
fire. After a great rattling and banging the Turks went out. After
this attack and defeat there was general rejoicing along the Greek
lines and satisfaction all over. The officers walked proudly, the
men in the trenches grinned. Then, mind you, just at this time,
late in the afternoon; after another successful day, came orders to
retreat.... I send this from Volo and before you print it the Turks
will be here.

On another occasion, in "The Blue Badge of Cowardice" (9:44–48), Crane
expressed it succinctly, angrily, and outright, almost as if he himself had been
personally insulted: "Back fell the Greek army, wrathful, sullen, fierce as any
victorious army would be when commanded to retreat before the enemy it
had defeated." Crane is clearly on the side of Greece; of that nation and its
literature he clearly had "a great idea."

Crane's disillusionment takes other and varied forms throughout his
war reports from Greece, and many times, its form is one of contrast between
the Greece of which he had had "a great idea" and the Greece he saw before
him. In describing "a certain part of the Greek nature" foreign to "the Anglo-
Saxon," Crane mentions "a battery of howitzers on a hill above the mosque
and the bullet-swept square. The captain of this battery walked out to his
position at middle-rear. He addressed his men. His chest was well out, and
his manner was gorgeous. If one could have judged by the tone, it was one of
the finest speeches of the age. It was Demosthenes returned and in command
of a battery of howitzers" (9:32–33). William Spofford locates "more than
fifty-five instances" of Crane's using or describing oratory.[8] In every instance,
insincerity is implied, along with puffery, egotism, and lying. Dredging up
Demosthenes for this comparison would indicate that already Crane's idea
of ancient Greece was being modified by what he was seeing of its modern
counterpart, but it also sheds a certain classical light on Crane's considerable
use of the notion of oratory in other works, particularly *The Red Badge*.

Still, on the rare occasion that Crane could report even a minor victory,
as toward the end of "A Fragment of Velestino" (9:27–44), his positive image
of Greece is reinforced by the centuries that lay behind Greek civilization
and pervaded, for example, the evening after a victorious day. Reading the
description immediately evokes Greek shepherds resting above the plains of
Troy:

There were some mountaineer volunteers in great woolly grey
shepherds' cloaks. They were curious figures in the evening light,
perfectly romantic if it were not for the modernity of the rifles

and the shining lines of cartridges. With the plain a sea of shadow below them, these men sang softly the wild minor ballads of the hills. As the evening deepened many men ... slept, but these grey-cloaked mountaineers continued to sing.... They sang of war, and their songs were new to the sense, reflecting the centuries of their singing, and as the ultimate quiet of night came to the height this low chanting was the only sound. [9:44]

In "Death and the Child," a youth named Peza becomes caught up in this Greek war song, only to have its tempo change to that of a horrifying dirge. Initially meeting a young veteran officer who, as Eric Solomon says, "accepts the role of Virgil to Peza's Dante,"[9] Peza is guided to "the top of a great hill," where he begins observing the inferno below: "Before them was a green plain as level as an inland sea" (5:124). Like the ocean of "The Open Boat," this "inland sea," this battlefield, provides the archetype of unconsciousness, the "cave" of "Death and the Child." Surrounded by mountains, the plain also contains "little black lines from which floated slanting sheets of smoke.... It was war" (5:124–135). Although Peza here does much observing, and no doubt becomes more conscious as a result (he is "edified, aghast, triumphant"), Peza is less prescient than the narrator who mocks him: "It was not a battle to the nerves. One could survey it [the battlefield] with equanimity, as if it were a tea-table" (5:124–25).

So Peza "bounded" down the hill toward the battle. The young officer finally leaves Peza with some soldiers at a place where there may soon be some heavy fighting. In the process Peza learns several things: (1) "the accidental destruction of an individual, Peza by name, would perhaps be nothing at all"; (2) that his death "would be as romantic, to the old standards, as death by a bit of falling iron in a factory"; (3) that the peasant soldiers were generally much more calm than he; (4) that after entering the battle zone, acting like "a corpse walking, on the bottom of the sea," and conceding that the wounded men may, like him, have "dreamed at lightning speed until the capacity for it was overwhelmed" (5:130), he finally realizes that "pity had a numerical limit." He no longer says, "those poor people," as he had in the beginning. Peza has a vision of finally reaching the "bottom of the abyss" when he finds himself below the battle: "In the vale there was an effect as if one was then beneath the battle. It was going on above somewhere. Alone, unguided, Peza felt like a man groping in a cellar."

That there is no transcendence, temporary or otherwise, in "Death and the Child" is made clear by the fact that Peza runs, like Henry, only never to return. Moreover, Henry had run from a real danger, an enemy with guns. Peza runs from an hallucination about dead men. Still, Peza's vision is much more horrifying than Henry Fleming's. And last, there occurs one of Crane's final descriptions of hell, a description more horrifying in the circumstances than those hells described in "An Experiment in Misery," *Maggie*, *The Red Badge*, and several other stories. It is also more obviously classical. Having come to a place where he might soon be in battle, Peza is armed with a dead man's rifle, which has the "crawling and frightful"movements of a "serpent" (5:139), and the cartridge bandoleer of another, which makes him feel "that the dead man had flung his two arms around him" (5:138). All dressed up for war with rifle, shells, and a new white hat, Peza faces the final confrontation which must be overcome before transcendence is possible:

> He looked behind him, and saw that a head by some chance had been uncovered from its blanket. Two liquid-like eyes were staring into his face. The head was turned a little sideways as if to get a better opportunity for the scrutiny. Peza could feel himself blanch; he was being drawn and drawn by these dead men slowly, firmly down as to some mystical chamber under the earth where they could walk, fearful figures, swollen and blood-marked. He was bidden; they had commanded him; he was going, going, going.
>   ... the man in the new white hat bolted for the rear. [5:139]

If Peza had lost some "egotism" by obeying the young officer's commands, he would have been annihilated by obeying these commandments, but perhaps would have achieved a kind of transcendence. But he doesn't, and once again Crane exhibits his fundamental belief that "conceit is the very engine of life."

Peza survives, climbing the mountain again, but neither pretending to see that the world was a world "for him," as does Henry Fleming, nor thinking that he could then be an "interpreter," but rather to lie gasping "in the manner of a fish" (5:141).

The child who had watched the battle from afar and who had been throughout a human personification of nature—indifferent or at most mildly interested in the goings on in the valley—is also a more devastating symbol in that he is probably doomed to repeat Peza's experience, as are all children in any age. When the child asks "Are you a man?" the answer is dearly "yes." Crane's idea of the human condition has changed. Henry Fleming, for example, is defeated because he can't sustain his vision. According to Holton, on the other hand, "it is Peza's very capacity to apprehend which has defeated and dehumanized him."[10] One can agree that Peza is defeated by his apprehensions without believing that he has also been dehumanized

by them. The human condition seems to be one of confronting reality and
then running from it in horror. The act of facing the horror and transcending
makes epic heroes heroes, because in doing so they become somewhat more
than human. It is in the failure, in the tragedy of not quite transcending reality
after the pain and struggle, that one is reminded of the hero's humanity.

When Crane returned from reporting the Greco-Turkish War, he said
that *The Red Badge* "is all right."[11] But it wasn't, for the very metaphor that
manifests Henry Fleming's heroism—his impression of an individual blade
of grass—becomes the metaphor for Peza's defeat: Peza "knew that the
definition of his misery could be written on a wee grass-blade" (5:141).

TURNING OUTWARD

After "The Open Boat" and "Death and the Child," Crane either grew tired
of his self-imposed task of exposing the innumerable illusions by which men
live or he began to see possibilities in a new area based more upon affirmation
than upon denial. After his Greek experience, he seemed never again to be so
sure of himself. Perhaps he could not be sure that even his repudiations had
been correct. To deny the epic, for example, requires certainty that the epic
is wrong. In life, one may proceed by saying that something is or is not true,
but Crane's art of denial, his repudiations of the accumulated assumptions of
millennia, becomes ambivalent in "The Open Boat" and downright horrifying
in "Death and the Child." Perhaps Holton is right and Crane "turned away,"
but perhaps Crane simply no longer had a strong commitment to the belief
that certain things were false.

Whatever the reason, Crane's quarrel with epic and its illusions
disappears from his work after 1898, and he seems to have spent his
remaining time, as Stallman and Liebling say, either writing the sort
of thing that would get him out of debt or casting about in a somewhat
confused attempt to work his way out of artistic uncertainty.[12] Much may be
accounted for by the simple fact that after reporting the Spanish-American
War, Crane was very sick. Even more than in the earlier stories, a riot of
shifting points of view, wrong interpretations, and unanswered questions fill
the later stories. "War Memories," for example, lacks any epic background,
and yet its sentences are continually placed in the interrogative, more so
even than in *The Red Badge*.

The difference is that the unifying power of epic is gone.

By repudiating the epic and all it stands for—nationalism, patriotism,
the greatness of individual and collective man, the existence of supernatural
powers that care and protect and guide—Crane, in his life and in his best
work, faced the horror of a meaningless universe as squarely as anyone has.

That he took no respite, in spite of malaria and tuberculosis, is perhaps unparalleled. It probably shortened his life.

While few deny that Crane's art broke down after the great period of 1897 to early 1898, some of the later pieces may illuminate where he might have gone had he lived long enough to pick up the pieces. Since Crane apparently belonged to the group of American writers whose "quest for a supreme fiction" is a driving force, he had to go beyond his repudiations. Although the lines are far from clear-cut, the evident distinction between his best works and the lesser, particularly the later, works indicates that he did. The best works tend to conform to a definition of modernism given by Altieri: modern literature tends, albeit often negatively, toward "impersonality (i.e., formalism, overtly mythical [epical] themes and constructs, the use of persona, and a stress on complex and paradoxical statements)."[13] Nagel has said that "the interpretive uncertainties of [Crane's] Impressionism foreshadow ... much of Post-Modernism."[14] While perceptive and true, this observation is so in part because both impressionism and modernism foreshadow the postmodern revolt. Crane is impressionistic throughout his career, and in that sense is postmodern. But Crane's great works, to the degree that they fit period definitions, are modern. His often bad later works tend to fit Altieri's definition of postmodernism as a movement emphasizing "the direct, the personal, the local, the anti-formal, and the topical."

Formalism in Crane—his use of myth, epic, and literary tradition in general—has been the subject of this book, but his use of persona and paradox are also well known. Maggie is not Crane, nor, certainly, is Henry Fleming, and while the correspondent in the dingey is in a way a Crane stand-in, he is so only as one undergoing the experience. The narrator of "The Open Boat," on the other hand, is the after-the-fact presence. The correspondent is decidedly a persona.

The personae of the best works tend to give way later to Crane surrogates, especially in some of the war stories, where the line between journalism and fiction grows fuzzy: Little Nell, Shackles, Johnnie, and Vernall.[15] In "Marines Signaling under Fire at Guantanamo" (6:194–200), even the surrogate is removed and the narrator is "I." While the "direct" tone advanced by some of these characters may be a result of the stories' closeness to newspaper dispatches, that tone does not necessarily explain such direct addresses to the reader as appear, for example, at the end of "War Memories": "The episode is closed. And you can depend upon it that I have told you nothing at all, nothing at all, nothing at all" (6:263).

"War Memories" also exposes some of Crane's rare personal moods, moods which sometimes verge on a nineteenth-century equivalent to contemporary "confessional" poetry. Most of Crane's readers knew who he was, knew he was covering the war, and could be expected to assume that Vernall, the "I" of the story and a correspondent, was Crane. What Vernall says is accurate, but not the kind of thing one reported about oneself to a nation sending the cream of its youth off to lick the Spanish. Having just made friends with one of those fine young men, a surgeon named Gibbs, Vernall soon finds Gibbs shot and dying, "dying hard. It took him a long time to die.... I thought this man would never die. I wanted him to die" (6:226–27). This statement is very personal, almost embarrassing in print even today, but certainly accurate. Yet it has little in it of the desire to shock so common in Crane, although that can be found easily enough even in the late writing.[16] Later he describes his great fear at the prospect of going on patrol the next day: "All that night I was afraid. Bitterly afraid. In the morning I wished for some mild attack of disease, something that would incapacitate me for the business of going out gratuitously to be bombarded" (6:228). Much of the remainder of the story is a description of fear and ineffectiveness. Crane was beginning, in the war stories drawn from experience, to write in a new subjective voice, so much so that he was often parodied for, of all things, egotism:

> I have seen a battle.
> I find it is very like what
> I wrote up before.
> I congratulate myself that
> I ever saw a battle.
> I am pleased with the sound of war.[17]

On occasion, however, Crane can be both personal and classical. That is, he can describe war in his own voice and be directly allusive, as in this description from "War Memories," where the correspondent has "a fine view of the Spanish lines": "There was a man in a Panama hat strolling to and fro behind one of the Spanish trenches, gesticulating at times with a walking stick! That was the strangest sight of my life—that symbol, that quaint figure of Mars.... He mystified us all" (6:245).

Perhaps what prompted many of the parodies was not Crane's egotism, although it was interpreted in this way, but rather the "anarchic individualism" so fundamental to postmodernism and vitally basic to Crane. His rejection of Christianity in *Maggie*, of literature and history in *The Red Badge*, of culture in *The Monster*, and of everything else in "The Open Boat" and "Death and the Child," and his insistence upon retaining what he called "the anarchy" of *The Black Riders*, attest convincingly to the ultimate rightness of Crane's confession to Nellie Crouse that he was "by inclination a wild, shaggy barbarian." A barbarian, too, in the classical Greek sense of "foreigner," Crane seemed always more at home walking the line between the anarchy of nihilism and the totalitarianism of late nineteenth-century American society; he seems to have been a cousin of chaos who only visited with mankind, a species to which at times he seems only distantly related.

The clearest tie between Crane and the postmodern, however, lies in the manner in which he falls directly in line with the tradition of American literature beginning, at least, with Whitman and moving to Wallace Stevens and beyond. In *The Fragile Presence*, Killinger speaks to the issue of the quest for a supreme fiction when he says that "the quest for a new transcendence *in* and *through* the materialities of human existence is unspeakably important."[18] In America this quest is perhaps first clearly articulated by Whitman—"The New World needs poems of realities"—most vividly stated by Stevens in "Not Ideas about the Thing but the Thing Itself"—and, according to Altieri, now resides in the "postmodern insistence that value is not mediated but stems from a direct engagement with the universal forces of being manifest in the particular."[19] In short, Crane's impressionism throughout most of his career deliberately and painfully avoids the notion of value; toward the end, that impressionism can be said to create it just as deliberately: a clear and direct movement in Crane from what became an aspect of modernism to what has been called an "insistence" of postmodernism.

A prerequisite for unmediated experience lies in a process Roy Harvey Pearce and others have called "decreation." Crane's art of repudiating epic is a holistic attempt to decreate not only literature but all human values: "human forms must first be destroyed if we are to be open to the true sources of value manifest in the natural process which create forms."[20] This, perhaps, is the ultimate goal of Crane's impressionism.

Attempts to participate in unmediated reality by finding some certainty in impressionistic experiences are everywhere in Crane; the complement of such participation, the extinction of ego, a special concern of much postmodernism, with rare exceptions comes late in Crane's career, for he first had to dispense with the egotistical selflessness of patriotism and the prideful humility of religion, as well as the egotism and pride necessary to one who undertook these repudiations. Mediated experiences with reality are everywhere in Crane and almost always provide sources for illusion and distortion. The old chieftain, long a British captive, in "The King's Favor" engages in this sort of illusion when he hears an old war song and has a vision of killing the British and being "again a great chief" (8:571). This story tries to evoke from readers, says Bergon, "those very states of wonder, awe, or transcendence which [Crane] habitually attributes to his characters."[21] Similarly, Maggie's "dream garden," Henry's Christian-inspired "visions of cruelty," and his Homeric pictures of deeds "paraded in wide purple and gold" are part of experience mediated by imagination and memory.

Occasionally, Crane presented impressionistic pictures that seem to have come close to passing beyond mediation. The early "Killing His Bear" describes a killing this way: "The little man saw the swirling fur over his gun barrel. The earth faded to nothing. Only space and game, the aim and the hunted. Mad emotions powerful enough to rock worlds, hurled through the little man, but did not shake the tiniest nerve" (8:251). Henry's vision of grass blades is another: "His mind took a mechanical but firm impression." There is mystery in all this. Scratchy is awed by his "glimpse at another world," and perhaps the Swede's "supreme cry of astonishment" is likewise partly the result of such a vision. Except for the earliest, in which the little man afterwards "ran up and kicked the ribs of the bear," these visions invariably produce selflessness. The Swede, in Frye's terminology, becomes a lightning rod for humanity. Scratchy relents: "I 'low it's off, Jack." And Henry, immediately after experiencing his one clear vision, leads the charge with a "delirium that encounters despair and death, and is heedless and blind to the odds. It is a temporary but sublime absence of selfishness" (2:105).

Selflessness, a manifestation of what psycho-criticism rather unnecessarily calls "ego annihilation" and "id destruction," mystified Crane. It seems to have been the one human quality he could not explain through his theory that "conceit" was "the very engine of life": "The final wall," he said on his deathbed, "is human kindness."[22] In postmodern literature selflessness is largely antihumanistic or nonhumanistic, but in Crane the question of whether it is humanistic or not is difficult to answer. To the degree that Crane is romantic, selflessness becomes antihumanistic. When he is being classical, it is, of course, humanistic. At such moments one must return to the picture of the "conceited" Swede outside the Palace Hotel. It is a picture, a metaphor for all of Crane's work: man implacably struggling against chaos, against the other.

There is no transcendence in Crane's work. In epic terms, the struggle is solely for consciousness; finally for Crane, transcending consciousness is not transcendence but a falling back and succumbing to false echoes in caves of unconsciousness. Still, in spite of this nihilistic view, there are numerous instances in the later stories of a kind of acceptance of man's struggle against "this booming chaos" (6:196). War is business. War is Henry Fleming "at a task ... like a carpenter who has made many boxes, making still another box, only there was great haste in his movements" (2:35). If Henry and the narrator seem repelled by this "business," the later war stories project the business of war with a sense of awesome mystery; it can even become very personal and "sublime":

There wasn't a high heroic face among them. They were all men intent on business. That was all. It may seem that I am trying to make everything a squalor. That would be wrong. I feel that things were often sublime. But they were *differently* sublime. They were not of our shallow and preposterous fictions. They stood out in a simple, majestic commonplace. It was the behavior of men. In one way, each man was just pegging along.... In another way it was pageantry, the pageantry of the accomplishment of naked duty. [6:249]

Although Crane manages to skewer "preposterous fictions," he is not primarily concerned with them, but rather with those men honestly, completely, "earnestly at work" (6:232).

The self-sacrifice and inexplicable kindnesses performed by men for no other reason than that they do perform them caused Crane to face a spectacle in which resentment toward a material and indifferent universe simply falls away, as does the antihumanism of romantic and postmodern visions. Crane at last comes as close to an epic transcendence as he ever does, and he does it by throwing away his art, much as Dante does when the character Dante arrives at the gates of paradise and is unable to describe it in words. Here is Crane: "One cannot speak of it—the spectacle of the common man doing his work, his appointed work. It is the one thing in the universe which makes one fling expression to the winds and be satisfied simply to feel" (6:249). Simply to feel. Crane seems to feel about such men, perhaps mankind, the way some romantic and postmodern writers feel about the material universe. Here, too, lies one result of the Arnold–Huxley controversy of classical versus scientific education. Rejecting the notion of order provided by classicism and the romantic notion of the material world as beneficent, Crane is left with his feelings.

Crane's later work is both hurried and harried, filled with experiments not so much of craft but of feeling. If the craft is disappointing, as in many of the late war stories and especially in most of the *Tales of Whilomville*, that loss is occasionally paid for by advances in feeling and perception. Before Stevens demanded it, Crane had "become an ignorant man again." And if he did not see the sun clearly "in the idea of it," nevertheless, he was moving forward at the end.

In spite of his time's occasional economic depressions and constant social exploitation, Crane lived in an age and a country of unbounded optimism. At the same time, he was born, lived, and died in a world and a time when it was increasingly possible for people to deny utterly the existence of the supernatural and at the same time to disavow the ultimate value of mankind.

Only toward the end did he begin to find that value, and the literature of this century is still following the path Crane walked. Fewer than twenty years before the Great War, less than half a century from the atomic age, Crane struggled in a world where belief in God and man was rapidly unraveling at the seams; the mass, on the other hand, was in a frenzy of physical, verbal, and written motion to sew those seams, to shore fragments against its ruin. Alone, unwilling to compromise, unable to find solace anywhere, Stephen Crane stared at the gaping holes in the world's fabric, saw through them the abyss, and searched there for patches.

NOTES

1. Gullason, "Tragedy and Melodrama," p. 245–53.
2. Kenneth T. Reed, "'The Open Boat' and Dante's *Inferno*: Some Undiscovered Analogues," *Stephen Crane Newsletter* 4 (Summer, 1970): 1–3; but see also Robert Meyers, "Crane's 'The Open Boat,'" *Explicator* 21 (April, 1963): item 60; Lloyd Dendinger, "Stephen Crane's Inverted Use of Key Images of 'The Rime of the Ancient Mariner,'" *Studies in Short Fiction* 5 (Winter, 1968): 192–94.
3. Donna Gerstenberger, "'The Open Boat': Additional Perspective," *Modern Fiction Studies* 17 (Winter, 1971–72): 558; but see also Bert Bender, "The Nature and Significance of 'Experience' in 'The Open Boat,'" *Journal of Narrative Technique* 9, no. 1 (1979): 70–79.
4. See not only Bender, but these: Robert Shulman, "Community, Perception, and the Development of Stephen Crane: *The Red Badge* to 'The Open Boat,'" *American Literature* 50 (November, 1978): 441–60; Joseph J. Kwait, "Stephen Crane, Literary Reporter: Commonplace Experience and Artistic Transcendence," *Journal of Modern Literature* 8, no.1(1980): 129–38.
5. Clark Griffith, "Stephen Crane and the Ironic Last Word," *Philological Quarterly* 47 (January, 1968): 83–91.
6. Holton, *Cylinder of Vision*, p. 194.
7. Berryman, *Stephen Crane*, p. 183.
8. William K. Spofford, "Crane's *The Monster*," *Explicator* 36, no. 2 (1978): 5–7.
9. Eric Solomon, *Crane: From Parody to Realism*, p. 108.
10. Holton, *Cylinder of Vision*, p. 191.
11. Stallman, *Omnibus*, p. xxvi.
12. Stallman, *Omnibus*, and A. J. Liebling, "The Dollars Damned Him," *New Yorker*, August 5, 1961, pp. 48–60, 63–66, 69–72; see also Stallman, "That Crane, That Albatross around My Neck: A Self-Interview by R. W. Stallman," *Journal of Modern Literature* 7 (February, 1979): 147–69.
13. Charles Altieri, "From Symbolist Thought to Immanence: The Ground of Postmodern American Poetics," *Boundary* 2, 1 (Spring, 1973): 605.
14. Nagel, *Stephen Crane and Literary Impressionism*, p. 175.
15. Little Nell appears in "God Rest Ye, Merry Gentlemen" (6:136–54); Shackles in "God Rest Ye" and "The Revenge of the *Adolphus*" (6:155–71); Johnnie in "This Majestic Lie" (6:201–21); Vernall in "War Memories" (6:222–63).
16. Mere shock value, and perhaps some verisimilitude, comes from the following in "War Memories": "I remember Paine came ashore with a bottle of whiskey which I took

from him violently" (6:227); Teddy Roosevelt, whom Crane knew, had called another Paine a "dirty little atheist"; but this passage was more probably addressed to a nation the majority of whose middle class spoke of drink as if it were as odious as murder.

17. From the *Lewiston* (Maine) *Journal* and reprinted in the *New York Tribune* (May 18, 1897); quoted in Stallman, *Biography*, p. 552. The *Buffalo Express* said a day earlier (also according to Stallman, *Biography*) that "Stephen Crane and Grover Cleveland are running a mad race in the use of the personal pronoun 'I,' with 'Steve' a neck ahead." The use of the "I" is of course not so much a measure of Crane's egotism as it is of his adherence to a credo of "personal honesty." It may also demonstrate that he is beginning to eschew the "impersonality" which characterizes modernism and coming closer to adopting the "personal" mode accepted by postmodernism. See also Bergon, *Crane's Artistry*.

18. John Killinger, *The Fragile Presence: Transcendence in Modern Literature* (Philadelphia: Fortress Press, 1973), p. 5.

19. Altieri, "Symbols of Thought," p. 612.

20. Ibid., p. 613.

21. Bergon, *Crane's Artistry*, p. 52.

22. *Letters*, p. 99.

AMY KAPLAN

The Spectacle of War in Crane's Revision of History

1

The year that saw the publication of *The Red Badge of Courage* to great acclaim on both sides of the Atlantic was reviewed as a time of "wars and bloodshed" by Joseph Pulitzer's New York *World*. The newspaper's year-end survey of 1895 recalled that "from Japan westward to Jackson's Hole, bloodshed has encircled the globe," and it listed some examples of contemporary wars:

> When the year 1895 dawned the Italians were engaged in a bloody war with the Abyssinians; Haiti was overrun by rebels, who had burned the capital, Port-au-Prince, and slaughtered many people; the French were preparing for their disastrous if victorious war in Madagascar; the Dutch were slaughtering the natives of Lombok, one of their dependencies in southeastern Asia; and rebellions were in progress in several of the South American countries.[1]

To newspaper readers in 1895, these outbreaks of international violence may have seemed remote from America's geographical borders and even more distant in time from the historic battlefields of America's last major conflict, the Civil War. Yet as the decade progressed, the United States ventured more

From *New Essays on* The Red Badge of Courage, edited by Lee Clark Mitchell, pp. 77–108. © 1986 by Cambridge University Press.

boldly into international disputes; after verging on military engagements with Italy, Chile, and Britain in the early 1890's, America fought a war against Spain in Cuba and the Philippines in 1898. Mass-circulation newspapers like the *World*, which had already made exotic battles in European colonies a staple for American consumption, had an enthusiastic audience feasting on the spectacle of the Spanish-American War. One year after covering the Greco-Turkish War, Stephen Crane landed in Cuba with the American marines as a special correspondent for Pulitzer. Dateline June 22, 1898, the *World* headline for the first major battle of the Spanish-American War read: "THE RED BADGE OF COURAGE WAS HIS WIG-WAG FLAG."[2]

What do these international wars have to do with *The Red Badge of Courage*, a novel begun in 1893 about an internecine conflict that took place thirty years earlier? Although Crane himself had not yet seen a battle when he wrote his book, the heightened militarism in America and Europe at the end of the nineteenth century shapes his novel as much as does the historical memory of the Civil War. Crane's novel participates in a widespread cultural movement to reinterpret the war as the birth of a united nation assuming global power and to revalue the legitimacy of military activity in general. The novel looks back at the Civil War to map a new arena into which modern forms of warfare can be imaginatively projected.

This conjunction of past and present may help explain the paradoxical status that *The Red Badge of Courage* has long held as *the* classic American Civil War novel that says very little about that war. Crane divorces the Civil War from its historical context by conspicuously avoiding the political, military, and geographical coordinates of the 1860s, and he equally divorces the conflict from a traditional literary context by rejecting generic narrative conventions. The novel reduces both history and the historical novel to what its main character thinks of as "crimson blotches on the page of the past." The illegibility of history in Crane's war novel has informed most critical approaches, which either treat it as a statement about war in general, turn war into a metaphor for psychological or metaphysical conflicts, reconstruct the absent historical referents of the Civil War battlefield, or decry the weakness of the historical imagination in American literature. Contrary to these critical assumptions, Crane wrenches the war from its earlier contexts, not to banish history from his "Episode" but to reinterpret the war through the cultural lenses and political concerns of the late nineteenth century.

If, on the battlefield of *The Red Badge of Courage*, Crane does not revisit old territory with a historical imagination, he does explore an unfamiliar social landscape reminiscent of the modern cityscape of his earlier writing and replete with similar social tensions. Like other well-known novels of its time, Crane's is a book about social change, about the transition not only from internecine to international conflict or from preindustrial to mechanized forms of warfare, but also from traditional to modern modes of representation. The novel implicitly contributes to and criticizes the contemporary militarization of American culture by focusing not on politics but on the problem of representing war. Crane transforms the representation of war from a shared experience that can be narrated in written or oral stories into an exotic spectacle that must be viewed by a spectator and conveyed to an audience. This transformation was to provide Crane with a lens for reporting the real wars he observed in Greece and Cuba only two years after writing his Civil War novel.

2

To read *The Red Badge of Courage* historically, it is necessary to understand how Crane's contemporaries were reinterpreting the Civil War, for Crane was not alone in divorcing the conflict from its historical context and formulating a new one. In the outpour of nonfiction and fiction in the 1880s, writers consistently avoided referring to political conflicts over slavery or secession in favor of the theme of national reconciliation.[3] In both genteel magazines and dime novels, the "road to reunion" took the form of glorifying the heroism and valor of the soldiers in both armies. Memoirs of the war depicted soldiers on both sides chatting and singing together on guard duty and cheering one another in the midst of battle as they rescued the wounded. Such memories led one author to conclude that "had the work of reconstruction been left to the fighting men of the North and South, much of the bitterness of that period would have been avoided."[4] The bonds between soldiers in the field were seen to outlast and transcend the political conflicts for which they fought.

Crane's source for *The Red Badge of Courage*, the popular *Battles and Leaders of the Civil War*, epitomized this trend. To instruct a new generation in the meaning of the war in 1884, the editors of *The Century Magazine* invited veterans from both the Union and Confederate armies to record in detail their memories of major battles with the purpose of facilitating mutual respect, "the strongest bond of a united people."[5] In their preface to the four-volume edition in 1887, the editors took partial credit for that fact that

> coincident with the progress of the series during the past three years may be noted a marked increase in the number of fraternal meetings between Union and Confederate veterans, enforcing the conviction that the nation is restored in spirit as in fact, and that each side is contributing its share to the new heritage of manhood and peace.[6]

These memoirs and meetings radically reinterpreted the meaning of the battlefield itself. No longer an arena for enacting political conflict, it became a site for transcending conflict through the mutual admiration of military prowess.

Fiction about the Civil War in the 1880s reinforced the theme of reconciliation by using romantic subplots to frame the battle scenes. In the traditional genre of the historical romance, heroism on the battlefield was rewarded by the love of the heroine at home; the plots often revolved around a love affair between a Union soldier and a Southern girl or around the division and reunion of kinsmen fighting on opposing sides. If memoirs hailed the reunion among men on the battlefield, fiction suggested that "neither the war nor reconstruction produced problems which could not be solved ... by an adequately consummated marriage."[7] During the postreconstruction period, both military histories and domestic fiction excised political conflict from the collective memory of the Civil War.

If the spirit of national unity could be abstracted from the devastating four-year conflict, the ideal of martial valor could be further abstracted from the goal of national unity. Participants and observers alike later viewed the battlefield of the Civil War as a testing ground for the virility and courage of the individual soldier, independent of any broader national aim. Oliver Wendell Holmes, Jr., for example, in his famous *Memorial Day Address* of 1895, lauded martial heroism as a value in itself, rather than as a means to a political or moral end. In the same year as the publication of *The Red Badge of Courage*, he stated:

> I do not know the meaning of the universe. But in the midst of doubt, in the collapse of creeds, there is one thing that I do not doubt ... and that is that the faith is true and adorable which leads a soldier to throw away his life in obedience to a blindly accepted duty, in a cause which he little understands, in a plan of campaign of which he has no notion, under tactics of which he does not see the use.[8]

By the 1890s, Holmes could wrench the battlefield from the social and historical context of the war in which he himself had fought, and could transform it into a figurative crucible for the test of individual manhood—a figuration that Crane's revisions put to the test.

Holmes reinterpreted the Civil War as a model for an emerging ethos that Theodore Roosevelt soon dubbed "the strenuous life." Whereas Holmes glorified the chastening discipline of the battlefield, others sought to revive those aristocratic and chivalric values repressed by the routinization of industrial life. The revival of the martial ideal, according to historian John Higham, was part of the broader "reorientation of American culture in the 1890s" toward the celebration of youth, combativeness, and muscularity.[9] This shift redefined masculinity in terms of aggressive and physical activism—now opposed to effeminacy—to supplant the older Victorian emphasis on self-discipline and responsibility—opposed primarily to childhood. Such a reorientation found a wide range of expressions, from the craze for outdoor activities and the movement to conserve the wilderness, to the intellectual recognition of the formative qualities of the frontier, to the popular enthusiasm for competitive athletics and spectator sports. A common denominator of these different cultural forms was the discovery of "the primitive" as a regenerative force against what some called the enervation of "overcivilization." "A saving touch of old fashioned barbarism," in the words of a sports enthusiast, could be found equally in the untamed wilderness, in the athletic arena, or on the battlefield.[10] Touching on all three realms, Crane reportedly confessed to Hamlin Garland that "his knowledge of battle had been gained on the football field, 'The psychology is the same. The opposite team is an enemy tribe!'"[11] Crane's vocabulary locates his Civil War battlefield at the intersection of militarism, athleticism, and primitivism in the 1890s.

In fiction, the discovery of the primitive and the celebration of the martial ideal joined together in trends as diverse as naturalism and the historical romance. The adventure tales of Robert Louis Stevenson were more widely read in the United States than in England, and Kipling remained one of the most popular writers in both countries throughout the 1890s. Kipling's *The Light that Failed* (1891), with its double focus on the bohemian artist in Europe and the imperial battlefields of the Orient, exerted a strong influence on American naturalists such as Crane, Norris, and London. While they explored the atavistic qualities of modern life and often universalized war as a metaphor for the social Darwinian struggle, the historical romance, which appealed to a similar ethos, underwent a popular revival on both sides of the Atlantic.[12] Sir Walter Scott's novels were reprinted and acclaimed not for their historicity but for their depiction of vigorous and virile action, and they were joined by new chivalric romances such as Robert Louis Stevenson's *Prince Otto* (1885), F. Marion Crawford's *Saracinesca* (1887), Anthony Hope's *Prisoner of Zenda* (1894), Richard Harding Davis's *The Princess Aline* (1895), and Charles Major's *When Knighthood Was in Flower* (1898).[13] Whether set in historical or mythical kingdoms, these novels stressed neither courtly behavior nor political intrigue, but the freewheeling and lawless spirit of the medieval knight, who best demonstrated his skill and valor through acts of raw physical violence.

In the 1890s, the figure of the medieval warrior combined primitive virility with an appeal to the contemporary concern for the purity of the Anglo-Saxon race. As Frank Norris claimed in his first novel, "somewhere deep down in the heart of every Anglo-Saxon lies the predatory instinct of his Viking ancestors—an instinct that a thousand years of respectability and tax-paying have not quite succeeded in eliminating."[14] According to historian Jackson Lears, the attraction to the medieval knight expressed a yearning for "real life," for a personal wholeness that could rejuvenate an insecure elite who felt threatened both by the "weightlessness" of their own lives and by the unruliness of the classes beneath them. Whereas the feudal lord appealed to readers with the iron fist he wielded over his vassals, bloody battles between knights in exotic lands compensated for the ennui resulting from the subordination of primal instincts to commercial needs.[15] In addition, reading about battles fought single-handedly with swords and brute strength fulfilled a longing for warfare untainted by the mechanization initiated in the Civil War and intensified during the half-century that followed.

Nevertheless, romances about crusaders, questing knights, and fantastic kingdoms did not only look back nostalgically toward a lost wholeness; they also projected fanciful realms for contemporary adventures and the exercise of military power. William Dean Howells was not the only critic to relate the "swashbuckler swashing on his buckler" to the arousal of jingoism and the clamor for foreign wars in the 1890s.[16] The lament for the closing of the frontier was often coupled with a call for opening new frontiers abroad to release the pressure of class conflict brewing at home, and the discovery of the primitive—in the wilds and within—similarly coincided with the discovery of primitive people to control in exotic places. Chivalric nostalgia existed side by side with the rationalization and modernization of the armed forces; the critique of overcivilization bolstered the onward march of "civilization," and the discovery of barbaric impulses within modern man would be enacted on a battlefield of "uncivilized" frontiers, such as Cuba and the Philippines.[17]

In his speech delivered in 1899, "The Strenuous Life," Theodore Roosevelt clearly summarized these connections between the Civil War, the martial ideal, and empire building. Opening with a reference to Lincoln and Grant, Roosevelt used the war as evidence of the "iron in the blood of our fathers" and called on his own generation to follow their example by embodying "those virile qualities necessary to win in the stern strife of actual life." The Civil War, he argued, placed "the mighty American republic once more as a helmeted queen among nations." His specific motive was to convince his audience to accept "the white man's burden" by annexing the Philippines, which had been recently occupied in the Spanish-American War. American "conduct toward the tropic islands," he claimed, was "merely the form which our duty has taken at the moment" to continue "the life of strenuous endeavor."[18] Roosevelt himself had just recently engaged in such a strenuous activity in the war with Spain by organizing and leading the volunteer regiment the Rough Riders, a collection of frontiersmen, displaced aristocrats, and Ivy League athletes. Stephen Crane, in his capacity as foreign correspondent, accompanied them on their well-publicized Cuban exploits, one of which he labeled a "gallant blunder."[19]

It is fitting that one of the best-sellers during the Spanish-American War was a novel about the Civil War, *The Song of the Rappahannock*, a book that rewrites *The Red Badge of Courage* by explicitly claiming that recruits did not act like Crane's hero. This novel, by Seymour Dodd, recapitulates those revisions of the Civil War we have traced through the 1880s and 1890s, which present not a "civil war" at all but a war that expunges internal conflicts. Dodd's preface reminds his readers that "memories of that older crisis can no longer be dividing or exclusive possessions, but each fragment of its story becomes part of the common heritage of American manhood." The second edition of the novel, published immediately after the Spanish-American War, spells out the fulfillment of this "heritage":

> on the heights of Santiago we see men of the South standing shoulder to shoulder with men of the North, mingling their blood victoriously under the old Flag, while the world looks on with admiration not unmixed with fear.[20]

Dodd's novel completes a circle of revisions that starts with the deletion of conflict from the Civil War battlefield by celebrating the martial valor of soldiers on both sides and ends with the fulfillment of the war's legacy by externalizing conflict as United States troops face foreign enemies abroad.

3

In *The Red Badge of Courage*, Crane not only contributes to the contemporary abstraction of the Civil War from its historical context but also takes the further step of challenging those popular tales that recontextualize the war. As Eric Solomon has established, parody provides a central narrative strategy in all of Crane's writing.[21] His war novel does more than parody either generic conventions or historical novels about the Civil War; it specifically parodies those narrative forms used to reinterpret the Civil War and to imagine new kinds of warfare in the 1890s.

The problem of reinterpreting the past to anticipate the immediate future is thematized in the first chapter of *The Red Badge of Courage*. Following the silent panorama of the battlefield in the opening paragraph, the novel bursts into a noisy state of anticipation: To plot in advance their upcoming initiation, recruits trade rumors about "brilliant campaigns" and veterans exchange tales of former battles to reimagine the enemy they will soon face. The central character, Henry Fleming, reexamines the stories he has heard about war in order to question what course his own actions might take. Throughout the first chapter, the narrator similarly evokes contemporary narratives of the Civil War and of the chivalric romance to test their applicability to his own story that lies ahead.

The second paragraph of the novel mocks the revival of the medieval romance by using chivalric rhetoric to describe the mundane activity of a soldier doing his laundry: "Once a certain tall soldier developed virtues and went resolutely to wash a shirt. He came flying back from a brook waving his garment, banner-like. He was swelled with a tale." The pose the soldier adopts of "herald in red and gold" is similarly deflated by his news, which sounds like small-town gossip, "heard from a reliable friend who had it from a truthful cavalryman who had heard it from his trustworthy brother." Both the medium and the message of these insubstantial rumors reveal the powerlessness of the recruits and the inadequacy of their tales to anticipate their fate.

The third paragraph of the novel suggests the social function of these chivalric stories for readers at the end of the century. The rumors of "a brilliant campaign" draw an audience of soldiers away from "a negro teamster who had been dancing upon a cracker-box." In the 1880s, tales of chivalric exploits similarly superseded the older narrative of emancipation at a time when reconciliation was effected at the cost of undoing the gains of former slaves after the war. In this only reference to blacks in the novel, Crane both divorces his own "episode" from any former stories about freeing the slaves and calls attention to the process whereby the history of emancipation had been reduced to a form of entertainment. The "deserted" teamster sits "mournfully down" to lament his loss of an audience and his own passing as a figure for the subject of emancipation from the narrative landscape of the Civil War battlefield.

In the first chapter, Crane similarly evokes and discards the domestic subplot, which provided an important structure in both Civil War romances and regional fiction. Thwarting Henry's expectation of a noble farewell, his mother deflates his romantic aspirations and reminds him that he is "jest one little feller 'mongst a hull lot'a others." When the regiment leaves his village, Henry catches a glimpse of a "dark girl," whom he thinks grows "sad and demure at the sight of his blue and brass." Like the "negro teamster," the "dark girl" mourns her own passing from the novel as a figure of the domestic subplot. Throughout the novel, domestic images resurface only to deflate the martial ethos rather than to validate it, as troops are compared to women trying on bonnets or to brooms sweeping up the battlefield.

In addition to rejecting these narratives of emancipation and domesticity, Crane parodies the memoirs of veterans that were so popular in the 1880s. The first chapter presents a commonplace scene in which Henry recalls chatting with a Confederate sentinel:

> "Yank", the other had informed him, "yer a right dum good feller." This sentiment, floating to him upon the still air, had made him temporarily regret war. (Chap. 1)

Here the familiar encomium for the valor of the enemy is reduced to barely articulate mutual recognition. Crane follows this set piece with the recruit's distrust of veterans:

> Various veterans had told him tales. Some talked of grey, bewhiskered hordes who were advancing, with relentless curses and chewing tobacco with unspeakable valor; tremendous bodies of fierce soldiery who were sweeping along like the Huns. Others spoke of tattered eternally-hungry men who fired despondent powder. (Chap. 1)

The veterans' accounts of the past prove no more reliable than the rumors that the recruits project about the future. These stories create a mythical alien enemy that no more prepares Henry for battle than the mirror image of the foe as a "dum good feller." Indeed, Henry finds that "he could not put a whole faith in veterans' tales, for recruits were their prey" (Chap. 1).

Crane's parody questions the pedagogical value of those memoirs that made up such popular works as *Battle and Leaders*. In a well-known letter, Crane dismissed these volumes for their content, for their lack of information about the subjective response to the battlefield—"they won't tell me what I want to know."[22] In the opening of his novel, he rejects them as a form, as a narrative mode inadequate not only for historical accuracy but also for the representation of warfare in the 1890s. More broadly, Crane undermines both the authority of veterans to transmit their knowledge to a younger generation of soldiers and the power of historical memory to assure continuity into the present.

Although the novel opens by dismissing equally the narrative of emancipation, the domestic subplot of fiction, and the memoirs of veterans, the chivalric narrative outlasts the others as the main character clings to it tenaciously. Like Emma Bovary or Lord Jim, Henry Fleming's inner aspirations are composed of ideas in the popular books he reads and clichés that circulate around him. Henry imagines himself most often as a medieval knight, who in his late-nineteenth-century manifestation combines violent adventure with primitive virility. If Henry's dreams are rendered as lurid chivalric exploits, his rational skepticism is also cast in the rhetoric of strenuosity. When Henry first considers enlisting, for example, he imagines battles to be "things of the bygone with his thought-images of heavy crowns and high castles" (Chap. 1). In Henry's suspicion of the present war, the narrator mocks the "warrior critique" of an overcivilized society by twice repeating the refrain-like formula: "Greeklike struggles would be no more. Men were better, or more timid. Secular and religious education had effaced the throat-grappling instinct or else firm finance held in check the passions." Like many of Crane's contemporaries, however, Henry hopes that the battle will prove him wrong and will thrust him beyond the mundane commercial world into a realm of primitive abandon.

Despite the narrative parody, Henry does find these hopes fulfilled on the battlefield, where he resurrects the image of the medieval warrior. As he anticipates the battle, for example, he imagines himself as a dragon fighter, and he later flees from "an onslaught of redoubtable dragons." When he does fight, after returning to the regiment, he sees himself as a medieval warrior who has finally penetrated the primitive depths:

> It was revealed to him that he had been a barbarian, a beast. He had fought like a pagan who defends his religion. Regarding it, he saw that it was fine, wild and, in some ways, easy. He had been a tremendous figure, no doubt. By this struggle, he had overcome obstacles which he had admitted to be mountains. They had fallen like paper peaks and he was now what he called a hero. And he had not been aware of the process. He had slept and, awakening, found himself a knight. (Chap. 18/17)

After the next fight, he feels that he has reached a frontier and entered "some new and unknown land" (Chap. 20/19). Crane represents Henry's battle experience as the return to a premodern era, as the exploration of an uncivilized frontier, and as the recovery of a primitive self in a dreamlike preconscious state. Crane's language becomes enmeshed in the rhetoric of strenuosity that it parodies as his narrative discovers the primitive and revives the martial ideal on the Civil War battlefield of the 1890s.

4

Lacking the familiar signposts of historical and geographical names and dates, Crane's battlefield does indeed appear as a timeless new and unknown land, divorced from any particular social context. Yet Crane delineates a social dimension of his landscape, which both explains the appeal of the chivalric revival for the youth of the 1890s and circumscribes its limits. The social geography of *The Red Badge of Courage* resonates with the tensions of the late nineteenth century, a period in which warfare provided the most common vocabulary for the violent class conflicts that erupted in America's cities. From the Great Railroad Strike of 1877 to the Haymarket Riot of 1886 to the Pullman Strike of 1894, labor struggles pitted workers against local police and state militias and threatened to engulf the entire nation in an apocalyptic battle. Problems and solutions alike were articulated in martial language: In Edward Bellamy's popular novel of 1888, *Looking Backward*, the army provided the model for a peaceful industrial utopia, and in 1894 Coxey's "army" of the poor marched in protest on Washington. Some social critics, such as the missionary Josiah Strong, blamed the intensity of urban conflicts on the closing of the frontier and advocated United States expansion abroad, with its concomitant militarism, as the only relief for these domestic social conflicts.

Although it is a critical commonplace that Crane uses war as a metaphor for city life in his urban writing, it is less noted that he inverts this metaphor in *The Red Badge of Courage*. He describes the battlefield with urban metaphors that overlay the countryside and leave only traces of the rural landscape. The approaching army is described as a train, for example; soldiers become "mobs" and "crowds," and officers are compared to political bosses cajoling the masses.[23] The battle itself is repeatedly called a vast "machine" that produces corpses and works according to mysterious orders. The main character moves from a farm into an army whose conditions resemble those of the industrial city of the late nineteenth century.[24] There he finds not the chivalric adventures he sought but the anonymous and "monotonous life in a camp" (Chap. 1). He also finds a social structure that is ridden with class tensions between officers and privates. Indeed, the novel represents more verbal expressions of hostility and physical acts of violence between members of the Union army than against enemy troops, who remain invisible on the battlefield. We see an officer beating a frightened recruit, for example; a fellow soldier wounds Henry; and he engages in hand-to-hand combat only with the corpse of the Union color bearer who refuses to loosen his grip on the flag.

These social conditions of army life overwhelm Henry with a sense not simply of overcivilized ennui but, more importantly, of powerlessness. Outrage against his impotence provides his strongest motivation for acting, both when he runs away and when he fights, and it takes specific shape in his hatred of his superiors, a hatred that far outstrips any emotion directed toward the enemy. Henry's final feats of heroism are spurred by his resentment toward the conversation he overhears between two officers; expecting "some great, inner historical things," he and his friend instead listen to the officers refer to the troops as "mule-drivers." For Henry, this shockingly confirms his mother's prediction: "he was very insignificant. The officer spoke of the regiment as if he referred to a broom" (Chap. 19/18). The officers' conversation pierces Henry's chivalric sense of self with language that recalls those figures rejected by the narrator in the first chapter. Henry and his comrades replace the black teamster as the work horses of the industrial army, and their heroism is deflated by the domestic reference to brooms. Henry and his friend cannot directly express their "unspeakable indignation" at the officer, except by fighting even more viciously, to the point where they seem "like tortured savages" (Chap. 20/19).

Although Henry resents the machinery of war and the powerlessness it entails and envisions himself as a primitive warrior to escape from this machine, his atavistic fantasies, rather than offering him an escape, entrench him more solidly in the machinery of the army. In the midst of the fight, the officers he resents so vehemently become his comrades-in-arms, and they transcend internal friction in the heat of the battle. When the colonel praises the youth and his friend for their fervor, "they speedily forgot many things. The past held no error and disappointment. They were very happy and their hearts swelled with grateful affection for the colonel and the lieutenant" (Chap. 22/21). In 1894, a year of violent strikes in the midst of a major depression, the popular syndicated version of *The Red Badge of Courage* ended here, with the privates reconciled with their superiors. Although it would be simplistic to reduce the novel to a social allegory, the tensions between officers and privates, between social classes, are externalized and transcended on the battlefield, and the mob of soldiers is channeled into the machine. War is transformed from a means of expressing conflict to a way of purging internal social conflict, which was the argument set forth for overseas expansion in the 1890s.

In the longer version of the book published in 1895, Henry moves beyond this social reconciliation to the more abstract harmony between the individual and the machine: "he emerged from his struggles, with a large sympathy for the machinery of the universe." Once Henry has proven his manhood on the battlefield, the "gigantic machine" no longer serves as a metaphor for war. Instead, it becomes a symbol of a cosmic order that gently embraces the individual soldier. The martial ideal plays a mediating role in this reconciliation. Mechanical order and primitive abandon are interdependent discourses; Henry's stories of chivalric heroism both fuel and are swallowed up by the machinery of modern warfare. Thus, by fusing industrial and chivalric language, Crane exposes the function of the revival of the martial ideal and shows that it criticizes a rationalized and hierarchical social order only to reinforce it.

5

The transition Henry makes from his local rural home to a distended industrialized army parallels the cultural course taken to revise the Civil War in the late nineteenth century—from a local internecine conflict to a model for international warfare. In charting these movements, Crane's narrative enacts an analogous transition from traditional to modern modes of representation. In the description of Henry's first battle, the narrator presents an excess of similes, as though he were frantically searching for the appropriate one. One of these compares Henry to an artisan "at a task. He was like a carpenter who has made many boxes, making still another box, only there was a furious haste in his movements" (Chap. 5). As the battle proceeds, however, the rhythm of the carpenter cannot keep up with such a relentless pace, and the artisanal imagery cannot sustain the representation of mechanized warfare. When Henry runs away after a lull in the fighting and then returns to observe it, the narrative moves from the carpenter/soldier producing his own coffin to the "grinding of an immense and terrible machine" that produces corpses. Just as Henry abandons his artisanal framework before he can return to the industrialized army, the narrator must abandon traditional narrative modes to develop new strategies for representing modern warfare.

If the first chapter of *The Red Badge of Courage* undermines the popular stories that revise the Civil War in the 1890s, the novel proceeds to question the viability of storytelling itself, to reject it as an outmoded narrative form. One of Crane's most hostile reviewers, General McClurg of the *Dial*, attacked the novel not only for its lack of patriotism, as Donald Pease has shown, but also for the fact that it has "absolutely no story," which McClurg elaborates as the absence of a traditional plot with logical sequence and causality.[25] Along with other reviewers, the general expected a story line that both embedded the battle in a political framework and rooted Henry's actions in a cohesive narrative pattern. Crane's refusal to tell a story, however, extends beyond the denial of a traditional plot to challenge the oral and written tradition of storytelling—a mode of communication, as Walter Benjamin has shown, linked to an artisanal preindustrial culture and inadequate to the representation of modern warfare.[26]

The first part of the novel, before Henry rejoins the battle, is filled with references to aborted forms of storytelling. When Henry finds his self-knowledge undermined by army life, he reassures himself that "like as not this here story'll turn out jest like them others did" (Chap. 1). But neither Henry's story nor Crane's novel turn out "like them others": When Henry runs away, he deviates from the traditional plot of heroism and from the role of "a man of traditional courage" (Chap. 3). In response, Henry then tries to bridge this gap by telling new stories. When he first enters the forest, for example, he weaves a Darwinian tale around a squirrel that runs from a tossed pine cone, only to have that story immediately undermined by the staring corpse in the middle of the woods—"The dead man and the living man exchanged a long look"—which usurps any possible exchange of experience through speech. Henry's reassuring tale is replaced by the fear that "some strange voice would come from the dead throat and squawk after him in horrible menaces" (Chap. 7). This pattern is repeated throughout the first half of the book: As soon as Henry tries to tell a tale, make a speech, or ask questions, the sight of corpses—staring, laughing, or shrieking—silences him. Jim Conklin's death, for example, both arouses and mocks Henry's desire to deliver any angry "phillipic." In the face of Conklin's grinning corpse, Henry can barely articulate "hell—," and then finds that "his tongue lay dead in the tomb of his mouth" (Chaps. 9, 10).

Stories in *The Red Badge of Courage* rarely communicate experience or forge solidarity among the soldiers; instead, they often appear as weapons and are described in martial metaphors such as "spears," "arrows," "missiles," and "shields." To defend himself against the attack he expects from his comrades Henry

> tried to be-think of him a fine tale which he could take back to his regiment and with it turn the expected shafts of derision.... He was much afraid that some arrow of scorn might lay him mentally low before he could raise his protecting tale. (Chap. 11).

Unable to control his tale, he imagines that his regiment will puncture his story by taunting him with his own name—"Where's Henry Fleming?"—thereby turning his name into "a slang phrase" (Chap. 11). By naming Henry in this manner for the first time in the novel, the narrator mocks the epic tradition that immortalizes the name of the hero by recounting his struggle with a foe. The youth's naming, in contrast, divorces the achievement of identity from the story of conflict and marks the failure of storytelling, which is reduced to the shorthand of the "slang phrase."

Soon after his naming, Henry receives his wound in response to another thwarted attempt to speak; the figurative attack of linguistic "arrows" and "shafts" turns into a literal attack with the butt of a rifle, which changes the course of the narrative. When Henry sees other men running with fright, he "had the impulse to make a rallying speech, to sing a battle-hymn but he could only get his tongue to call into the air: "Why—why—what—what's th' matter?" To find an answer, in the "centre of a tremendous quarrel," he grabs someone to speak to "face to face" (Chap. 13/12). But such direct communication proves impossible, because the youth can only stammer and the man can only respond by swinging his rifle. Henry's wound signifies the inefficacy of human speech on the battlefield. Although the air is filled with the noise of human voices, attempts to speak coherently are drowned out by the songs and "stentorian" speeches of guns, the prelinguistic shrieks of the fighting soldiers, the cursing of officers, and the laughter of corpses.

Crane further undercuts the power of storytelling through the figure of the "tattered man," who first appears among the wounded as a listener:

> There was a tattered man, fouled with dust, blood and powder stain from hair to shoes who trudged quietly at the youth's side. He was listening with eagerness and much humility to the lurid descriptions of a bearded sergeant. His lean features wore an expression of awe and admiration. He was like a listener in a country-store to wondrous tales told among the sugar-barrels. He eyed the storyteller with unspeakable wonder. His mouth was a-gape in yokel fashion. (Chap. 8)

This description caricatures the tattered man both as a country bumpkin and as a figure for the oral tradition of the tall tale. He sees the battlefield as an extension of his rural community, in which identities are clearly delineated and nothing appears incongruous or out of context. Adapting every occurrence to the stories he expects to hear, he assumes, given the context, that Henry has a hidden wound; he cannot imagine instead that Henry has a hidden story, which would remove him from the context of the other wounded soldiers. When the tattered man grows delirious from his wounds, he confuses Henry with the friend and next-door neighbor who fought beside him on the battlefield. By renaming Henry "Tom Jamison," the tattered man attempts to absorb Henry into a rural storytelling tradition, seeing a wound that isn't there and a neighbor he doesn't know. When Henry abandons the tattered man wandering in the fields, the narrative abandons this figure for the listener who can both absorb and partake in the story.

In the dismissal of the tattered man and the transformation of stories into weapons, Crane removes his own representation of war from the oral tradition, from the realm of "experience which is passed on from mouth to mouth."[27] He replaces the tattered man with the man with the "cheery voice" who, thriving on incongruity, magically leads the youth back to the regiment. This figure is described through a curious amalgamation of images from fairy tales and urban fiction. With "the keenness of a detective and the valor of a gamin," he weaves his way through the mazes of the battlefield as though they were city streets (Chap. 13/12). In contrast to the tattered man, he makes no attempt to ask Henry questions, to listen to his stories, or to create any bond between them, even though he speaks incessantly. In fact, Henry never even sees his face.

Despite his brief appearance, this faceless guide plays a pivotal role in the narrative. A figure for the author, he allows the story to start again, to be retold as a tale of courage. Through this garrulous and faceless character Crane makes the major turning point in his narrative gratuitous and parodies storytelling by exposing its arbitrariness. Drawn to Henry by his wound, the guide understands it at face value, and Henry's regiment immediately recontextualizes it as a sign of his fighting. Crane thus underscores the divorce of storytelling from cumulative experience by making his own tale revolve around this empty sign.

6

If Crane rejects storytelling as inadequate to narrate the experience of modern warfare, what other mode of narration does he put in its place? Critics tend to treat Crane's parody as the shedding of illusions to achieve a more realistic representation, whether of detailed sensory perceptions or of internal subjective impressions. Yet *The Red Badge of Courage* does not undercut the conventions of the story to represent a more immediate reality; rather, it frames a new sense of the real as a highly mediated spectacle. If Crane decontextualizes war as a subject for the storyteller, he recontextualizes it as an object to be viewed by a spectator. His spectacles of warfare are contained in the act of seeing, without hinting at a broader framework or a deeper meaning, and they do not outlast the moment in which they are glimpsed. Crane's emphasis on seeing in *The Red Badge of Courage* does not bring the war closer to the reader; instead, it distances the reader as a spectator of improvised sketches and theatrical scenes.

The first paragraph of the novel, which surveys the panorama of the battlefield, ends by drawing our attention to the act of seeing: "when the stream had become of a sorrowful blackness one could see, across, the red eye-like gleam of hostile campfires set in the low brows of distant hills." This anonymous "one" introduces the disembodied eye, which, like the faceless soldier, guides us through the battlefield. As the scene darkens, the enemy comes into view like stage lights in a theater. Conflict is theatricalized when the viewer cannot escape being seen as well; we look out at the landscape only to find hostile eyes staring back, just as Henry sees corpses glaring at him. The first paragraph, then, introduces the visual mode of representation that frames and competes with those parodied stories that immediately follow.

In describing the battle, the narrator repeatedly highlights his own composition of the scene. The shooting of a soldier, for example, is presented as "the instant's spectacle of a man, almost over it, throwing up his hands to shield his eyes" (Chap. 20/19); the retreating cavalry appears as a "sketch in gray and red dissolved into a mob-like body of men" (Chap. 4); and a sleeping soldier is framed as "the picture of an exhausted soldier" (Chap. 14/13). In many such passages the nouns—for example, "spectacle" "picture," or "sketch"—dominate the sentence grammatically and draw attention away from the activity of fighting to the act of seeing. This focus has the effect of freezing all motion within a static snapshot-like frame. In contrast to a story, which weaves together events and actions in a continuous narrative, Crane's spectacles isolate discontinuous moments of vision.

Crane's visual effects should be contrasted to those spectacles that have long filled the historical novel, where they are integrated with storytelling. In Scott's novels, descriptions of martial processions, chivalric contests, and heraldic displays implicitly tell a tale; visual details delineate the contours of a social order, and colorful spectacles enact broader political or moral dramas. Crane's notorious use of color—the subject of many contemporary parodies—can be seen to parody the traditional descriptions of the historical romance. We read, for example, of "columns changed to purple streaks," of a "yellow light thrown upon the color of his ambition," of a "vast blue demonstration," of a "black procession of oaths," and of "the red sickness of battle." Although these colors tease us with their vividness, they have less a mimetic than a curiously opaque effect. They conspicuously deny any narrative beyond themselves and excise all vestiges of storytelling from visual description.

In contrast to Scott, Crane's use of color is antiemblematic; the "red badge" itself flaunts its overt symbolic qualities, while at the same time being divorced from any meaningful context. In *The Red Badge of Courage* even the flag—the ultimate political emblem—lacks any referential stability. When, at the end of the first battle, Henry sees the flags, he "felt the old thrill at the sight of the emblems" (Chap. 5). Yet the noise of more distant battles immediately throws this vision out of focus to make him aware that "the war is not directly under his nose." When he does look around, he is surprised by the discrepancy between the tranquil landscape and the chaotic battlefield, a gap that the flag cannot fill by centering his dispersed vision or by endowing the action with political significance. When Henry grabs the flag in a later battle, it lacks its own reference until he "endowed it with power," just as others must invest his wound with significance. In the absence of a narrative or political context, the meaning of emblems must be improvised in the momentary drama.

The color bearer provides an appropriate figure for the narrator, whose visual representations are less descriptive and emblematic than theatrical. While they freeze the action of the battle, they call attention to the bold strokes of the narrator, to his own power to sketch the scene with bravado. In the highly debated simile, for example, at the end of Chapter 9—"the red sun was pasted in the sky like a fierce wafer"—the verb "pasted" draws attention to the theatricality of the narrator's gesture, as though the sun were used as a prop in a stage setting. This powerful yet elusive simile interrupts Henry's aborted attempt to speak heroically and usurps his undelivered phillipic with the narrator's own heroic gesture. In contrast to the youth's silence and immobility, the theatrical style of the narrator becomes the focus of the spectacle, and his composition of the scene provides the central heroic act.

Throughout the novel, the narrator places the reader in the position of a spectator by referring to the battlefield as a "stage" or a "tableau," and to the soldiers as actors, or by comparing them to football players. The characters themselves alternate between the roles of actor and spectator. When the recruits retreat during the first battle, for example, we read that they are "not even conscious of the presence of an audience" of veterans, and we watch an officer beat a recruit as the two are "acting a little isolated scene" (Chaps. 4, 5). When the fighting begins, we observe Henry watching the battle: "the youth forgetting his neat plan of getting killed, gazed spellbound. His eyes grew wide and busy with the action of the scene." His anticipation of the impending fight is compared to a child's anticipation of a circus parade (Chap. 5). When the battle stops, he immediately wants to "look behind him and off to the right and off to the left. He experienced the joy of a man who at last finds leisure in which to look about him" (Chap. 5). His pleasure stems not just from surviving the battle or fighting well but from surveying the scene, an act that provides a sense of control that storytelling lacks.

Immediately after Henry runs "like a blind man," he returns to the battlefield to see what he might be missing: "It is better to view the appalling than to be merely within hearing. The noises of the battle were like stones; he believed himself liable to be crushed" (Chap. 6). Not seeing is more threatening to his identity than not fighting. After retreating into the woods, he finds himself driven back to the battle to observe "the immense and terrible machine," for "its complexities and powers, its grim processes, fascinated him. He must go close and see it produce corpses" (Chap. 8). He does then witness such a production in the highly theatrical spectacle of Jim Conklin's death. Despite the horror of the scene, "he had a great desire to see, and to get news. He wished to know who was winning," as though he could contain the battle in the confines of a football game (Chap. 11). Henry's obsession with seeing suggests that he runs away, in part, to trade the role of actor for spectator, to gain both a sense of control and a vicarious thrill from observing the battle at a safe enough distance not to be crushed by it.

When Henry rejoins the fighting, he is described as a performer so absorbed in his role as to forget when the scene closes. While he continues to fire during the lull in the battle, his comrades become "spectators" watching him (Chap. 18/17). Only by fighting in an isolated scene separated from the context of a surrounding battle can Henry secure a reputation for himself among his fellow soldiers, who "now looked on him as a war devil." Henry does not achieve this identity through confrontation with the enemy—who has stopped firing—but by acting in an improvised one-man show before the audience of his regiment. Their awestruck glances replace the staring corpses and reverse his earlier fear of his name becoming a slang phrase.

Henry's desire for vengeance against the officer who called him a mule driver is similarly expressed in theatrical terms. To retaliate against the man who had "dubbed him wrongly" he cannot imagine speaking back—or even fighting back—but he can envision his revenge in the picture of his own dead body: "his corpse would be for those eyes a great and salt reproach" (Chap. 23/22). This vision has more power for Henry than the thought of proving himself through his action or using speech to rename himself.

When Henry reenters the fray, he does not give up his desire to see. While holding the flag he has just taken in battle, he stops to survey the panorama of the battlefield:

> The youth, still a bearer of colors, did not feel his idleness. He was deeply absorbed as a spectator. The crash and swing of the great drama made him lean forward, intent-eyed, and his face working in small contortions. Sometimes, he prattled, words coming unconsciously from him in grotesque exclamations. He did not know that he breathed; that the flag hung silently over him, so absorbed was he. (Chap. 23/22)

His absorption in the act of seeing makes communicative speech both impossible and unnecessary. By grabbing the flag, he has earned not only proof of his fighting prowess but also the right to see, so that, as color bearer, he plays the role of both spectator and actor. He gains the leisure to stand still and observe the fighting around him at the same time that he serves as the focal point for the rest of the troops. He can, for the first time, safely see and be seen.

Memory in *The Red Badge of Courage* is also theatricalized. Henry reviews his battle experiences as though he were observing an array of pictures rather than narrating a sequence of events. After the first battle, for example, we watch him "standing as if apart from himself" while "he viewed the last scene" (Chap. 4). After another battle, he finds "considerable joy in musing upon his performances during the charge.... He recalled bits of color that in the flurry had stamped themselves unawares upon his engaged sense" (Chap. 23/22). The recollection of these "bits of color" protects him from hearing "the bitter justice in the speeches of the gaunt and bronzed veterans" who call up tales of less sanguine memories.

In Henry's final assessment of his experience, he continues to consider his acts "in spectator fashion." Henry's "procession of memory" is described as though

> his public deeds were paraded in great and shining prominence. Those performances which had been witnessed by his fellows marched now in wide purple and gold, hiding various deflections. They went gaily with music. It was pleasure to watch these things. He spent delightful minutes viewing the gilded images of memory. (Chap. 25/24)

This spectacle of heroism is interrupted, however, by "the dogging memory of the tattered soldier." His memory evokes a narrative of events that disrupts the colorful procession. Yet Henry succeeds in translating this story of the past into the language of spectatorship:

> he saw his vivid error and he was afraid that it would stand before him all of his life. He took no share in the chatter of his comrades, nor did he look at them or know them save when he felt sudden suspicion that they were seeing his thoughts and scrutinizing each detail of the scene with the tattered soldier. (Chap. 25/24)

Once Henry contains the tattered man in the frame of a theatrical scene and cuts him off from a memory that can be recounted in a story, he can "put the sin at a distance" and find "in it quaint uses."

The theatrical quality of Crane's battlefield has important implications for the definition of manhood in *The Red Badge of Courage*. Critics have long debated whether or not Henry becomes a man by proving himself on the battlefield and whether he achieves a deeper self-knowledge. We can place this question in the context of the 1890s if we recall that to Crane's contemporaries, such as Holmes and Roosevelt, the battlefield provided an arena for recovering the whole self in acts of primitive virility, shorn of the veneer of bourgeois life. Crane shows, on the contrary, that the self realized through the spectacle of the battle is highly theatrical, and thus inherently tentative and unstable. Although *The Red Badge of Courage* is about the growth of a youth, it does not tell the story of a self that evolves from cumulative experience; rather, it displays a self that must be repeatedly improvised before the observer. In the novel, manhood does not emerge in the medium of conflict, from the classical struggle with a foe; instead it takes shape in the medium of the spectacle, from the relationship to a spectator. For Henry to become a man or to have a self, he needs to imagine an audience watching him, and can only represent his actions in the eyes of others, whether in the glances of his fellow soldiers, in the praises from the colonel, or in the fantasy of his own corpse viewed by the officer. This need for an audience helps explain why, when he runs away, he imagines himself being seen and laughed at by corpses; their stares preserve Henry's identity and keep him from his often expressed fear of being "swallowed up," a fate that for him is worse than death. Thus Crane's representation of war as a spectacle both adopts and subverts the interpretation of the battlefield as a crucible for virility, as well as the concept of manhood as an internal primal quality. The constant need for an audience on the battlefield both destabilizes and resocializes the identity of the "real man."

Martial valor has traditionally depended on the display of the soldier before an audience, whether through military parades, or chivalric contests, or in the written heroic record. In *The Red Badge of Courage* Crane undermines these traditional forms of spectatorship with his repeated references to the newspaper as the modern lens for composing and viewing the spectacle of war. When Henry runs away from the battle, he wonders about the form that the representation of his actions might take, and realizes that

> individuals must have supposed that they were cutting the letters of their names deep into everlasting tablets of brass or enshrining their reputations forever in the hearts of their countrymen, while, as to fact, the affair would appear in printed reports under a meek and immaterial title. (Chap. 8)

Immediately after reflecting about the ephemeral nature of the newspaper report, he comes upon an isolated field strewn with corpses that seems to provide evidence of this idea:

> On the far side, the ground was littered with clothes and guns. A newspaper, folded up, lay in the dirt. A dead soldier was stretched with his face hidden in his arm. (Chap. 8)

The description draws our vision to the newspaper before we notice the corpse. This narrative placement of the newspaper suggests its mediatory function in modern warfare, a role initiated during the Civil War—one of the first major wars to be reported on a mass scale—and intensified during the international wars of the late nineteenth century. Indeed, the newspaper becomes the disembodied eye that confers an identity on the fighting men and produces a spectacle for readers far away from the front. The placement of the newspaper in the landscape suggests that soldiers too rely upon the paper to read about themselves on the battlefield, and they thereby become both performers in and spectators of the same drama. Yet the appearance of the newspaper in this field of corpses also underscores its incongruity, as it lies on the ground cut off both from a living audience and from a meaningful context.

Crane's revision of the history and story of the Civil War as a spectacle links his imaginative rendition of a war he never experienced to his later career as a foreign correspondent, covering the Greco-Turkish and Spanish-American wars in the late 1890s. Crane reportedly jumped at the chance to see a real war in order to prove that *The Red Badge of Courage* was "all right."[28] Although he may have found that these wars verified his realism, his reports and fiction also show that the framework of the spectacle established in the novel provided a lens peculiarly suited to view international warfare in the 1890s.

"Jingoism is merely the lust of the spectator," wrote a British contemporary of Crane's, J. A. Hobson, in one of the first major studies of imperialism. Hobson compared the vicarious aggression of a spectator at a sporting event to the emotions of the jingoist, who remains "unpurged by any personal effort, risk or sacrifice, gloating over perils, pains and slaughter of fellow men who he does not know, but whose destruction he desires in a blind and artificially stimulated passion of hatred and revenge."[29] "The lust of the spectator" is both gratified and further aroused only in the act of watching, which distances the viewer while tantalizing him with the possibility of action. According to Hobson, who served as a journalist in the Boer War, the newspaper plays a crucial domestic role in arousing the spectatorial lust that supports imperial ventures in remote territories. Coinciding with the development of a mass circulation press in Britain and the United States, the international conflicts of the late nineteenth century created a new need for foreign correspondents to bring home the meaning of wars that "did not directly concern the future of the two countries where the major reading-public resided."[30]

In America in the 1890s, the so-called yellow press of Hearst and Pulitzer was notorious not only for sensationalistic coverage of the Cuban rebellion and the subsequent Spanish-American War, but also for staging many of the spectacles they reported. When in 1896 the illustrator Fredric Remington complained to Hearst from Havana that nothing was happening, Hearst reportedly responded, "You furnish the pictures and I'll furnish the war."[31] To keep his promise, Hearst filled his front page with pictures of Spanish atrocities at the same time that he started the modern sports page.[32] Both Hearst and Pulitzer made the news they reported by sending reporters on special spy missions, by leading rescue campaigns of Cuban ladies, or by using their own yachts—carrying their reporters—to capture Spanish refugees.

These spectacles often featured the reporter himself as their chief actor. During the international wars between the Civil War and World War I, the foreign correspondent came into being as a professional writer with a public persona. Bylines changed from "from our own correspondent" to the attribution of personal names, and headlines sometimes included the name of the reporter, as in the case of a celebrity like Crane: "STEPHEN CRANE AT THE FRONT FOR THE WORLD," "STEPHEN CRANE'S VIVID STORY OF THE BATTLE OF SAN JUAN," and "STEPHEN CRANE SKETCHES THE COMMON SOLDIER."[33] Reporters often made themselves or their colleagues the heroes of their stories and the act of reporting the main plot. This focus turned writing into a strenuous activity and the reporter into a virile figure who rivaled the soldiers. If the private, Henry Fleming, tries to become a spectator of the same battle he fights, reporters, the professional spectators, often tried to become actors by engaging in combat. Crane himself both played and parodied the figure of the heroic correspondent by flaunting his indifference to bullets under fire and by capturing a Puerto Rican town in a mock invasion. The theatrical style of *The Red Badge of Courage* anticipates the aggrandizement of the act of reporting to overshadow the action on the battlefield.

By dramatizing the exploits of the reporter, newspapers transformed political and military conflicts in foreign colonies into romantic adventures in exotic landscapes. In addition, Crane suggests in his novel *Active Service*— based on his experience in the Greco-Turkish War—that the reporter also provided an important spectatorial function for the soldiers on the field, who

> when they go away to the fighting ground, out of the sight, out of
> the hearing of the world known to them and are eager to perform
> feats of war in this new place they feel an absolute longing for a
> spectator.... The war correspondent arises, then, to become a sort
> of cheap telescope for the people at home; further still, there have
> been fights where the eyes of a solitary man were the eyes of the
> world; one spectator whose business it was to transfer, according
> to his ability, his visual impressions to other minds.[34]

This "cheap telescope" proved especially important on the battlefield of
colonial territories, where enemy combatants often were both physically
and ideologically invisible. Reports from Cuba commented on the difficulty
American troops had in seeing the Spanish fighters, who sniped at them
through the thick brush. After Spain surrendered, America's former allies,
the Cubans and even more so the Filipinos, turned their guerrilla warfare
against the Americans now occupying their lands. Whereas the European
Spaniards were represented as equal, if hated, foes, the Cuban and Filipino
guerrillas, even as allies, were represented not as soldiers fighting a real
war but as criminal elements to subdue.[35] In the face of such invisible and
shifting allies and enemies, the political context of the war often blurred. The
reporter redrew the contours of a foreign terrain by dramatizing American
action and identity in the eyes of the audience at home rather than in relation
to a shadowy and less than human enemy. The promise of being seen through
the medium of the newspaper compensates for the confusion and the fear of
not seeing.

In *The Red Badge of Courage*, Crane had already developed the mechanisms
of this cheap telescope by rendering the enemy invisible on the battlefield of
the Civil War and by making the soldier's identity more contingent on an
audience than on conflict with the foe. Many of Crane's newspaper reports
call attention to the spectacular nature of the battles through techniques
similar to those we have seen in his novel. In Crane's story of the Rough
Riders' "gallant blunder," for example, their noise and bravado appear to be
directed more toward making an impression on a domestic audience than
toward using effective strategy against the enemy, and in his vivid report of
the regulars charging up San Juan Hill, Crane offers the readers cues for
cheering, as though he were describing a football game.[36]

If his newspaper reports utilize this cheap telescope, many of Crane's
later stories about war test its ramifications and its limits. Much of his late
fiction explores the boundary line between action and spectatorship and the
consequences of crossing it. The correspondent in "Death and the Child,"
for example, loses his mind when he tries to step over that line; he takes up

arms to join the battle, only to hallucinate that the gun is strangling him. In "The Open Boat," the correspondent finds himself thrust into the role of actor in a classic adventure tale, only to share impotence and blindness with the other men in the boat.

In preparing Crane to view modern wars as spectacles, *The Red Badge of Courage* also taught him the incompatibility of the spectacle with traditional forms of storytelling, a gap only deepened by the newspaper version of the "story," which subordinates narrative context to theatrical effects. The impossibility of narrating experience frames Crane's "War Memories," his fictionalized memoir of the Spanish-American War. "War Memories" opens with a reporter's lament about the difficulty of getting at the "real thing," because, he continues, "war is neither magnificent nor squalid; it is simply life, and an expression of life can always evade us. We can never *tell* life, one to another, although sometimes we think we can" (emphasis added).[37] Yet if "telling" life in a coherent narrative is impossible, displaying it through fragmented scenes structures Crane's retrospective on the war. "War Memories" ends with a procession of wounded soldiers, who parade into town from the battlefield and file past a hotel veranda, "suffering from something which was like stage-fright."[38] Fixing the reader in the position of spectator, the narrator calls attention both to his own theatricality and to its limits as he draws the curtains on the last line: "The episode was closed. And you can depend upon it that I have told you nothing at all, nothing at all, nothing at all."[39] Like Henry's recollection of the battle, Crane's "War Memories" of his activity as a correspondent form a fragmented spectacle, which he refuses to contextualize within the narrative of experience or history.

The link between Crane's revision of the Civil War and his representation of international warfare in the 1890s may help explain the unique position of *The Red Badge of Courage* in literary history, not only as the classic novel about the American Civil War but also as a paradigm of the modern American war novel. The popularity of Crane's book in both England and America in the 1890s can be understood in the context of the heightened militarism in both cultures, enacted on the battlefields of colonial territories. If those British reviewers were correct who read *The Red Badge of Courage* as a critique of jingoism, of the spectatorial lust that facilitated imperial warfare, its critique must be an imminent one that emerges from a narrative structure engaged in producing the spectacle of modern warfare.[40]

In his legacy to the century he did not live to see, Crane not only redefined the war novel through the focus on the psyche of the individual soldier but also "invented the persona of the war correspondent for the novelist" of the twentieth century.[41] The components of this figure who straddles the boundary line between spectator and actor are already present in *The Red Badge of Courage*. There Crane not only outlined a hero and a narrative strategy to be fleshed out by American writers from Ernest Hemingway to Norman Mailer, but his revision of the Civil War also shaped both the experience and the representation of those remote wars that American writers have pursued throughout the twentieth century. It is Crane's anticipation of the modern spectacle of war, more than his historical veracity, that allowed Hemingway to write in 1942 that *The Red Badge of Courage* was the only enduring "real literature of our Civil War."

NOTES

1. Quoted in Charles H. Brown, *The Correspondents' War: Journalists in the Spanish-American War* (New York: Scribners, 1967), p. 1.

2. Stephen Crane, *Reports of War*, ed. Fredson Bowers (Charlottesville: University of Virginia Press, 1971), p. 487.

3. Paul H. Buck, *The Road to Reunion, 1865–1890* (Boston: Little, Brown, 1937), chaps. viii/xi.

4. George Williams, "Lights and Shadows of Army Life," *Century Magazine* 28 (October 1884): 810.

5. Editors, *Century Magazine* 28 (October 1884): 944.

6. Robert U. Johnson and Clarence C. Buel, eds., *Battle and Leaders of the Civil War*, 4 vols. (New York: The Century Co., 1887–8), preface.

7. Robert A. Lively, *Fiction Fights the Civil War* (Chapel Hill: University of North Carolina Press, 1957), p. 57.

8. Quoted in George M. Fredrickson, *The Inner Civil War: Northern Intellectuals and the Crisis of the Union* (New York: Harper & Row, 1965), p. 170.

9. John Higham, "The Re-Orientation of American Culture in the 1890's," in *Writing American History: Essays in Modern Scholarship* (Bloomington: Indiana University Press, 1970), pp. 73–102.

10. Quoted in Higham, "The Re-Orientation," p. 86.

11. John Berryman, *Stephen Crane* (New York: Meridian Books, 1962), p. 78.

12. On the similarities between naturalism and the romance, see T. J. Jackson Lears, *No Place of Grace: Antimodernism and the Transformation of American Culture, 1880–1920* (New York: Pantheon Books, 1981), pp. 103–7.

13. James D. Hart, *The Popular Book: A History of America's Literary Taste* (1950; rpt. Berkeley: University of California Press, 1963), chap. 11.

14. Quoted in Larzer Ziff, *The American 1890's* (Lincoln: University of Nebraska Press, 1966), p. 265.

15. Lears, *No Place of Grace*, chap. 3.

16. William Dean Howells, "The New Historical Romances," *North American Review* 171 (December 1900): 935–6.

17. David Axeen, "'Heroes of the Engine Room': American 'Civilization' and the War with Spain," *American Quarterly* 36 (Fall 1984): 481–502.

18. Theodore Roosevelt, *The Strenuous Life: Essays and Addresses* (New York: The Century Co., 1900) pp. 1–21.

19. Stephen Crane, "Roosevelt's Rough Rider's Loss Due to A Gallant Blunder," *New York World*, June 25, 1898, reprinted in Crane, *Reports of War*, p. 146.

20. Seymour Dodd, *The Song of the Rappahannock* (New York: Dodd, Mead, 1898).

21. Eric Solomon, *Stephen Crane: From Parody to Realism* (Cambridge, Mass.: Harvard University Press, 1966), pp. 1–18.

22. R. W. Stallman and Lillian Gilkes, *Stephen Crane: Letters* (New York: New York University Press, 1960), p. 17.

23. These examples were pointed out by Kenneth Haltman in an unpublished paper.

24. In an 1896 *New York Times* review of *The Red Badge of Courage*, Harold Frederic suggests that this sense of an urban environment structures our reading experience when be compares the characters to strangers on a train: "not a word is expended on telling where they come from, or who they are. They pass across the picture, or shift from one posture to another in its moving composition, with the impersonality of one's chance fellow-passengers in a railroad car." Harold Frederic, "Review," *New York Times*, January 26, 1986. Reprinted in *Stephen Crane: The Critical Heritage*, ed. Richard Weatherford (London: Routledge & Kegan Paul, 1973), p. 117.

25. General Alexander C. McClurg, letter to the *Dial*, April 16, 1896; rpt. in Weatherford, *Stephen Crane*, pp. 138–41. Donald Pease, "Fear, Rage, and the Mistrials of Representation in *The Red Badge of Courage*," in Eric Sundquist, ed., *American Realism: New Essays* (Baltimore: Johns Hopkins University Press, 1982), pp. 155–75.

26. Walter Benjamin, "The Storyteller," in *Illuminations*, ed. Hannah Arendt (New York: Schocken Books, 1969), pp. 83–109. Benjamin discusses the challenge presented by the technological and mass qualities of the World War I battlefield to the traditional experience transmitted through stories.

27. Ibid., p. 84.

28. Berryman, *Stephen Crane*, p. 174.

29. J. A. Hobson, *Imperialism: A Study* (1902; reprinted Ann Arbor: University of Michigan Press, 1972), p. 215.

30. Phillip Knightley, *The First Casualty: From Crimea to Vietnam: The War Correspondent as Hero, Propagandist and Myth Maker* (New York: Harcourt, Brace, Jovanovich, 1975), p. 42.

31. Frank Luther Mott, *American Journalism: 1690–1960* (New York: 1962), p. 529.

32. Higham, "The Re-Orientation," p. 84.

33. Crane, *Reports of War*, pp. 487, 492, 495.

34. Stephen Crane, *The Third Violet and Active Service*, ed. Fredson Bowers (Charlottesville: University Press of Virginia, 1976), p. 172.

35. Axeen, "'Heroes of the Engine Room,'" pp. 499–510.

36. Crane, *Reports of War*, pp. 146, 154–65.

37. Stephen Crane, "War Memories," in *Wounds in the Rain* (1900), reprinted in *Tales of War*, ed. Fredson Bowers (Charlottesville: University Press of Virginia, 1970), p. 223.

38. Ibid., p. 263.

39. Op. cit.

40. For examples of this reading, see Weatherford, ed., *Stephen Crane*, pp. 99, 105, 127.

41. Martin Green, *The Great American Adventure* (Boston: Beacon Press, 1984), p. 169.

CHRISTOPHER BENFEY

Introduction to
The Double Life of Stephen Crane

Stephen Crane's extraordinary career was once the stuff of legend. A hundred years later we are still trying to sort out the facts of his life from the fictions. Crane was the most vivid and innovative writer to emerge in the United States during the 1890s. Today he is remembered mainly as the author of *The Red Badge of Courage*, a novel that is inflicted on high-school students as though it were documentary coverage of the Civil War. It fooled some of Crane's contemporaries too; at least one veteran claimed, "I was with Crane at Antietam." Crane, who was born in 1871, enjoyed the confusion.

In his time Crane was one of the most visible American writers, and one of the most talked about. As a young reporter of New York slum life he once caused a scandal by defending a prostitute in court against a policeman's charges. Later he was a highly paid war correspondent, covering conflicts in Greece and Cuba for the papers of Pulitzer and Hearst. (They knew his celebrity value; his account of the first major battle of the Spanish-American War carried the headline THE RED BADGE OF COURAGE WAS HIS WIG-WAG FLAG.) During the last year of his life he took refuge, from creditors and hangers-on, in a huge Elizabethan manor house in the south of England. There he lived quietly with his common-law wife, Cora Taylor, the former madam of a Jacksonville brothel called the Hotel de Dream. But shrewd witnesses

From *The Double Life of Stephen Crane*, pp. 3–12. © 1992 by Christopher Benfey.

lived nearby; for his close friends and neighbors in England included Joseph Conrad, Ford Madox Ford, and Henry James.

Crane was twenty-three in the fall of 1895, when *The Red Badge of Courage* was published. An impoverished newspaper reporter living in New York, he watched the machinery of fame that had been perfected by his bosses go to work for him. *The Red Badge* was a bestseller in the United States, and inspired among English critics what H. G. Wells called an "orgy of praise." During the next few years Crane worked as a journalist in New York and England, trying to keep the promise of his early work. "People may just as well discover now," he complained in 1896, "that the high dramatic key of *The Red Badge* cannot be sustained." While he recovered the intensity of *The Red Badge* in at least a dozen dazzling short stories, as well as in some of his cryptic poems, the hectic pace of Crane's life caught up with him. Exhausted from covering the Spanish-American War and claiming to be "disappointed with success," Crane died of tuberculosis in a sanatorium in the Black Forest on June 5, 1900. He had managed to see the new century—just, though he had not yet reached his twenty-ninth birthday.

To his contemporaries Crane's short life had some of the allure of pulp fiction; "he actually lived what his average countrymen collectively dreamed," J. C. Levenson has written. If the lives of writers tend to be conspicuous for their lack of outward event (one thinks of the quiet lives of Hawthorne or Dickinson or Wallace Stevens), Crane's life sometimes seems nothing but outward event—one wonders when he found the time to write.

The shape of Crane's career has a peculiar fascination for the biographer. If most writers tend to write about their experience, however disguised, Crane did the reverse: he tried to live what he'd already written. *Maggie*, his first, and affecting, novel about a "girl of the streets," shows more curiosity than knowledge; a few years after writing it Crane fell in love with a real-life madam. His acquaintance with conflict was limited to football when he wrote *The Red Badge of Courage*; he became a war correspondent in Cuba and Greece to see, he told Joseph Conrad, whether *The Red Badge* was accurate. He wrote several shipwreck narratives before he managed to find himself aboard a foundering steamer. Even in his newspaper work he sometimes lacked the patience to wait for something to happen. On one occasion he "covered" in great detail a fire in the Bowery, and was much praised for his vivid account; he'd made it all up.

The biographer's major task, in making sense of Stephen Crane, is not the tedious and often unconvincing effort to tie the work, however tenuously, to possible models in the life, tracing every fictional mother to the novelist's mother, and every artist to the novelist-in-disguise. The challenge, instead, is to make sense of Crane's fascinating attempts to live his fictions, to make his life an analogue of his work.

For Crane lived his life backwards, or rather he wrote it forwards. While Crane's case is particularly extreme (and all the more visible for being so literal—no metaphorical shipwrecks for him), I suspect that this pattern is more common among writers than might be supposed. Indeed, one might push the generalization further. We are mistaken when, in trying to understand an author's career, we take the "real life" for granted, and look for its imprint in the "imaginary life" of the subject's writings. For surely this is the wrong way around; what solidity, and givenness, there is in a writer's life exists first in the writings. The problem is to see how the work of art shaped the writer's life.

In a further turn of the screw, some of Crane's best-known works are about people who try—usually in vain—to live according to the shapes of their own previously imagined stories, stories that are in turn often based on the popular culture of the nineteenth century. Maggie believes a knight will come to her rescue, as so often happens in the melodramas she sees on stage; Henry Fleming assumes the Civil War will correspond to his own fantasies of heroism, drawn from epics and soldiers' yarns; the Swede who visits the Blue Hotel is convinced that he'll die in the manner of gunmen in dime westerns. In Crane's world, written narratives tend to precede experience, rather than the reverse.

This doesn't mean that we can dispense with psychological explanations in making sense of Crane's life and work. On the contrary, we must deal with a psyche so powerful that it shaped events according to its own, mainly literary, patterns. Crane probably came to this practice early, growing up in a religious household devoted to the written word, and found it confirmed in a newspaper world that emphasized getting the story even if one had to foment it.

To some extent, of course, we all try to live our fantasies. But the sheer extremity of Crane's write-it-then-live-it procedures deserves special attention. John Berryman said of Crane's hunger for danger: "after imagining it for a masterpiece he needed to feel [it], and to see what he would do with it." Or, as Crane himself remarked in one of his sketches, "when a man gets the ant of desire-to-see-what-it's-like stirring in his heart, he will wallow out to sea in a pail."

Crane's ancestry did not promise a life of adventure. He was born in Newark, New Jersey, in 1871, the youngest of fourteen children, of whom nine survived infancy. On his mother's side of the family, Crane wrote, "everybody as soon as he could walk became a Methodist clergyman—of the old ambling-nag, saddlebag, exhorting kind." His mother married a minister of the same faith, who wrote reformist tracts on the dangers of dancing and drinking. He died when Crane was eight, a loss crucial to the child's growing sense of his world. Crane's industrious but overextended mother wrote for Methodist journals to support the family and lectured for the New Jersey Woman's Christian Temperance Union. Thus, Crane's parents were both writers; he grew up in a world in which words were powerful. Biographers have tended to dismiss Crane's parents as slightly comical characters. One aim of this book is to reunite, so to speak, the prodigal son and his parents.

Like the careers of other highly visible and self-dramatizing writers, Crane's has seemed to crystallize around a series of near-legendary incidents. During the years between his arrival in New York City in 1891 at the age of nineteen and his death nine years later, his life (like his novels) was curiously *episodic*, as though he were intentionally living a narrative plot. The chapters of his life—from scandal to shipwreck to love and war—tend to have clear beginnings and endings.

Crane's life was at once so productive and so short that it's easy to forget that he could have been a twentieth-century writer. He was born in 1871, the same year as Dreiser. Willa Cather, Gertrude Stein, and Robert Frost were born during the following three years. Only Crane's amazing precocity makes us think of him as belonging to the generation that preceded theirs.

But for a writer of Crane's proximity to our own time (had he lived to be seventy he would have died in 1941), we know remarkably little about his day-to-day existence; indeed, we know even less than earlier students of Crane's life thought they did. The astonishing fact is that for seven decades much of the scholarship on Crane's life and work has been based on a fraud. The single greatest bar to a right understanding of Stephen Crane's life is the work of his first biographer, Thomas Beer, on whose vivid and remarkable book all later biographers have depended heavily. In the writing of biography, invention is supposed to play a subsidiary role; in Beer's *Stephen Crane* (1923) it was primary. Beer was never quite above suspicion; doubts were raised early on—especially during the 1950s—about this detail or that one: Was the singer Helen Trent (of whose existence no evidence has come to light) really one of his first loves? Had Crane really counted the great painter Albert Pinkham Ryder among his drinking buddies? Did he really write a story, the manuscript of which has been lost, called "Vashti in the Dark," about a Methodist minister who finds that his wife has been raped by a black man, and kills himself in grief?

But the extent of Beer's invention has only quite recently been clarified, thanks to the detective work of Stanley Wertheim and Paul Sorrentino, who edited Crane's correspondence, and the analysis of John Clendenning. Beer's book on Crane, it now seems fair to say, is a tissue of lies, a forgery through and through. But having discovered so much, we find that we know far less than we thought we did about the enigmatic Crane, and especially about his childhood and early youth. For with regard to those years, Beer was the major, almost the only, source. As for the extraordinary letters Beer quotes at length, containing some of Crane's most bracing, and most often quoted, literary and philosophical opinions, they too are apparently forgeries—brilliant forgeries, one feels compelled to add. (Beer's drafts of these letters have come to light, allowing us to appreciate his mastery of the forger's art.) We must now forget that Crane claimed he got his artistic education on the Bowery, that he thought *War and Peace* went on and on like Texas, that he said that while Robert Louis Stevenson had passed away, he hadn't passed away far enough.

Half the clues to Crane's life have gone up in smoke. Under such circumstances, to try to make sense anew of Crane's career is particularly challenging. The disappearance of so much biographical detail shifts the balance—the documentary balance, so to speak—back toward Crane's writings, where of course it should have been all along.

"Each generation has something different at which they are all looking," Gertrude Stein observed. The generation that came of age during the 1890s—the generation of both Stein and Crane—shared Crane's mania for risk. The usual diagnosis is that prosperity resulting from industrialization removed the monied classes from the immediacy of life. ("Secular and religious education had effaced the throat-grappling instinct," Crane wrote in *The Red Badge*, "or else firm finance held in check the passions.") How much earlier this immediacy of life was present was much debated, as the vogue shifted from medieval knighthood to the equally chivalrous cowboys in Owen Wister's *The Virginian* and Frederic Remington's illustrations. Wister's friend Theodore Roosevelt (who admired Crane) offered a cure with his cult of "strenuousness," and William James looked for a "moral equivalent of war" in peacetime. There was widespread fear that the lower classes, still exposed to the vivifying diet of risk, were getting stronger and the ruling classes weaker—a dangerous situation in the eyes of establishment figures like Roosevelt and Remington.

While Crane shared this sense of malaise, he also questioned it. One of his early poems is a shrewd critique of the strenuous ethic, as well as an anxious meditation on his own action-obsessed life:

THERE WAS A MAN WHO LIVED A LIFE OF FIRE.
EVEN UPON THE FABRIC OF TIME,
WHERE PURPLE BECOMES ORANGE

AND ORANGE PURPLE,
THIS LIFE GLOWED,
A DIRE RED STAIN, INDELIBLE;
YET WHEN HE WAS DEAD,
HE SAW THAT HE HAD NOT LIVED
    (*The Black Riders*, LXII)

The fear expressed in the last line would seem more appropriate when voiced, as it is in Henry James's *The Ambassadors*, by a provincial like Lambert Strether; it sounds odd from Crane, whose life was packed with those intensities that Strether was afraid he'd miss. The indelible red stain is, presumably, Crane's own written works, including *The Red Badge of Courage*, as though his writing somehow canceled out his life.

What Crane is reacting to is his suspicion that "real life" had itself become unreal by the 1890s. The strenuous life of the West, as portrayed by Wister, Remington, and Roosevelt, already seemed conventionalized, sentimentalized, lost to real experience. Crane's obsessive search throughout the 1890s was to find a way to become absorbed in the actual lives of the people he wrote about without lapsing into artifice and theatricality. Crane's stated allegiance to William Dean Howells's variety of literary realism was always less an aesthetic conviction than a commitment to intense experience. While he dutifully concurred in Howells's ambition to "picture the daily life in the most exact terms possible," the lives that interested Crane were those of people caught in extreme situations, too absorbed in their difficulties to indulge in hypocrisy and selfishness.

It was ultimately *inner* experience that Crane was after; the fear in his poem is that of an inner life lost. But it is precisely Crane's psyche that has proved baffling and unavailable, not least because he indulged in none of those apparent revelations of private life so dear to biographers: diaries, journals, intimate letters, memoirs, autobiographies. As a result of this paucity of self-exposure, we're in the dark about some of the most basic things about Crane. His feelings about his parents, for example, and his childhood in general are virtually a blank. The precise tenor of his relations with Cora remain an enigma; their letters have never come to light. We don't know, for example, whether they ever considered having children, or were capable of having them. We don't know when Crane contracted tuberculosis, or when he knew he was dying of it. And there are months in his life when we have virtually no idea where he was or what he was doing. One is faced with these mysteries in addition to the usual cruxes, such as how this boy, recently escaped from college, managed to write the greatest war novel by an American.

Stephen Crane comes across, nearly a hundred years later, as a figure of extraordinary personal magnetism. This pull comes partly from the surface of his own writings—those flashing, ironic, crystalline constructions that have so successfully resisted the clumsy advances of academic criticism. And part of the magnetism comes from the man himself, as he appears (and disappears) in the distorting mirrors of personal reminiscence and anecdote. Crane was talked about almost from the beginning of his career, and written about from the end. This elusive, angular, underweight, physically unobtrusive figure was singularly blessed, and cursed, with the gift of being noticed.

Crane was aware of his mercurial existence; he seemed almost to revel in it. "I cannot help vanishing and disappearing and dissolving," he told an editor in 1897. "It is my foremost trait." The lack of conventional biographical "material"—other than his own extensive published works—is worth thinking about. For Crane was a man who, in peculiar ways, vanished into his own fictions. He once excused himself for not writing long descriptions home of what he saw and did in England: "I write myself so completely out ... that an attempt of the sort would be absurd."

Equally absurd is the frequent tendency, by Crane's biographers and critics, to slide over our ignorance and pretend that we know more about this enigmatic life than we do. In this book I have tried instead to preserve the mystery, to highlight what we don't know, while at the same time providing a key for what we know.

That key is a simple one, though complex in its application. For Crane's double life was not so much duplicitous as strangely *duplicate*. His fictions were not retrospective; they were eerily predictive. The question is why he felt it necessary to try to live what he had already so masterfully imagined. He planned his life; he seemed to plan his death. It was the most deliberate life imaginable.

NOTES

"Brevity," Crane once told Cora, "is an element that enters importantly into all pleasures of life." To avoid cluttering my text with numerals and distracting injunctions to read other things, I have kept scholarly apparatus minimal. Crane's writings are short and easy to track down. Unless another source is given, all quotations from Crane's works are drawn from the readily available Library of America edition: *Stephen Crane: Prose and Poetry*, edited by J. C. Levenson (New York: 1984). Other materials by Crane are taken from *The Works of Stephen Crane*, edited by Fredson Bowers (Charlottesville: The University Press of Virginia, 1969–76), ten volumes, referred to in the Notes, with volume and page number, as "V." Quotations from Crane's letters and correspondents come from *The Correspondence of Stephen Crane*, edited by Stanley Wertheim and Paul Sorrentino (New York: Columbia University Press, 1988), two volumes.

INTRODUCTION
(numbers refer to pages in the text)

3. Colonel John L. Burleigh, quoted in R. W. Stallman, *Stephen Crane: A Biography*, rev. ed. (New York: Braziller, 1973), p. 181.

4. H. G. Wells, "Stephen Crane from an English Standpoint," in Stephen Crane, *The Red Badge of Courage*, ed. Sculley Bradley, Richmond Groom Beatty, E. Hudson Long (New York: Norton, 1962), p. 205.

4. J. C. Levenson, "Stephen Crane," in *Major Authors of America*, ed. Perry Miller (New York: Harcourt, 1962), vol. 2, p. 385.

5. See Larzer Ziff, "Outstripping the Event: Stephen Crane," in Ziff, *The American 1890's* (New York: Viking, 1966). Of Crane's journalism, Ziff remarks: "Stephen Crane's expectations had a way of outstripping the event ... [he] developed a set of responses that anticipated the reality" (p. 186).

6. See Miles Orvell, *The Real Thing* (Chapel Hill: University of North Carolina Press, 1989). Orvell argues that Crane's characters take their cues from popular culture, trying to fit their lives to its patterns.

—John Berryman, *Stephen Crane* (New York: Sloane, 1950), p. 97.

8. Thomas Beer, *Stephen Crane* (New York: Alfred A. Knopf, 1923).

—See Stanley Wertheim and Paul Sorrentino, "Thomas Beer: The Clay Feet of Stephen Crane Biography," in *American Literary Realism* 22, no. 3 (1990): pp. 2–16; and John Clendenning, "Thomas Beer's *Stephen Crane*: The Eye of His Imagination," in *Prose Studies* 14, no. 1; (May 1991), pp. 68–80.

9. See Alan Trachtenberg, *The Incorporation of America: Culture and Society in the Gilded Age* (New York: Hill and Wang, 1982), pp. 109, 141, for the generation of the 1890s.

PAUL SORRENTINO

Stephen Crane's Struggle with Romance *in* The Third Violet

Stephen Crane's *The Third Violet* (1897) has often been dismissed as a failed attempt to write popular romance. Commercially unsuccessful, it received mixed reviews: American critics thought it a "vacuous trifle," "as inane a story of summer resort flirtations as was ever written," and "a book with badness written large all over it"; to the English the book kept Crane "in the front rank of English and American writers of fiction" and made him "the author who will introduce the United States to the ordinary English world."[1] Crane's own responses range from characterizing it as "serious work" to condemning it as "even worse" than any of his other books.[2] Though occasionally praised—Ford Madox Ford called it his favorite of Crane's books and Christopher Benfey has more recently ranked it "among Crane's unfairly forgotten works"[3]—it has generally been dismissed as a partly autobiographical potboiler lacking a coherent plot, a clear purpose, and developed characterization. To Edwin H. Cady, for example, "The failure to face and develop the conflicts of class and convention, of sex and of art against society, destroys the novel and strips its deficiencies of all concealment."[4] John Berryman asks, "What made Crane think he could write effectively at length about a courtship resists inquiry."[5] But *The Third Violet* is more than a potboiler; it deserves renewed attention as Crane's thoughtful response to the Realism War of the late nineteenth century. A self-conscious parody of the romance novel that fictionalizes

From *American Literature*, Vol. 70, No. 2 (June, 1998), pp. 265–291. © 1998 by Duke University Press.

Crane's struggles with his own identity and with the profession of authorship, the book provides additional evidence about Crane's literary interests and opinions.

The Third Violet has its roots in Crane's October 1894 interview of William Dean Howells, "Howells Fears the Realists Must Wait," which focused on the battle in the literary marketplace between realistic and romantic fiction. According to Cady, the interview "elucidated Howells' theory more plainly and effectively than perhaps any other single statement—including Howells' own."[6] Crane asked Howells whether or not he had recently "observed a change in the literary pulse of the country.... Last winter, for instance, it seemed that realism was almost about to capture things, but then recently I have thought that I saw coming a sort of a counter-wave, a flood of the other—a reaction, in fact."[7] The romantic novels of this counter-wave were unrealistic, Howells argued, because they lacked proportion and perspective, and equated life with "Love and courtship": "Life began when the hero saw a certain girl, and it ended abruptly when he married her." A realistic novel keeps love in perspective and sees it as simply one of "these things that we live in continually" (617). The most influential American critic of romance, Howells had depicted the stereotypical romance novel as *Tears, Idle Tears* and "slop, silly slop" in *The Rise of Silas Lapham*, and he later coined the expression *romanticistic novel* to characterize a genre that "professes like the real novel to portray actual life, but it does this with an excess of drawing and coloring which are false to nature ... and endeavors to hide in a cloud of incident the deformity and artificiality of its creations."[8]

Recognizing the potential loss of income risked by ignoring popular taste, Crane speculated in the interview whether realistic novels would be "a profitable investment." If fiction is a commodity, then the value of one's stock in the literary market depends on public acceptance. Though Howells encouraged the realistic writer to remain "true to his conscience," he acknowledged that the battle between private vision and public demand would be "a long serious conflict." Given popular taste, realists faced a dilemma: Should they strive for an honest interpretation of reality or cater to public demand for romance and become, in Howells's words, "public fools" acting like "trained bear[s]" (616)?[9]

As a child, Crane learned about the dangers of romance from his father. A prominent Methodist author and clergyman, the Reverend Jonathan Townley Crane sounds much like Howells in a tract criticizing idle reading:

> [N]ovel-readers spend many a precious hour in dreaming out clumsy little romances of their own, in which they themselves are the beautiful ladies and the gallant gentlemen who achieve

impossibilities, suffer unutterable woe for a season, and at last anchor in a boundless ocean of connubial bliss.... It is a vice of novelists as a class, to exalt love and matrimony above all else, and thus create in susceptible youth the habit of thinking and dreaming of matrimony above all else."[10]

Long before meeting Howells, Crane knew about the falseness of romance, experimenting only briefly with what he called his "clever Rudyard-Kipling style" (*C*, 1:63).

Describing his quest for realism as "more of a battle than a journey," he wrote in spring 1894:

> I developed all alone a little creed of art which I thought was a good one. Later I discovered that my creed was identical with the one of Howells and Garland and in this way I became involved in the beautiful war between those who say that art is man's substitute for nature and we are the most successful in art when we approach the nearest to nature and truth, and those who say— well, I don't know what they say. They don't, they can't say much but they fight villianously [*sic*] and keep Garland and I out of the big magazines. Howells, of course, is too powerful for them.
>
> If I had kept to my clever Rudyard-Kipling style, the road might have been shorter but, ah, it wouldn't be the true road.... And now I am almost at the end of it. (*C*, 1:63)

Crane later asserted, "the nearer a writer gets to life, the greater he becomes as an artist, and most of my prose writings have been toward the goal partially described by that misunderstood and abused word, realism" (*C*, 1:232). Crane's pursuit of a career as a writer, however, was periodically frustrated by publishers. In 1893, when no one would publish his first book, *Maggie*, he printed it privately at his own expense; in 1894 negotiations over the publication of *The Black Riders and Other Lines* temporarily stalled because Crane and the publisher disagreed "on a multitude of points"; and in the same year he became convinced that S. S. McClure, who had held the manuscript of *The Red Badge of Courage* for six months without taking action, was a "Beast" who had kept him "near mad" and "in one of the ditches" of poverty (*C*, 1:73, 79). By the time of the interview with Howells in October 1894, professional setbacks had stretched Crane's patience. Although he was only two months away from national recognition with the newspaper publication of *The Red Badge of Courage*, he was still a year away from commercial success and the international acclaim brought by the book publication of his war novel. Appropriately, Crane initially titled *The Third Violet*, a fictionalized account of his professional struggles, "The Eternal Patience."[11]

On the surface, *The Third Violet* exemplifies what Howells criticized during the interview—a story in which boy meets girl, boy pursues girl, and boy and girl live happily ever after. Billie Hawker, a struggling artist in New York City, returns to his parents' farm in the country to paint and there becomes infatuated with Grace Fanhall, a wealthy aristocratic socialite vacationing for the summer at a local inn. Unfortunately, Hawker handles the courtship awkwardly, and he becomes distressed when faced with a rich rival, Jem Oglethorpe. Teasing and satirical comments from George Hollanden, a writer also staying at the inn, upset Hawker further, though he is relieved when his rival departs. The novel then shifts abruptly to New York City and the Bohemian rooms of Hawker and his artist friends. Hawker finds his attraction to Grace complicated by Florinda O'Connor, a local model who loves him. Confused about his feelings, he treats Florinda coolly, but his friends tease him about his relationships with two women. After a certain amount of anguish and self-pity, Hawker visits Grace in her Manhattan brownstone and tells her he has treasured two violets she gave him while they were in the country. To his surprise she gives him a third, and the novel ends with the two apparently happily together.

Much of the novel's dialogue focuses on the difficulty authors and painters face in balancing popular taste and personal vision. Like Crane just before publication of *The Red Badge of Courage*, Hawker is on the verge of fame, but he struggles with the debate articulated by Oglethorpe, who contends that the best artists are those who earn the most money, and Hollanden, who says they are the worst.[12] After studying art in Paris, Hawker returns to America but finds that to survive he must cater to the marketplace by painting designs for tomato cans.[13] Though forced to equate art with advertising, he privately adheres to the realist credo of painting "the ordinary thing" (296). But anxiety about demeaning work intensifies Hawker's social awkwardness; as he gets off the train in the opening scene, he accidentally hits the nephew of Grace Fanhall with an easel, a symbol of his profession. Hawker's clumsiness foreshadows his awkwardness with Grace and his difficulty in integrating his profession and his social life. Similarly, his anxiety mars his work and affects his relationships with other artists. He becomes upset while "discussing art with some pot-boiler" (356), who, like Oglethorpe, defines art solely in terms of commercial success, and he approaches his craft violently. Painting "with a wild face like a man who is killing" (337), Hawker envisions a "burning" sky colored with "powder smoke," as though a weapon had been fired. When Hollanden questions the accuracy of Hawker's depiction of the setting, Hawker screams, "[S]hut up or I'll smash you with the easel" (337–38). The association between artistic creation and violence suggests Hawker's internal battle: Should he pursue his personal vision of truth or should he be content to continually replicate the same forms on cans? In chapter 1, when Hawker rides a carriage to his parents' farm, he gets off at a literal crossroads, which metaphorically suggests the crossroads he has come to in his professional development. He could follow the path of Purple Sanderson, who struggled before achieving fame and wealth as an artist, or he could follow Hollanden, who began his writing career "with a determination to be a prophet" but devolved into "being an acrobat, a trained bear of the magazines, and a juggler of comic paragraphs" (293–94).[14]

Crane reached his own crossroads while writing *The Third Violet* in fall 1895. A celebrity after the appearance of *The Red Badge of Courage*, he wavered between commitment to a vision and the lure of public acclaim. On the one hand, he was delighted with the "passionately enthusiastic" reviews of his war novel and capitalized on his fame by touring Virginia for a proposed series of articles on Civil War battlefields for the McClure Syndicate (*C*, 1:144). On the other, he feared the public's obsession with the "damned" and "accursed" *Red Badge of Courage*, and he hoped that readers might "discover now that the high dramatic key of The Red Badge cannot be sustained" (*C*, 1:161, 191). He worried that instant fame might "turn [him] ever so slightly from what [he] believe[d] to be the pursuit of truth" (*C*, 1:192). To the editor of a magazine he wrote, "Now that [*The Red Badge of Courage*] is published and the people seem to like it I suppose I ought to be satisfied, but somehow I am not as happy as I was in the uncertain, happy-go-lucky newspaper-writing days. I used to dream continually of success then. Now that I have achieved it in some measure it seems like mere flimsy paper" (*C*, 1:233). As he had learned during his interview with Howells, the anticipation of success can easily divert one from the pursuit of one's artistic vision. For Crane, however, the real danger was ultimately "not the world ... but man's own colossal impulses more strong than chains" (*C*, 1:187). He knew that the pursuit of fame for its own sake—an "appetite for victory, as victory is defined by the mob"—could sidetrack him from "a sincere, desperate, lonely battle to remain true to [his] conception of [his] life and the way it should be lived" (*C*, 1:186, 187).

Ironically, Crane's fame made him as much a marketable commodity as his successful novel. While Crane was writing his novel criticizing the commodification of art, Elbert Hubbard, one of the 1890s' greatest hucksters, was planning a banquet for December 1895, ostensibly to honor the author of the acclaimed war novel but actually to publicize his Society of the Philistines and its iconoclastic magazine, *The Philistine*. A master of advertising, Hubbard released Crane's letter of acceptance to newspapers without asking his permission; mailed seven hundred invitations, most of them complimentary; and printed three souvenir pamphlets. Rather than a tribute to Crane, the banquet deteriorated into a drunken roast of the guest of honor and left him feeling deceived and disillusioned. Treating Crane as a commodity, Hubbard had packaged and sold him to the public.[15]

Crane responded to the battle between realism and romance—and his own anxiety about the profession of authorship—by parodying the romance novel in *The Third Violet*. Eric Solomon has argued that Crane frequently uses parody to establish "a dialogue between the parodied tradition and his new realism," but he considers *The Third Violet* a potboiler written to capitalize on the success of love stories.[16] The novel, however, is more than hack work; rather than accepting romantic clichés, Crane treats them ironically to expose their artifice. While visiting the waterfall near Hemlock Inn, for example, Hawker recounts to Grace the sentimental Indian legend of the "red-stained crags" (296):

> "Once upon a time, there was a beautiful Indian maiden, of course. And she was, of course, beloved by a youth from another tribe who was very handsome and stalwart and a mighty hunter, of course. But the maiden's father was, of course, a stern old chief, and when the question of his daughter's marriage came up, he, of course, declared that the maiden should be wedded only to a warrior of her tribe. And, of course, when the young man heard this he said that in such case he would, of course, fling himself headlong from that crag. The old chief was, of course, obdurate, and, of course, the youth did, of course, as he had said. And, of course, the maiden wept." After Hawker had waited for some time, he said with severity: "You seem to have no great appreciation of folk-lore." (299)

The stubborn parent, the handsome impetuous hero, and the beautiful weeping heroine are stock characters in romance. Grace's lack of interest is, therefore, no surprise, for Hawker's introductory "Once upon a time" and his repeated "of course" remind her of the formulaic nature of the plot. A romance plot does not imitate "the ordinary thing"; it imitates another romance plot.

After Hawker and Grace return to New York City, Crane echoes the waterfall scene in Grace's home, where "great folds of lace swept down in orderly cascades, as water trained to fall mathematically" (366), an image that also suggests the predictability of clichéd plots. Crane again parodies the romance tradition by alluding to an imaginary sentimental drama, "Hearts at War,"[17] in an awkward exchange between Hawker and Grace:

[W]hen she entered the room he said: "How delighted I am to see you again."

She had said: "Why, Mr. Hawker, it was so charming in you to come."

It did not appear that Hawker's tongue could wag to his purpose. The girl seemed in her mind to be frantically shuffling her pack of social receipts and finding none of them made to meet this situation. Finally Hawker said that he thought "Hearts at War" was a very good play.

"Did you?" she said in surprise. "I thought it much like the others."

"Well, so did I," he cried hastily. "The same figures moving around in the mud of modern confusion. I really didn't intend to say that I liked it. Fact is—meeting you rather moved me out of my mental track."

"Mental track?" she said. "I didn't know clever people had mental tracks. I thought it was a privilege of the theologians."

"Who told you I was clever?" he demanded.

"Why—" she said, opening her eyes wider. "Nobody."

Hawker smiled and looked upon her with gratitude. "Of course! 'Nobody!' There couldn't be such an idiot. I am sure you should be astonished to learn that I believed such an imbecile existed. But—"

"Oh," she said.

"But I think you might have spoken less bluntly."

"Well," she said, after wavering for a time, "you are clever, aren't you?"

"Certainly," he answered reassuringly.

"Well, then?" she retorted with triumph in her tone. And this interrogation was apparently to her the final victorious argument.

At his discomfiture, Hawker grinned. (366–67)

The title "Hearts at War" describes not only a major subject in romance—emotional conflict during courtship—but also the tense and clumsy conversation between Hawker and Grace. Like his dog, who vies for attention by "wagging his tail" (367), Hawker wags his tongue with dialogue he hopes will attract Grace. When words fail him and he acts with "dramatic impulsiveness" (366), she "frantically" searches for the proper response to his behavior. Not surprisingly, he immediately changes his opinion of "Hearts at War" when Grace points out that it has a clichéd plot. Her statement that she "thought it much like the others" refers to romance's continual retelling of the same story, what he calls "the mud of modern confusion" that prevents seeing reality clearly. Hawker's sudden shift is less a statement about the play than an unsuccessful attempt to ingratiate himself. When he demands to know who called him "clever," Grace hesitates, then, like a heroine in sentimental drama, melodramatically opens "her eyes wider" and satisfies him with a simple "Nobody"—to which he replies, "Of course! 'Nobody!'" As in the Indian legend, the phrase "of course" signifies the clichéd nature of the dramatized situation between this hero and heroine. Grace's response is the proper one any time hearts are at war in romantic stories. Grace triumphs in this battle because she exposes Hawker's attempt to be verbally "clever"; his "discomfiture" is like that of his dog, who upon being rejected acts "'like a man suddenly stricken with age,' as the story-tellers eloquently say" (367). In both waterfall scenes, then, the storyteller ironically appropriates the romantic plot but becomes trapped by his own language and artifice. In retelling a legend from folklore, Hawker fails to convince Grace of its accuracy; in the reenactment of a play involving hearts at war, his inconsistency in point of view undermines his reliability as a character and narrator.

The last chapter of *The Third Violet* also exemplifies Crane's subversion of romantic clichés. Hawker says to Grace, "'adios' now for fear that I might leave very suddenly. I do that sometimes" (385). This announcement prompts Grace to give Hawker a third violet, which he accuses her of having flung at him. In no time at all, not only the flower but heightened emotions are flying in the air, which leads Hawker to ask defensively:

> "Now you are enraged. Well, what have I done?"
>
> It seemed that some tumult was in her mind, for she cried out to him at last in sudden tearfulness: "Oh, do go. Go. Please. I want you to go."
>
> Under this swift change, Hawker appeared as a man struck from the sky. He sprang to his feet, took two steps forward and spoke a word which was an explosion of delight and amazement. He said: "What?"
>
> With heroic effort, she slowly raised her eyes until, a-light with anger, defiance, unhappiness, they met his eyes. Later, she told him that he was perfectly ridiculous. (387)

Readers have usually interpreted the last line as meaning that sometime after the emotional explosion the two lovers joked about their own silliness and ended up living happily ever after, like so many other romantic characters who lived once upon a time.[18] But the line could also be read as Grace's later realization that Hawker was indeed "perfectly ridiculous." After upsetting

Grace, he denies responsibility for the situation—"what have I done?"—and acts as though "struck from the sky." The metaphorical bolt of lightning, however, elicits no epiphany, no sudden recognition about his relationship with Grace; instead, he merely responds with another question, a bathetic "What?" Hawker's behavior is no surprise, for he has frequently been insensitive and self-absorbed. When he rides with Grace to Hemlock Inn on his father's ox wagon, he thinks only of himself and fears that local socialites will consider him simple and rustic. Later, when Florinda asks Hawker, "what makes you so ugly" (356) and "what makes you so mean to me" (361), he can respond only with denial and a question: "I am not ugly, am I?" (356) and "I'm not mean to you, am I?" (361). Ironic comments such as "[p]robably he saw a grievance in her eyes" and "[h]is tone seemed tender" (356) suggest that his social awareness around Florinda is only temporary and tentative; when he feels threatened by her comments concerning his gloves, he slanders the Irish: "I suppose your distinguished ancestors in Ireland did not educate their families in the matter of gloves" (357). Throughout the novel Hawker's repeated boorishness signals his insecurity about his family's poverty, about his social awkwardness, and about his professional future. Because nothing in the story argues unambiguously for a happy ending with the eventual union of Hawker and Grace, only a reader's expectations of romance raise that possibility. Nineteenth-century readers of romance had become conditioned to expect that the "all-sufficiency of love" would overcome "social or psychological barriers,"[19] but in *The Third Violet* Hawker remains trapped by self-imposed barriers. The novel's ironic ending undercuts the neat plot line of a clichéd formula and exposes its unreality.

Besides parodying hackneyed plot devices, Crane undermines the romantic myth of the artist's life. Grace accepts the stock view of the artist's studio as a haven of mutual "sympathy" and "appreciation" (302) where artists lead "a lazy, beautiful life ... lounging in ... a studio, smoking monogrammed cigarettes and remarking how badly all the other men painted" (375). Because she believes this vision gives one "something to think of beyond just living," Grace concludes that "[i]t must be finer at any rate than the ordinary thing" (296). Ironically, "something ... beyond just living" suggests a romanticized view, whereas the portrayal of the "ordinary thing" is precisely what Howells was advocating. Grace's romantic view of artists is constantly challenged by the daily existence of Hawker and his colleagues, who spend much of their time playing cards on credit and worrying about paying for food and rent. The titles of the magazines they occasionally do hack work for—*Monthly Amazement*, *Eminent Magazine*, and *Gamin*—suggest the precarious nature of a profession in which one might descend from being an eminent artist to making a living as a sensation monger. The image of poker chips—"a stack of blues" (345)—to be used for hiring a model implies that their profession is a gamble. Rather than depicting artists as immune to life's vagaries, Crane portrays them as ordinary people in ordinary situations.

Because of Crane's attraction to realism, it is no surprise that he criticizes romantic clichés as unrealistic; but there is some question about what it meant to define realism in terms of its ability to accurately reflect the world. Despite Howells's theoretical pronouncements on the nature of realism, it is difficult to categorize realists because they chose such vastly different subjects and used vastly different styles. American realism, as Amy Kaplan has argued, is "not a seamless package ... but an anxious and contradictory mode which both articulates and combats the growing sense of unreality at the heart of middle-class life. "[20] By the time Crane was writing *The Third Violet*, the contextual theory of knowledge and the pluralistic metaphysics of Pragmatism were so pervasive in American thought that it would have been naive to assume that realists could objectively mirror reality. Given this intellectual climate, Crane might easily have perceived reality as, in Patrick Dooley's words, "the totality of conflicting, ongoing, interpenetrating experiences."[21] Although Crane professed "that the most artistic and the most enduring literature was that which reflected life accurately" (*C*, 1:230), his use of disjointed plots, shifting perspectives, and limited points of view implies epistemological uncertainty and the existence of multiple realities. Curiously, as he depicts romance as unrealistic in *The Third Violet*, he anticipates the self-conscious, antirealist novel of the twentieth century, with its treatment of life itself as a fiction. As defined by Robert Alter, the self-conscious novel

> systematically flaunts its own condition of artifice and ... [in] so doing probes into the problematic relationship between real-seeming artifice and reality.... [F]rom beginning to end, through the style, the handling of narrative viewpoint, the names and words imposed on the characters, the patterning of the narration, the nature of the characters and what befalls them, there is a consistent effort to convey to us a sense of the fictional world as an authorial construct set up against a background of literary tradition and convention.[22]

Though *The Third Violet* is not so consistently self-conscious as, say, Joyce's *Ulysses* or John Fowles's *The French Lieutenant's Woman*, Crane's exposure of the technical trappings of fiction making, combined with his parody of romance, undermines the ontological distinction between fact and fiction.[23]

Crane's inclination to accept an indeterminate universe clarifies an important difference between his practice of realism and Howells's theory. In an extremely revealing metaphor, Howells compares an author's attempt to write realistically with that of an artist painting a cyclorama:

> I think the effect is like that in those cycloramas where up to a certain point there is real ground and real grass, and then carried indivisibly on to the canvas the best that the painter can do to imitate real ground and real grass. We start in our novels with something we have known of life, that is, with life itself; and then we go on and imitate what we have known of life. If we are very skillful and very patient we can *hide the joint*. But the joint is always there, and on one side of it are real ground and real grass, and on the other are the painted images of ground and grass. I do not believe that there was ever any one who longed more strenuously or endeavored more constantly to make the painted ground and grass exactly like the real.... But I have to own that I have never yet succeeded to my own satisfaction.... At the same time I have the immense, the sufficient consolation, of knowing that I have not denied such truth as was in me by imitating unreal ground and grass, or even by copying the effect of some other's effort to represent real ground and real grass.[24]

Howells's metaphor implies that the real and fictional worlds of ground and grass are clearly distinct, that the purpose of art is to imitate life, and that the task facing an artist is to hide the point at which art and life join. The more technically proficient the painter, the more realistic the art. For Crane, however, the problem is not technical but ontological. Both worlds are imaginative constructions, mimesis has meaning only insofar as the fiction of literature approximates the fiction of life, and the task of the self-conscious artist is to explore the joint, the ontological space in which fact and fiction are indistinct.

In *The Third Violet*, Crane uses self-conscious characters, narrative frames, and word play to expose, rather than hide, this joint. Throughout, characters discuss their situations as though they see themselves as being in a fiction. When Grace and Hawker contrast realistic and romanticized perceptions of an artist's life, for example, she recognizes her own "point of view" and identifies as a "story" his autobiographical account of an unheroic life, about which he privately laments to Hollanden, "What in thunder was I invented for" (376, 383). Perceiving himself as an invention, Hawker bemoans his fictional status. Similarly, just before the picnic scene, when Hollanden realizes that Hawker is thoroughly infatuated with Grace, he immediately identifies Hawker's "dramatic situation" (291, 292) with that of other lovers in romance. A writer himself, Hollanden depicts Hawker's anxiety about rival suitors as a play:

> "The woods must be crowded with [rivals]. A girl like that, you know. And then, all that money. Say, your rivals must number enough to make a brigade of militia. Imagine them, swarming around. But then it doesn't matter so much," he went on cheerfully. "You've got a good play there. You must appreciate them to her—you understand—appreciate them kindly like a man in a watch-tower. You must laugh at them only about once a week and then very tolerantly, you understand—and kindly and—and appreciatively." (292)

When Hawker inquires about his rival, Hollanden fictionalizes Oglethorpe as an antagonist with "of course ... train loads of money" (306)—the phrase "of course" emphasizing the formulaic portrayal of the rival suitor—and reminds Hawker of his role in the play: "Under the circumstances you are privileged to rave and ramp around like a wounded lunatic" (306). As a character in Hollanden's romantic drama, Hawker must observe the dictates of the form. So clichéd are romantic plot and characterization that when Hollanden suggests that Oglethorpe's wealth might be irrelevant, Hawker chastises him for not keeping "to the thread of the story" (306).

In creating characters aware of their own fictionality, Crane has nested literary frames within one another: the narrator of the novel tells a story about artists, one of whom fictionalizes others in a drama. The embedding of one version of representation within another creates a separate joint for each frame and makes problematic the relationship between fact and fiction. Rather than asking readers to accept *The Third Violet* as a reflection of reality, "the ordinary thing" (296), Crane disrupts expectations by focusing on the fiction-making process. Hollanden consciously writes into existence another reality for Hawker, Fanhall, and Oglethorpe, but this imaginative construction is yet another romance. Thus the romance form of the book titled *The Third Violet* frames the "real" world of Hawker and his friends, which frames Hollanden's romantic play. Hollanden further elaborates the framing by embedding a pictorial representation of Hawker: "Heavens! Of all pictures of a weary pilgrim" (307). This use of literary and pictorial frames exposes multiple joints, creates narrative distance, and further prevents readers from knowing which is the "real" world. Is it their own world once they stop reading the book, is it Crane's or the narrator's interpretation of events, is it the daily world of these characters, or is it Hollanden's dramatized or pictorial version? Is it possible that, rather than there being one "real" world, every world is a fictional construction? According to Jorge Luis Borges, such questions "disturb" us because they "suggest that if the characters of a fictional work can be readers or spectators, we, its readers or spectators, can be fictitious."[25]

Hawker himself relies on frames to create another reality. When he first encounters Grace, he envisions her as an object in a "frame of light" suitable for painting: "Wouldn't I like to paint her" (282, 281). Later, he and another artist, Pennoyer, allude to the literal "frame-maker," who constructs frames for portraits, but Crane then shifts to a figurative consideration of framing. When Pennoyer leaves, Hawker works on his "unfinished 'Girl in Apple Orchard,'" a secret portrait of Grace inspired by their visit to the country.[26] Surrounded by paintings on the studio wall, his previous attempts to portray life accurately, Hawker romanticizes the urban Grace by reimagining her as a rural girl, a comfortable reality for him given his own rustic background. His attempt to frame a new reality for her is tinged with guilt, however, because he realizes that in re-creating Grace as a figure in romance he is being false to the realistic vision of the paintings on the wall, which "in heavy gilt frames contemplated him and the violets" that she had given him (347). His internal battle reminds the reader of the problematic relationship between fact and fiction; the changing definition of the word *frame*—associated first with a person, then an object, and finally a concept—suggests the capability of language to signify multiple realities. In the unsettled world of *The Third Violet*, definitions of words—like *fact, fiction,* and *frame*—are indeterminate.

As do his frames and characterization, Crane's wordplay, especially his use of puns, exposes the technical trappings of fiction and represents reality as ultimately a linguistic construction. While discussing art, Grace suggests to Hawker that it "must be finer at any rate than the ordinary thing"; that is, she believes art should go beyond simple daily life and strive for an ideal. Acting authoritatively like a Muse of the arts, Hawker "mused for a time. 'Yes. It is— it must be,' he said. 'But then—I'd rather just lie here'" (296). His position is literally prone, but figuratively he acknowledges that it would be easier to lie about his aesthetic position to please Grace. When their conversation becomes heated, he tries to ingratiate himself with "a graceful tribute" (298), but his words, like his actions, ultimately fail to construct a satisfying reality or to portray a man at peace with himself. Shortly thereafter, while taking a boat ride on the lake, Hawker responds to Grace's interest in artists by describing his experience painting still life:

"But, still, the life of the studios—" began the girl.

Hawker scoffed. "There were six of us. Mainly we smoked. Sometimes we played hearts and at other times poker—on credit, you know—credit. And when we had the materials and got something to do, we worked. Did you ever see these beautiful red and green designs that surround the common tomato can?"

"Yes."

"Well," he said proudly, "I have made them. Whenever you come upon tomatoes remember that they might once have been encompassed in my design. When first I came back from Paris I began to paint, but nobody wanted me to paint. Later, I got into green corn and asparagus—"

"Truly?"

"Yes, indeed. It is true."

"But, still, the life of the studios—" (302)

Hawker's suggestion that tomatoes might later remind Grace of his painting raises the subject of the ability of art to imitate life, but the wordplay on "Truly" and "true" calls into question not only Hawker's painting but also the truth status of art itself. The narrator further emphasizes the slipperiness of language by punning on "still" as an adjective and adverb in "still life" and "still, the life," by framing the dialogue with the twice-repeated phrase "But, still, the life of the studios," and by earlier depicting the evening setting as artificial, an "embroidered" night (302).[27]

Hawker's conversation with Hollanden similarly focuses on how language shapes reality. When they visit a Bohemian café and Hawker apparently complains about the food and service, Hollanden criticizes him for trying to be "correct" in order to "achieve a respectability": "It is a fact that there are indications that some other citizen was fortunate enough to possess your napkin before you, and moreover you are sure that you would hate to be caught by your correct friends with any such consomme in front of you as we had to-night. You have got an eye suddenly for all kinds of gilt. You are in the way of becoming a most unbearable person" (370, 371). Hollanden fears that his friend will become like the smug Lucian Pontiac, another painter who has become commercially successful. Having "spent many years in manufacturing a proper modesty with which to bear his greatness" (372), Pontiac has fabricated a persona and knows how to behave in front of "correct friends." Like Pontiac, Hawker wishes to construct a public self by saying and doing the appropriate thing. Hawker's sudden obsession with appearances, "all kinds of gilt," is meant to create guilt in those who fail to please others; but as he himself realizes, hiding behind an illusion is "unbearable." Implicitly, Hawker struggles with the incompatibility of two artistic visions: the financially comfortable world of romance, which caters to public demand; and the precarious, but more honest, commitment to one's own interpretation of reality. Crane's phrase "men of war" (372) refers not only to customers in the café arguing vociferously in the background but also to the literary battle being fought within Hawker.

The dialogue between Hollanden and other tourists also illustrates the capacity of language to refer to itself. When asked what makes "literary men so peculiar," Hollanden assumes "an oratorical pose on a great weather-beaten stone" and elaborately explains how he set out to be a literary "prophet" but "ended in being an acrobat, a trained bear of the magazines, and a juggler of comic paragraphs." When the elder Miss Worcester criticizes his "personal history" for being full of "whoppers" that "tangle us up purposely" and concludes that not "a word of it is true," he replies, "What do you expect of autobiography?" Hollanden's account—delivered in the character of a master of words, an orator—reveals how he has been created by his own language. When he failed to become a literary prophet, "in defense" he "created a gigantic dignity ... to delude the populace," using the maxim "that each wise man in this world is concealed amid some twenty thousand fools" to construct a cynical persona. Aware of the falseness of his pose, he acknowledges that he will "never disclose to anybody" that he is not a priceless pearl of art and philosophy" (293–95). Ironically, he does precisely that when, like a prophet speaking in parables, he alludes to the biblical pearl of great price (Matthew 13:45–46). It is thus no wonder that Miss Worcester criticizes him for wordplay that tries "to make us think and then just tangle[s] us up purposely" (a reaction similar to that Christ received when speaking in parables). Dismissing objections to his account of himself, Hollanden defensively reiterates, "This is autobiography." In one sense, the word *this* refers to his account, but it also refers to the language that constitutes his response. Because autobiography, like a novel, is a linguistic creation, it too is a fiction. Hollanden invents his life just as one invents any literary representation, but his language hides as much as it reveals his identity. Because of his "whoppers," it is difficult to expose the joint at which the real Hollanden becomes the fictional and to decide whether one identity is more true than the other. The statement "This is autobiography" is true only insofar as Hollanden exists in language. Strip away his words, and he ceases to exist. Hollanden's reality is thus only language, as is everything else in *The Third Violet*—Florinda's apartment building "with fire escapes written all over the face of it" (361) and Grace's home with its "poetry of a prison" (366), for example. According to William H. Gass, within a linguistically constructed universe, all "literature is language, ... [and the] stories and the places and the people in them are merely made of words."[28]

Through allusion a novel can be aware not only of itself but of another text. In *Adventures of Huckleberry Finn*, for example, Twain alludes to *Don Quixote* to heighten the contrast between Huck's realistic outlook and Tom's romantic escapades. The allusions in a text comment on the action, and in so doing they are embedded into, or framed by, the larger text. Although every allusion is not a statement about the relationship between fact and fiction, some of those in *The Third Violet* are part of Crane's larger commentary on this subject. Perhaps as importantly, these allusions reveal hitherto unknown information about his reading and interests. At one point his artists perceive themselves as characters in a poem. When Hawker visits his friends, he asks,

> "How's the wolf, boys? At the door yet?"
> "'At the door yet?' He's half way up the back stairs and coming fast. He and the landlord will be here to-morrow. 'Mr. Landlord, allow me to present Mr. F. Wolf of Hunger, N.J. Mr. Wolf—Mr. Landlord.'"
> "Bad as that?" said Hawker.
> "You bet it is." (346)

The allusion may be to Charlotte Perkins (Stetson) Gilman's poem "The Wolf at the Door," an allegorical representation of poverty as "a hot breath at the keyhole," that Crane might easily have known.[29] First published in *Scribner's Monthly* in January 1894, it was reprinted in Gilman's first collection of poetry, *In This Our World* (1893; rev. ed., 1895), which met with international approval, including that of Howells. The allusion allows artists in the novel to fictionalize themselves in a poem and to transform the fictional wolf into a character, Mr. F. Wolf, in their world. Though the artists are certainly being playful, their banter frames one form of representation with another and merges fact and fiction.

The most striking example of Crane's exposure of the process of fiction making—one that combines framing, wordplay, and self-conscious characters—reveals another of Crane's interests overlooked by previous scholars: opera. While working for his brother Townley's news bureau in Asbury Park, New Jersey, in 1890, Crane met soprano Louise Gerard and her husband Albert Thiess, and briefly reported on her career, later converting his note into an article, "The King's Favor." Four years later he summarized Gerard's career for two musical journals. Crane also reported on opera in New Orleans, and his farcical play "The Ghost" drew on the light operas of Gilbert and Sullivan. He occasionally referred to opera in his work, and he apparently wrote the libretto for a lost opera called *Dolores*. It is not surprising, then, to find allusions to Verdi's *La Traviata* and *Il Trovatore* in *The Third Violet*. Crane had ample opportunity to see a performance of Verdi's *La Traviata*. One of Verdi's best-loved operas, it was performed throughout the United States in the late nineteenth century and at the New York Metropolitan annually between 1893 and 1896, years during which Crane spent half of his time in New York City. Almost as popular, *Il Trovatore* was featured at the Met five times between 1894 and 1896.[30] But even if he had never attended a performance of either work, allusions in his novel reveal that he was familiar with them. The plot of *La Traviata* was extremely well known, and its score was frequently played on home pianos.[31]

Crane uses Verdi's operas in his novel to further blur the distinction between fact and fiction. Both *La Traviata* and *The Third Violet* employ rival suitors, a contrast between country and city life, and a floral motif, especially of violets. *Florinda*, the name of the artist's model in Crane's novel, suggests *Flora*, the name of the mezzo-soprano in Verdi's opera; and the prima donna Violetta (an Italian variant for violet) is, like Florinda, a popular figure in demi-mondaine city life. Both Violetta and Grace Fanhall give flowers to their suitors, and Violetta lives in the "home of the Graces."[32] In addition, Hawker portrays himself as Alfredo, the tenor in *La Traviata*, and his heightened emotions recall those of many an operatic character. When Hawker returns to his studio, he whistles "an air from 'Traviata'.... This air was as much a part of Hawker as his coat" (355). If clothes make the man, then the aria suits him fine, for it is Alfredo's "Di quell' amor," which expresses his love for Violetta and is the central melody of the opera. Shortly after Hawker's whistling, a fellow painter comments, "[I]f a man loves a woman better than the whole universe, how much does he love the whole universe?" (358), a question that alludes to the aria's opening lines: "All that hath life hath its breath, its breath from thee, Love, thou'rt the soul of the life, the life universal."[33] Crane similarly alludes to *Il Trovatore*. When Hawker visits Grace to announce his planned departure from the city, he sees men shoveling snow: "The noise of their instruments scraping on the stones came plainly to Hawker's ears in a harsh chorus, and this sound at this time was perhaps to him a miserere" (385), an allusion to the workers who swing their hammers to the Anvil Chorus in *Il Trovatore*, and to the "Miserere" aria, which expresses the tenor's love.[34] Unfortunately, when Hawker's attempt to say good-bye creates tension between Grace and himself, he misinterprets her offer of a third violet as a gesture of condescension: "I don't wish you to feel sorry for me. And I don't wish to be melodramatic. I know it is all commonplace enough, and I didn't mean to act like a tenor. Please don't pity me" (386). In keeping with the spirit of an aria, characters "put on a good many airs," speak "airily" or "with an air," and don "the air" of someone "grievously wronged" (312, 313, 318, 353).

Like Crane, Verdi found contemporary forms of artistic representation confining and unrealistic. In *La Traviata*, Verdi questions the artificiality and rigid formal structure of traditional opera, its preference for heroic, patriotic subject matter, and its emphasis on music over story; he adapted the form so that *La Traviata* became "the first important opera in which stiff forms were bent in response to the naturalistic demands of contemporary theater."[35] Crane bends the romance form in a similar way to expose its artificiality, but by embedding within his subversive romance an opera that undermines its own tradition, he reiterates the difficulty of separating fiction from reality. Is the "real" Hawker the one constructed by the narrator, or is he the one who reads himself into an opera?[36]

Ironically, as Crane parodied romance and questioned epistemological and ontological assumptions, he constructed his own life as a romantic tale. Scholars have often noted the autobiographical elements in *The Third Violet*, which reflects Crane's time in Sullivan County, his friendship with artists in New York City, his anxiety about the profession of authorship, and his infatuation with Nellie Crouse, a prim, thoroughly conventional young woman whom he had apparently met only once at a tea party.[37] Infatuated with Crouse, Crane started an intense letter-writing campaign in late December 1895—days after finishing *The Third Violet*—that lasted about two and a half months. She initially responded with long letters and a photograph, but her interest waned, and the correspondence stopped. The connection between the novel and the letters to Crouse is complicated. Crane sent the manuscript to Ripley Hitchcock at Appleton on 27 December 1895, four days before he wrote the first known letter to Crouse, but she was certainly on his mind twelve months earlier, when they met in January, well before he started writing the novel. During their correspondence in early 1896 he could conceivably have been revising the manuscript at the request of Hitchcock, who suggested changes in dialogue and in the portrayal of Grace Fanhall. Unfortunately, because no manuscript of *The Third Violet* exists, it is impossible to know what sorts of editorial changes, if any, Crane made while writing to Crouse. However, the similarities between the language, characterization, and themes of the novel and those of the letters suggest that they are fictional and real-life mirrors of Crane's struggles with his private and public personae. If one reads the letters to Crouse along with *The Third Violet*, it is clear that Crane was writing the subject matter and themes of the novel into his own life, and thus writing himself as hero into a "real-life" romance and opera, again blurring the distinction between fact and fiction.

Crane's seven fervent letters are by turns satirical, melodramatic, and bitterly ironic, as he assumes different roles in order to woo Crouse. Among his longest and most revealing letters, these show him struggling with the conventions of courtship, with the tension between artistic integrity and the demands of a literary marketplace, and with the international acclaim resulting from the book publication of *The Red Badge of Courage*—topics also central to *The Third Violet*. Like Hawker, Crane assumes poses that variously reveal and hide his true feelings. When Crouse disapproves of his calling himself a "chump" and "a blockhead"—epithets also used for Hawker—he becomes a refined critic with "a considerable liking for the man of fashion if he does it well" (*C*, 1:200). Crane's shifting roles, like Hawker's, reflect his awkwardness in courtship; but unlike Hawker, Crane recognizes his own shortcomings: "I reach depths of stupidity of which most people cannot dream. This is usually in the case of a social crisis. A social crisis simply leaves me witless and gibbering. A social crisis to me is despair" (*C*, 1:184).[38]

As did Hawker with the Indian legend and Hollanden with his imaginary play, Crane parodies the clichéd plots of romance novels in his correspondence with Crouse: "Once upon a time there was a young woman but her sister married a baronet and so she thought she must marry a baronet, too. I find it more and more easy to believe her stupid" (*C*, 1:181). Similarly, just as Hawker melodramatically envisions himself as a character in literature—in his case, the tenor in *La Traviata*—Crane projects himself into one of his own short stories. When he sent Crouse a copy of "A Grey Sleeve," written between the time they met and the time he began writing her, he was hoping for more than her opinion of it. A sentimental, melodramatic love story about a Union officer and a Confederate woman who fall in love after seeing each other only once, the story captures Crane's idealized view of his relationship with Crouse. With the Civil War as backdrop, he could gauge her response to their relationship, just as Hawker did with the play "Hearts at War." Crane's own shifts in attitude toward "A Grey Sleeve"—he ranged from calling it "not in any sense a good story" to labeling it "charming" (*C*, 1:171, 180)—is similar to Hawker's abrupt turnabout toward the play. Rather than remaining true to their own visions, both suitors end up trying to please their audiences. Curiously, then, while Crane was parodying the literary form of romance and questioning the nature of reality in *The Third Violet*, he was so infatuated with a woman he barely knew that he read himself into a previously written short story and inscribed himself as a lover in his correspondence.

At some point, however, Crane realized how embarrassing his posturing for Nellie had been, and he wrote himself out of the romance with the final words of his last letter to her: "[M]y pen is dead. I am simply a man struggling with a life that is no more than a mouthful of dust to him" (*C*, 1:208). Crane was never good at saying good-bye. As he wrote to Hitchcock close to the time of his last letter to Nellie, "I cannot help vanishing and disappearing and dissolving. It is my foremost trait" (*C*, 1:213)—words reminiscent of Hawker's announcement to Grace of his departure: " 'adios' now for fear that I might leave very suddenly. I do that sometimes." Realizing that his stilted assertions of virtue had made him seem "perfectly ridiculous," Crane knew that his romance with Nellie would end unhappily, and he fled into the arms of Amy Leslie, whom he had met in 1895 sometime between his initial meeting with Crouse and his writing of *The Third Violet*. There is a tragic irony here, for Crane, a tenor who enjoyed singing, chose as his next lover a flamboyant woman who had become famous as an opera soprano. Just as Hawker had envisioned himself as the tenor in *La Traviata*, Crane sought his own prima donna in Leslie. But this real-life opera was to end, like so many fictional ones, sadly "more by fate or chance than from any desire of" Crane (*C*, 1:297). Fact and fiction were again interchangeable.

The Third Violet appeared at a crucial point in Crane's life. Struggling with the profession of authorship and the battle between realistic and romantic fiction, Crane wrote the novel as a public criticism of popular fiction in America and as a private diary of his professional, philosophical, and emotional development. Like Hawker, in the fall of 1895 Crane was at a crossroads; on the verge of fame, he faced the dilemma Howells had raised during the interview. Would he remain committed to artistic truth or end up a "trained bear" writing to delight an audience? Haunted by the "accursed" *Red Badge of Courage*, Crane found his later work unfavorably compared to his war novel, and in the last year and a half of his life he relied increasingly on hack work to pay ever-mounting bills. The man who set out to subvert the romance tradition found himself in his final days—literally on his deathbed— again parodying it in *The O'Ruddy*. Crane could have remembered Howells's words during the interview: "A writer of skill cannot be defeated because he remains true to his conscience. It is a long serious conflict sometimes, but he must win, if he does not falter" (617). Crane may have occasionally stumbled in his battle, but he remained true to his conscience.

NOTES

1. Richard M. Weatherford, ed., *Stephen Crane: The Critical Heritage* (London: Routledge, 1973), 206. Stanley Wertheim and Paul Sorrentino, eds., *The Crane Log: A Documentary Life of Stephen Crane, 1871–1900* (New York: G. K. Hall, 1994), 258, 261.

2. *The Correspondence of Stephen Crane*, ed. Stanley Wertheim and Paul Sorrentino, 2 vols. (New York: Columbia Univ. Press, 1988), 1:191, 292. Further references to this volume are noted parenthetically in the text as *C*.

3. Ford Madox Ford, "Stevie & Co.," *New York Herald Tribune*, 2 January 1927, sec. 7, p. 6; Christopher Benfey, *The Double Life of Stephen Crane* (New York: Knopf, 1992), 148.

4. Edwin H. Cady, *Stephen Crane*, rev. ed. (Boston: Twayne, 1980), 147–48.

5. John Berryman, *Stephen Crane* (New York: Sloane, 1950; reprint, Cleveland: World-Meridian, 1962), 122.

6. Edwin H. Cady, *The Realist War: The Mature Years (1885–1920) of William Dean Howells* (Syracuse: Syracuse Univ. Press, 1958), 217.

7. Stephen Crane, "Howells Fears the Realists Must Wait," in *Prose and Poetry*, ed. J.

C. Levenson (New York: Library of America, 1984), 617. Subsequent references to Crane's works are to this volume and are cited parenthetically in the text.

8. William Dean Howells, *Selected Literary Criticism, Volume 3: 1898–1920*, in *A Selected Edition of W. D. Howells*, ed. Donald Cook et al., 30 vols. (Bloomington: Indiana Univ. Press, 1968–), 30:218. Though the words *romance, romantic,* and *sentimental* have a long critical history, I am using the terms in the way that Crane and Howells would have understood them. Romances, or romantic novels, typically focused on love, adventure, or combat; relied on clichéd plots; and emphasized action over character. Crane and Howells criticized such novels because their purpose was to offer an escape from daily realities and because they relied on melodrama and sentimentality to solicit an emotional response out of keeping with the action.

9. Crane's interview of Howells can be read as a response to F. Marion Crawford's *The Novel: What It Is* (1893; reprint, Westport, Conn.: Greenwood, 1970), which was probably Crawford's response to Howells's earlier criticism of romantic fiction in *Criticism and Fiction* (1891). One of the most popular writers of romantic fiction, Crawford clearly articulated in *The Novel* a description of, and justification for, the romantic fiction he himself wrote: "So far as supply and demand are concerned," he asserted, "books in general and works of fiction in particular are commodities and subject to the same laws, statutory and traditional, as other articles of manufacture" (12).

10. Jonathan Townley Crane, *Popular Amusements* (New York: Carlton, 1869), 136, 142.

11. R. W. Stallman, *Stephen Crane: A Critical Bibliography* (Ames: Iowa State Univ. Press, 1972), 225. Crane was probably aware of a novel by Howells similar in theme to his own. Howells's *The World of Chance*, published a year before the interview, tells of an aspiring young novelist who, with manuscript of a novel in hand, comes to New York City from the Midwest to earn fame as a professional writer. Like Howells's fictional character, Crane also came to New York City with manuscript in hand and supported himself as a freelance writer. If Crane knew of Howells's novel, which seems likely given the friendship between the two and Crane's admiration for the Dean's work, Crane must have wondered about the role of chance in his own life.

12. Compare Crane's comments on the connection between art and income: "Before 'The Red Badge of Courage' was published I often found it difficult to make both ends meet. The book was written during this period. It was an effort born of pain, and I believe that this was beneficial to it as a piece of literature. It seems a pity that this should be so,—that art should be a child of suffering; and yet such seems to be the case. Of course there are fine writers who have good incomes and live comfortably and contentedly; but if the conditions of their lives were harder, I believe that their work would be better" (*C*, 1:230–31; for related comments see also 232, 323).

13. Contemporary readers would have understood Hawker's anxiety about the place of art in advertising. With the rise of nationally marketed newspapers and magazines in the late nineteenth century, readers became increasingly aware of the importance of illustrations in advertisements. Among the early ads to combine visual and verbal text were those for food products, of which soup was the first canned food product to be nationally advertised. In 1895, the year that Crane was writing *The Third Violet*, the Joseph Campbell Preserve Company began selling the now-famous can of Campbell's Tomato Soup. Between 1895 and 1898 a tomato was the dominant image on the can; see Campbell's Soup Company, *Chronology: Campbell's Soup Company* (Camden, N.J.: Campbell, 1994), 1. For a discussion of the kinds of jobs painters took to support themselves while learning their craft, see H. Wayne Morgan, *New Muses: Art in American Culture, 1865–1920* (Norman: Univ. of Oklahoma Press, 1978), 23–25.

14. Marston LaFrance first noticed that Crane used the image of the "trained bear" in both the interview and his novel; see *A Reading of Stephen Crane* (Oxford: Clarendon Press, 1971), 175.

15. See Paul Sorrentino, "The Philistine Society's Banquet for Stephen Crane," *American Literary Realism* 15 (autumn 1982): 232–38.

16. Eric Solomon, *Stephen Crane: From Parody to Realism* (Cambridge: Harvard Univ. Press, 1966), 130.

17. Though a play with this title may exist, my research and conversations with historians of American theater have failed to find evidence of it. Crane probably invented the title.

18. See Cady, *Crane*, 147; Lillian Gilkes, "*The Third Violet, Active Service*, and *The O'Ruddy*: Stephen Crane's Potboilers," in *Stephen Crane in Transition: Centenary Essays*, ed. Joseph Katz (DeKalb: Northern Illinois Univ. Press, 1972), 113; Solomon, *Stephen Crane: From Parody to Realism*, 144.

19. John C. Cawelti, *Adventure, Mystery, and Romance: Formula Stories as Art and Popular Culture* (Chicago: Univ. of Chicago Press, 1976), 42.

20. Amy Kaplan, *The Social Construction of American Realism* (Chicago: Univ. of Chicago Press, 1988), 9.

21. Patrick Dooley, *The Pluralistic Philosophy of Stephen Crane* (Urbana: Univ. of Illinois Press, 1993), 46.

22. Robert Alter, *Partial Magic: The Novel as a Self-Conscious Genre* (Berkeley and Los Angeles: Univ. of California Press, 1975), x–xi. For a discussion of Crane and postmodern theory, see James B. Colvert's "Stephen Crane and Postmodern Criticism," *Stephen Crane Studies* 1 (spring 1992): 2–8; and "Stephen Crane and Postmodern Theory," *American Literary Realism* 28 (fall 1995): 4–22, especially his summary of the critical views on Crane's epistemology (21 n. 7).

For other recent uses of the word *self-conscious* to describe Crane, see Donald Pizer, "Maggie and the Naturalistic Aesthetic of Length," *American Literary Realism* 28 (fall 1995): 58–65; and Michael Davitt Bell, *The Problem of American Realism: Studies in the Cultural History of a Literary Idea* (Chicago: Univ. of Chicago Press, 1993), 132.

23. Compare Crane's novel with Joseph Conrad's *Lord Jim* and Ford Madox Ford's *The Good Soldier*, novels in which self-conscious narrators tell convoluted narratives to imitate the convoluted nature of moral and psychological realism; in *The Third Violet* self-consciousness is occasionally the subject matter as well as the technique of the novel.

24. Howells, *Selected Literary Criticism*, 222–23.

25. Jorge Luis Borges, *Labyrinths: Selected Stories and Other Writings*, ed. Donald A. Yates and James E. Irby (New York: New Directions, 1964), 196.

26. Hawker may have begun "Girl in Apple Orchard" before going to the country and meeting Grace, which would suggest that the girl in the painting was initially a generic figure or someone else; but if this is so, it seems fairly clear, given the association of violets with the painting and Hawker's obsession with Grace, that she is now the girl in the painting.

27. The scene also typifies Hawker's struggle to maintain a consistent point of view and to be honest with Grace. When she admires his painting of cows in the snow, he describes it as possibly his best work; but when she confesses that her opinion is based on that of others, he responds "with dogged shakes of the head" that "[i]t wasn't any good" (303).

28. William H. Gass, *Fiction and the Figures of Life* (New York: Knopf, 1970), 27.

29. Another possible source is William Dean Howells's *A Hazard of New Fortunes*,

in which Basil March rationalizes that charitable contributions to the poor would not necessarily "keep the wolf from their doors" (*A Selected Edition of W. D. Howells*, 16:66). Gilman's poem, however, is a more likely source. Crane could have read the poem in *Scribner's Monthly*, or Howells, knowing that Crane considered himself a poet, might have recommended that he read *In This Our World*.

30. Irving Kolodin, *The Metropolitan Opera, 1883–1939* (New York: Oxford Univ. Press, 1940), 606.

31. Michael Saffle, Professor of Music History, Virginia Tech, interview with author, 15 May 1996.

32. Giuseppe Verdi, *La Traviata*, Kalmus Vocal Scores (New York: Kalmus, n.d.), 7.

33. Ibid., 40.

34. The passage may also refer to Psalm 51 (50 in the Vulgate), which is known as the "Miserere." One of the penitential psalms, it begins, "Have mercy on me, O God."

35. Joseph Kerman, "The Uses of Convention," in *The Opera News Book of "Traviata,"* ed. Frank Merkling (New York: Dodd, 1967), 24. *La Traviata* was influenced by the adaptation by Dumas *fils* of his novel *The Lady of the Camillias*. Focusing on contemporary subject matter, the play also challenged conventional expectations of its audience. Interestingly, Crane's novel, Verdi's opera, and Dumas's play are autobiographical, were written quickly, challenged literary convention, and focused on flowers as the central image.

36. Although Crane's treatment of clichés draws attention to his technique of fiction making, Corwin K. Linson, in *My Stephen Crane* (ed. Edwin H. Cady [Syracuse: Syracuse Univ. Press, 1958]), claims that "[h]is was not a studied technique, he was not self-conscious about it" (30). A contemporary reviewer for *Godey's Magazine*, however, recognized the craftsmanship in *The Third Violet*: "Now he has given out a book absolutely devoid of flesh and blood, and yet a remarkable piece of purely literary craft; as a study in handling and technical originality it is something unprecedented. But it is all handling. The story is of the slightest possible texture, and it is rather uncertain how it all ends" (Weatherford, *Crane*, 214–15). See also J. C. Levenson's introduction in *"The Third Violet" and "Active Service,"* in *The Works of Stephen Crane*, 10 vols., ed. Fredson Bowers (Charlottesville: Univ. Press of Virginia, 1969–76), 3:xi–xl, for a discussion of stylistic technique in *The Third Violet*.

37. On the relation of the novel to Crane's life, see William L. Andrews, "Art and Success: Another Look at Stephen Crane's *The Third Violet*," *Wascana Review* 13 (spring 1978): 71–82; Christopher Benfey, *The Double Life of Stephen Crane*, 140–70; R. W. Stallman, *Stephen Crane: A Biography*, rev. ed. (New York: Braziller, 1973), 295–97.

38. Another of Crane's letters, written to an admirer around the time of his last letter to Crouse, reveals his response to someone who idealized him as a romantic hero:

> I cannot for a moment allow you to assume that I am properly an ideal. Ye Gods! I am clay—very common uninteresting clay. I am a good deal of a rascal, sometimes a bore, often dishonest. When I look at myself I know that only by dint of knowing nothing of me are you enabled to formulate me in your mind as something of a heroic figure. If you could once scan me you would be forever dumb.... I am glad to write to you and tell you the truth as I know it. Of course, I wish ... I could tell you that I am a remarkable person but, alas, poor romance, I am most hideously ordinary. (1:209)

GEORGE MONTEIRO

The Drunkard's Progress

Thus alcohol stands indicted as an impostor. He who is fully under its influence may be happy after a fashion, but his enjoyment is based upon a mockery. He feels like a giant, while he is really shorn of his natural force. He drivels the veriest nonsense, while he thinks he reasons better than Plato. His maudlin attempts at smartness are the feeblest and the flattest of human utterances; but they seem to him wit almost superhuman. When he is so far gone as to stammer in his speech and totter in his gait, and be helpless in mind and body, his sense of his wisdom, his strength, his greatness, and his goodness is at its highest point.

—Rev. J. T. Crane, *Arts of Intoxication* (1870)

Much has been said about our negligence in rendering our homes attractive, and our cuisine appetizing; and not always without reason. We therefore recommend that in our unions essays be read on the science and art of making home outwardly wholesome and attractive, books on that subject be circulated, and all possible efforts be made to secure a more scientific attention to the products of the kitchens, and a higher aesthetic standard for the parlor.

—WCTU "Plan of Work" (1874)

From *Stephen Crane's Blue Badge of Courage*, pp. 48–59. © 2000 by Louisiana State University Press.

And we cry till our bitter crying the nation alarms
For the sons Intemperance is stealing out of our arms!
　　　—Josephine Pollard, "Stolen; or, the Mother's Lament" (1882)

1

There are nine steps in "The Drunkard's Progress," according to a nineteenth-century temperance print. Step 1 depicts the young man taking "a glass with a friend." In step 2 the incipient drunkard takes "a glass to keep the cold out." In step 3 he has had "a glass too much." In step 4 he is "drunk and riotous." With step 5, he attains "the summit"; sitting down now with "jolly companions," he is the "confirmed drunkard." Now begins the descent. With step 6 he comes to "poverty and disease." At step 7 he is "forsaken by friends." Step 8, taken in "desperation," leads him into "crime." In Step 9 he turns his gun on himself and blows his brains out, committing, as the label says, "death by suicide." Although not every one of the steps corresponds exactly with the steps of George Kelcey's rise and fall as a drinker, the correspondence overall is close enough to suggest that Crane had one such temperance paradigm in mind when he constructed the plot of *George's Mother*.

When we consider what might be called the work's ethos, moreover, we find that it has strong affinities with the documented principles of the American temperance movement. What I have in mind, particularly, are two documents dating from the early years of the Woman's Christian Temperance Union that can be brought to bear on *George's Mother*. The first document is "Which Shall Win?"—a piece by Frances E. Willard, the WCTU's longtime president. The second one is the text of a resolution passed by the WCTU at its second national convention. In tandem they provide a useful perspective on Crane's intentions in the second of his Lower East Side novellas.

Miss Willard, quoted from an 1877 temperance reader, argues:

The grog-shop is a two-edged sword, and cuts both ways at once. It is a rotating machine for the snaring of souls. It catches our young men and boys before they reach the church and Sabbath-school—while they are on their way—and they never reach its doors, or else it catches them as they return, and mars or neutralizes the blessed lessons there imparted. Between the two there is the old "irrepressible conflict" over again. It is war to the knife, and the knife to the hilt, and only one can win. And in the warfare, we of Christ's army are outnumbered. There are twelve saloons to every church; twelve bar-keepers to every minister.

> The church opens its blessed doors two or three days in the
> week; the saloon grinds on and on with its mill of destruction all
> the days of every week; all the months of every year.... They have
> studied carefully the tastes, tendencies, and preferences of our
> boys and young men, their natural and innocent taste for variety,
> fondness for amusement, preference for young company, and
> they pander to all these in ways that take hold upon death.[1]

Miss Willard, soon to be the WCTU's president, was present at its second
convention, held in Cincinnati in 1875, which passed the following resolution:
"That since women are the greatest sufferers from the liquor traffic, and
realizing that it is to be ultimately suppressed by means of the ballot, we, the
Christian women of this land, in convention assembled, do pray Almighty
God, and all good and true men, that the question of the prohibition of the
liquor traffic shall be submitted to all adult citizens, irrespective of race, color
or sex."[2] Among the suffering women, of course, were wives, mothers, and
daughters. "Do you hear the cry of the women— / Of the women whose
hearts are broken?" asks one temperance poem calling for the dawning
of a better day, "Of a day when wives' and mothers' sadness / Shall be all
forgotten in their gladness."[3] The suffering of one daughter in a home of
alcoholics Crane undertook to dramatize in *Maggie: A Girl of the Streets*.
The suffering of a temperance-worker mother he undertook in *Maggie's*
companion piece, *George's Mother*. "Our women believe that special efforts
should be made to help the mother in her unequal warfare with the dram-
shop for the preservation of her boy," wrote Frances E. Willard in 1888,
"[for] it is plainly perceived by them that something is wrong in the popular
division of responsibility by which, although the father may be a moderate
drinker, the failure of the boy to grow up good and pure is adjudged to be his
mother's fault."[4] Many of Crane's readers have seen *George's Mother* as a try
at adjusting this moral balance in the mother's favor and have stopped right
there. But other readers have looked more deeply for evidence of Crane's
more complex intentions.

Edward Garnett, for instance, sees *George's Mother* as no more
hospitable to the mother than to her drunkard son. In Crane's picture of the
mother, writes Garnett, "all the mysterious craving of maternal love, its fierce
pleasure in self-sacrifice, its self-regarding heroism, and self-denial based on
its egotistic interest, is presented with an unerring truthfulness that leaves
nothing further to be said."[5] Maxwell Geismar insists that in this work, in
which "the alcoholic and oedipal worlds are interchangeable," Crane gives us
in the mother an "aging, sick, ugly symbol of maternal love [that] combine[s]
the offices of nursemaid and mistress."[6] Eric Solomon says that *George's*

Mother shows "two characters as similar in their fantasies and their egos yet seriously in conflict in their views of the proper life." When the mother dies, concludes Solomon, "the conflict is over, and neither side has won. The dreams have failed, and love has died."[7]

Brenda Murphy offers the most detailed account of the pernicious, self-destructive war the little woman who is George's mother wages on the prodigality of her own self-destructive son. Detecting the irony implicit in Crane's original title for the story, *A Woman Without Weapons*, Murphy demonstrates convincingly that not only does the mother possess an arsenal of weapons but that she uses them skillfully enough to emerge in death (her death is the final weapon) as victor. "George's mother has succeeded in wresting her son from the forces of sin. It matters little to her 'moral victory' that she may have destroyed both of them in the process."[8]

One can only speculate why Crane changed the title of his book. If *George's Mother* gives the son and the mother close to equal billing, perhaps *A Woman Without Weapons* implies that the book is principally the mother's. Indeed, most readers see the novella, more or less, as the dramatization of the downward course traveled by an alcoholic son, greatly to the crushing disappointment of his earnest, well-meaning mother. In this, Crane's story recreates the paradigmatic story of a mother's defeat by her son's alcoholism, as it is told in "Stolen; or, the Mother's Lament," a temperance-reader poem voiced through the mother:

> They have stolen my child!—they have stolen my child, I say!
> My beautiful boy!—my precious one!—they have stolen away!
> And the earth is a heap of ashes, the sun is no longer bright,
> Since out of my home and my heart has vanished their chief
>   delight.
> . . . .
> It was not done in a moment, with a sudden wrench or blow
> As Death knows how to rob us of treasures we prize below,
> But it came with the trail of a serpent—the soft, insidious thing!
> And it spoke to my son like a siren, while it plunged in my heart
>   its sting!
> . . . .
> I kept the old house cheerful with pictures and works of art,
> With books, and a thousand nameless things that gladden the
>   youthful heart;
> And though I'd no daughters to aid me in this delightful task,
> I tried to be sister, and mother, and all that a child could ask.

I noticed his anxious brow—for a mother's gaze is keen—
And I missed the honest look in his eyes I had always seen;
While into his voice came a harsher tone, and he seemed to avoid
    my sight,
For he knew that my heart was set on his doing exactly right.

O Love! is there any cross that can give thee such pain as this?
O Love! can aught else so embitter thy cup of bliss,
As to see the child thou hast nourished and cherished with tend'rest
    care,
Torn out of thy holy embrace by the tempter's snare?
. . . .
Who robbed me of this my joy, and took from my side the sire
Who wept o'er the empty chair that stood by the table or fire,
Until, grown weary with waiting for a change that never came,
He sickened, and under the daisies we buried his grief and shame?
. . . .
The serpent stole into my Eden—why not into yours?
Not even the bond of affection our treasure secures;
The child at your knee, full of prattle, whose future you can not
    divine,
May prove just as guilty a sinner, as wretched a wanderer as mine![9]

Continuing through several additional stanzas, each contributing to a generalized condemnation of the evils of drink, this poem laments the fate of a woman not without weapons but with weapons that, save possibly for prayer, have failed her. Notice that like George's mother, the mother in this poem follows Frances Willard's domestic motto of "home protection" through cleaning and decoration of her son's home—but to no avail. When Crane dropped his original title, there was some loss—perhaps a certain flair—but the logic of his double-focus narrative—on both mother and son—dictated some sort of change. George's mother is no stranger to a good fight. She has fought intemperance as a member of the Woman's Christian Temperance Union. When Charley Jones, the old acquaintance who will shepherd George along the primrose path to better society and "improved" drinking, first encounters George, he starts out by treating him to a drink. As natural as this moment might seem to today's reader, it had particular importance to Crane's contemporaries. The national meeting of the WCTU in 1874, in its "Plan of Work," provided for an "Anti-Treat Pledge," explaining: " 'Come, let's take something together,' has been to thousands the keynote of destruction. We are laboring for the organization of a league which shall enroll as members those, who, though not ready to sign the pledge, are willing to refrain from 'putting the bottle to their neighbor's lips,' by pledging their honor that they neither 'be treated' nor 'treat.' "[10] This ritual of treating, while seemingly promoting camaraderie, is deeply pernicious in that it vastly increases the amount of consumption, "since a man is expected to buy a round of drinks for every round he has received."[11] The thematic connection is then made perfectly clear when Jones asks George about his mother. " 'How is th' ol' lady, anyhow?' continued Jones. 'Th' last time I remember she was as spry as a little ol' cricket, an' was helpeltin' aroun' th' country lecturin' before W.C.T.U.'s an' one thing an' another.' "[12] These credentials serve, of course, to bolster the reader's respect for her skill in the war she conducts on behalf of her son's sobriety and Christian salvation. She herself seems to be aware, moreover, that she is far from being a helpless woman without weapons.

So common was the notion that each temperance fighter was engaged in nothing short of a war and that all methods and devices for carrying on that war were nothing less than weapons that the instruction manual published by the United Society of Christian Endeavor carried the title *Weapons for Temperance Warfare*. Presenting "Some Plans and Programmes for use in Young People's Societies, Sunday-schools and Christian Temperance Unions," this vade mecum carried an epigraph on its title page from John B. Gough (elsewhere called "the Cold-Water warrior"[13]), reading: "Fight the drink! Fight it, fight it wherever we find it, fight it in the social circle, fight it in the dram-shop, fight it at home, fight it abroad. I expect to my dying day to fight the drink with every lawful weapon." The book, dedicated to Frances E. Willard, whose message in 1896 to the Temperance Committees "suggested the preparation" of "This Little Volume," also reproduces Miss Willard's inspiring message, mixing Christianity with temperance:

> Only a clear brain can think God's thoughts after him.
> Only a steady hand can glorify the divine Carpenter by faithful industry.
> Only a heart unhurried by artificial stimulants can be loyal in its love toward Christ and humanity.
> I beseech you to be incessant and ingenious in your efforts to teach total abstinence for the sake of Head, Hand, and Heart; and to take as your watchwords
>   HOME PROTECTION
>   AND
>   THE LIQUOR TRAFFIC MUST BE DESTROYED
> Yours in the purpose to glorify God in our bodies and our spirits, which are his.[14]

When the motto "home protection" was criticized as "organized mother love," Miss Willard countered by advocating proudly what she called the "politics of the mother heart,"[15] words that express the implicit creed by which George's mother lives and fights.

Weapons for Temperance Warfare, drawing on columns originally published in the *Sunday School Times*, offers practical advice on how to carry on war against the armies of intemperance. There are pieces on pledge signing, temperance budgets, and facts and figures. There are drawn-out plans and detailed sample programs for temperance meetings. There are suggestions for choosing the most useful biblical texts and the most appealing gospel hymns. In its list of hymns "especially adapted for use in temperance meetings" appear "Yield Not to Temptation," "Throw out the Life-Line," and "Where Is My Boy Tonight?"—each dealing with the basic material of Crane's story of a boy and his mother. The hymn Crane has George's mother sing is by Isaac Watts:

> Am I a soldier of the cross?
>   A follower of the Lamb!
> And shall I fear to own his cause,
>   Or blush to speak his name?
>
> Must I be carry'd to the skies,
>   On flow'ry beds of ease?
> Whilst others fought to win the prize,
>   And sail'd through bloody seas?
>
> Are there no foes for me to face?
>   Must I not stem the flood?
> Is this vile world a friend to grace,
>   To help me on to God?
>
> Sure I must fight, if I would reign;
>   Increase my courage Lord;
> I'll bear the toil, endure the pain,
>   Supported by thy word.
>
> Thy saints, in all this glorious war,
>   Shall conquer, though they die;
> They view the triumph from afar,
>   And seize it with their eye.

When that illustrious day shall rise,
   And all thy armies shine
In robes of victory through the skies—
   The glory shall be thine.[16]

Entitled "Holy Fortitude; or, The Christian Soldier" and listed as a hymn of warfare, it was a favorite among temperance workers as well as Methodists.[17]

Echoing the language of "Warfare," George's mother sees herself as truly a crusader. To fight against George's intemperance is to do the Christian God's work. Her opponent is the dragon of alcoholism that the ironically named George (recalling the saint) does not have the will to defeat.[18] This crusade will be fought in the home, the church, the saloon. This war will not be fought by George but over him.

2

The *Illustrated London News* called *George's Mother* "a more than commonly able temperance tract." It allowed that Crane's novella rapidly, though convincingly, sketched "a very commonplace 'Rake's Progress'—the descent of a young New York working man, by means of friendly clubs and saloon-haunting, from dignity, self-respect, and the estate of the dutiful son to becoming a 'tough,' and breaking the heart of his old mother." "Mr. Crane's vein of bitter irony is to be seen in the maudlin friendship of the bar-loafers," continues the review, "but in the picture of the little brown old mother there is heart also."[19]

The promising suggestion that *George's Mother* recalls Hogarth's "Rake's Progress" has not been much explored by scholars.[20] What can be looked at here is the way George Kelcey's social progress (up and down) ties in, roughly, with his progress through drink (up and down). Just as George moves, in order, from the street to the saloon, the backroom, Bleecker's apartment, and the club's room above the saloon, he then reverses the procedure by returning, in order, to the saloon, the street, and, finally, the vacant lot where he becomes part of the street gang.

His is not the progress of a rake, exactly, but that of a drunkard. Initially, George accompanies an old acquaintance to "a little glass-fronted saloon that sat blinking jovially at the crowds." Charley Jones, ordering whiskey for himself while George drinks beer, exchanges a few words with the barkeep and then addresses his new friend: " 'This is th' hang-out fer a great gang,' said Jones, turning to Kelcey. 'They're a great crowd, I tell yeh. We own th' place when we get started. Come aroun' some night. Any night, almost. T'-night, b'jiminy. They'll almost all be here, an' I'd like t' interduce yeh. They're a great gang! Gre-e-at!'" That evening George returns to the saloon and is introduced to Bleecker. Shortly thereafter Bleecker and his crowd repair to the backroom to hold their private drinking party. Charley Jones drinks whiskey, but while George is also drinking, we are not told what he drinks. Bleecker works his spell over George, who not only "admired Bleecker immensely" but "developed a brotherly feeling for the others." Back home, in bed, George "had a pleasurable consciousness that he had made a good impression upon those fine fellows. He felt that he had spent the most delightful evening of his life." The next time he runs into Jones, he is told that Bleecker will host "a blow-out" the next night and that he "expressly" wants George to come. George arrives at Bleecker's "apartments," is introduced to the other guests, and, along with them, is offered drink. "There were upon it [the table] a keg of beer, a long row of whiskey bottles, a little heap of corn-cob pipes, some bags of tobacco, a box of cigars, and a mighty collection of glasses, cups, and mugs." Kelcey takes a mug of beer. Later he switches to whiskey. When, still later, he trips over a pair of outstretched legs and strikes his head, he reacts by pouring himself "an extravagant portion of whiskey." Kelcey gets very drunk, wants to sing a song, but instead passes out.

He awakens the next morning to a scene of widespread destruction. "After the tumults of the previous night the interior of this room resembled a decaying battle-field. The air hung heavy and stifling with the odors of tobacco, men's breaths, and beer half filling forgotten glasses. There was ruck of broken tumblers, pipes, bottles, spilled tobacco, cigar stumps." It is of particular interest that Crane makes so much of pipes, tobacco, and smoke. During the earlier private party in the backroom of the saloon, the entrapped men have been described as garlanded by smoke: "the tobacco-smoke eddied about the forms of the men in ropes and wreaths. Near the ceiling there was a thick gray cloud."

As early as 1883 the WCTU had targeted tobacco as a grave danger to temperance, forming in that year a department called Effort to Overthrow the Tobacco Habit.[21] By 1895 the *Union Signal*, a WCTU publication, was arguing for everyone's "right to fresh air" and advocating that "smokers be permitted to smoke only in such places and ways as would not interfere 'with the rights and freedoms of any other individual.'"[22] One temperance piece attacks the widespread use of tobacco by pretending to extol its personal and social advantages:

How sweet it makes the breath! What a clean and wholesome odor lingers behind in the garments of those who use it! But one of the most conspicuous advantages accruing to mankind from smoking is its unselfishness; for, in this respect, it presents itself in striking contrast to the injurious habit of drinking. A man calls for a glass of ale, and there he sits, a selfish being, with perhaps a dozen or more around him, yet none but himself derive the least pleasure from the foaming beverage before him. Not so the smoker. He can purify and sweeten the air of the largest room; and, let it be ever so crowded, all present have a share of his smoke to enjoy. All present depart freshened and sweetened by the emanations from his pipe.[23]

On the morning after the drunken celebrations at Bleecker's place, George awakens with a strong thirst. But when he finally manages to get himself a drink of water, it is "an intolerable disappointment. It was insipid and weak to his scorched throat and not at all cool." Bleecker invites him to go out for a cocktail. George makes "a movement of disdain for cocktails" but accompanies Bleecker to the street. Once outside, he goes his own way, parting company from his host of the night before, "the only man of them who knew much about cocktails."

It is not much later that George begins to wonder whether he still cares for beer. He recalls that "he had been obliged to cultivate a talent for imbibing it.... He was born with an abhorrence which he had steadily battled until it had come to pass that he could drink from ten to twenty glasses of beer without the act of swallowing causing him to shiver. He understood that drink was an essential to joy, to the coveted position of a man of the world and of the streets. The saloons contained the mystery of a street for him. When he knew its saloons he comprehended the street. Drink and its surroundings were the eyes of a superb green dragon to him. He followed a fascinating glitter, and the glitter required no explanation." Bleecker and the boys form a club with dues set at a dollar a week. The saloon keeper donates "half the rent of quite a large room over the saloon." On leaving one meeting of the club, Kelcey's legs are described as being "like whalebone when he tried to go up-stairs upon his return home, and the edge of each step was moved curiously forward."

In time George loses his job and, in need of money, approaches his friends Bleecker, Jones, and O'Connor for a loan. They do not lend him the money, and he discovers that now he is "below them in social position." But the seeds for new friendships and loyalties had already been sown when he helped the street tough Fidsey Corcoran beat up a man the latter had provoked into fighting. As George nears his home after being rebuffed by his erstwhile drinking friends, he encounters Fidsey and another member of the street gang. They invite George to partake of a "big can" of beer they have sneaked away from a "new barkeep." An argument breaks out, but it does not keep any one of them from his "smoke" at the can. Somehow Fidsey and the boys maneuver Kelcey into confronting one Blue Billie. But George avoids fighting when a little boy delivers the message that George's mother is sick. She dies shortly after George gets there. The reader last sees George, defeated and alone, as he sits staring at the wallpaper. "The pattern was clusters of brown roses. He felt them like hideous crabs crawling upon his brain."

Much of what George has done self-destructively, when not out of sheer fecklessness, he has done vindictively. When he thinks of getting drunk he relishes in anticipation the effect his actions will have, presumably, on his mother. Invited to Bleecker's party, he thinks of himself as "a very grim figure." "He was about to taste the delicious revenge of a partial self-destruction. The universe would regret its position when it saw him drunk."

The mother's arsenal of weapons will prove inadequate to the formidable task of wrenching George away from drink. Her boy is not amenable to "home protection," the bedrock of Miss Willard's temperance program.[24] Consequently, when all the cleaning and decorating and special cooking she can accomplish fails to reform George, this "poor, inadequate woman, of a commonplace religiosity" (as William Dean Howells called her)[25] turns to the church. By weeping at his truculent refusal to accompany her to prayer meeting, Mrs. Kelcey manages to get him there. But sadly for her, this one visit serves merely to confirm George's belief that he is damned. George is uncomfortable, angry, "wild with a rage in which his lips turned slightly livid." Yet his interest is piqued when "one by one people arose and told little tales of their religious faith. Some were tearful and others calm, emotionless, and convincing. Kelcey listened closely for a time. These people filled him with a great curiosity. He was not familiar with their types." At last, the clergyman, described as "a pale-faced, but plump young man in a black coat that buttoned to his chin"—reminiscent of the clergyman who, fearing for his respectability, spurns Maggie—speaks. "Kelcey was amazed, because, from the young man's appearance, he would not have suspected him of being so glib; but the speech had no effect on Kelcey, excepting to prove to him again that he was damned." The clergyman has spoken (though not to George), but he has not, as the temperance manuals preached, reached down to those young men who, going "down in evil ways," are "not riding a docile, well-broken steed" but "are on a monster, wild and blood-thirsty, going at a death rate."[26]

To his mother's bitter disappointment, George does not return to prayer meeting. It is only as his mother lays dying in the next room that standing before George is "the pale-faced but plump young clergyman."[27]

" 'My poor lad—' began this latter." It is too late. Crane has had it both ways. The church has been ineffectual. And George, inadvertently in league with his mother's destructive impulses, has destroyed himself. Ironically, in the end the "woman without weapons" has apparently all the weapons she needs to vanquish her son.

NOTES

1. Frances E. Willard, "Which Shall Win?" in *Readings and Recitations, No. 1,* ed. L[izzie] Penney (New York: National Temperance Society and Publication House, 1877), 9–10.

2. Anonymous, *A Brief History of the Woman's Christian Temperance Union,* 2nd ed. (Evanston: Union Signal, 1907), 12.

3. Caroline A. Soule, "The Cry of the Women," in *Readings and Recitations, No. 1,* 12.

4. Frances E. Willard, *Woman and Temperance: or, The Work and Workers of the Woman's Christian Temperance Union* (Hartford: Park Publishing, 1883), 237.

5. Edward Garnett, "Two Americans," *London Speaker,* 30 (Aug. 6, 1904), 436–37. This review is reprinted in George Monteiro, "Stephen Crane: A New Appreciation by Edward Garnett," *American Literature,* 50 (Nov. 1978), 465–71.

6. Maxwell Geismar, *Rebels and Ancestors: The American Novel, 1890–1915* (Boston: Houghton Mifflin, 1953), 94, 95.

7. Eric Solomon, *Stephen Crane: From Parody to Realism* (Cambridge, Mass.: Harvard University Press, 1966), 60, 66.

8. Brenda Murphy, "A Woman with Weapons: The Victor in Stephen Crane's *George's Mother,*" *Modern Language Studies,* 11 (Spring 1981), 92.

9. Josephine Pollard, "Stolen; or, the Mother's Lament," in *Readings and Recitations, No. 4,* ed. L[izzie] Penney (New York: National Temperance Society and Publication House, 1882), 83–87.

10. Quoted in Helen E. Tyler, *Where Prayer and Purpose Meet: 1874—The WCTU Story—1949* (Evanston: Signal Press, 1949), 30.

11. John W. Crowley, *The White Logic: Alcoholism and Gender in American Modernist Fiction* (Amherst: University of Massachusetts Press, 1994), 30. Crowley makes his point in a chapter on Jack London's *John Barleycorn* (1913).

12. Stephen Crane, *George's Mother,* in *Bowery Tales,* Volume I of *The University of Virginia Edition of the Works of Stephen Crane,* ed. Fredson Bowers, intr. James B. Colvert (Charlottesville: University Press of Virginia, 1969), 113–78.

13. For John B. Gough pictured as "the Cold-Water warrior," see W. J. Rorabaugh, *The Alcoholic Republic: An American Tradition* (Oxford and New York: Oxford University Press, 1979), 98.

14. Belle M. Brain, *Weapons for Temperance Warfare* (Boston and Chicago: United Society of Christian Endeavor, 1897), [1], [3], [5].

15. Quoted in Mark Edward Lender and James Kirby Martin, *Drinking in America: A History* (New York: Free Press/London: Collier Macmillan, 1982), 107.

16. *The Psalms, Hymns, and Spiritual Songs, of the Rev. Isaac Watts, D.D.,* ed. Samuel Worcester (Boston: Crocker and Brewster, 1838), 563.

17. John Julian, ed., *A Dictionary of Hymnology* (New York: Dover, 1957), 55; and Willard, *Woman and Temperance,* 312, 350. Interestingly, in chapter 5 of Mark Twain's *Adventures of Tom Sawyer* a minister reads this hymn in "a peculiar style which was much

admired in that part of the country. His voice began on a medium key and climbed steadily up till it reached a certain point, where it bore with strong emphasis upon the topmost word and then plunged down as if from a spring-board" (Mark Twain, *Mississippi Writings*, ed. Guy Cardwell [New York: Library of America, 1982], 38).

18. Crane's obituary in *Publishers' Circular* actually listed him as the author of a book entitled *St. George's Mother* ("Mr. Stephen Crane," 72, June 9, 1900, 629). Curiously, there exists a later book by J[oseph] Johns entitled *St. George and the Dragon: England and the Drink Traffic* (London: S. W. Partridge [1907?]).

19. Anonymous, [*George's Mother*]. *Illustrated London News*, 109 (Oct. 3, 1896), 439.

20. Alice Hall Petry argues for Hogarth's influence on *Maggie: A Girl of the Streets*, especially on Crane's portrait of the mother, in "*Gin Lane* in the Bowery: Crane's *Maggie* and William Hogarth," *American Literature*, 56 (Oct. 1984), 417–26. Gerard M. Sweeney extends her argument in "The Syphilitic World of Stephen Crane's *Maggie*," *American Literary Realism*, 24 (Fall 1991), 79–85.

21. *Brief History*, 39.

22. Ruth Bordin, *Woman and Temperance: The Quest for Power and Liberty, 1873–1900* (Philadelphia: Temple University Press, 1981), 109.

23. Anonymous, "The Logic of Smoking," in *Readings and Recitations, No. 5*, ed. L[izzie] Penney (New York: National Temperance Society and Book Publications, 1884), 73.

24. She inscribed photographs of herself "Yours for Home Protection, Frances E. Willard"; see Bordin, *Woman and Temperance*, 44.

25. W. D. Howells, "New York Low Life in Fiction," *New York World* (July 26, 1896), 18.

26. Rev. T. De Witt Talmage, "True Help," in *Readings and Recitations, No. 3*, ed. L[izzie] Penney (New York: National Temperance Society and Publication House, 1879), 18.

27. In Crane's work the adjectives "pale-faced" and "plump" are usually denigrating.

ROBERT M. DOWLING

Stephen Crane and the Transformation of the Bowery

In the late seventeenth century, a rural path known as Bowery Lane (from the Dutch word *bowerij*, or farm) was put to use as the main postal route from New York to Boston. The lower mile of this, situated in the heart of Manhattan's Lower East Side, became known simply as the Bowery. Due to its heavy commercial traffic and proximity to immigrant neighborhoods, the Bowery rapidly swelled into a celebrated urban boulevard, rivaling the already famous Broadway to its west. And with the construction of the Great Bowery Theater in 1826, the Bowery and thereabouts became New York's theatrical center, both on the stage and off. The area was packed to the point of bursting with cheap theaters, burlesque shows, dance halls, brothels, basement-level dives, and beer halls that seated up to two thousand patrons. It competed with Broadway, but did not cater to a Broadway crowd; it was notoriously flamboyant and alive with action; it was the epicenter of working-class culture and openly advertised itself as such, basing its appeal on picaresque urban experience and melodramatic spectacle.

By 1871, the year Stephen Crane was born, the Bowery as it was known worldwide had all but vanished. And with the construction of the Third Avenue elevated train seven years later, the boulevard was transfigured beyond recognition. The sun was blocked out by the tracks, and the streets were showered with hot oil and coal. By 1893, the year Crane published the vanity

From *Twisted from the Ordinary: Essays on American Literary Naturalism*, edited by Mary E. Papke, pp. 45–62. © 2003 The University of Tennessee Press.

edition of his first novella, *Maggie: A Girl of the Streets*, the Bowery was already the infamous Bowery, once again conspicuous but now for alcoholism, poverty, homelessness, and crime. The streets were filled with hoboes and rival gangs. The number of prostitutes drew sailors by the thousands. The area was no longer a bastion of republicanism, and its inhabitants were continually being inveigled into accepting an oppositional system of social behavior. They were helpless in a cycle of cultural prostration seemingly indefinite in origin. As T. J. Jackson Lears postulates in "The Concept of Cultural Hegemony," "most people find it difficult, if not impossible, to translate the outlook implicit in their experience into a conception of the world that will directly challenge the hegemony culture" (596). For the majority of New Yorkers grappling with the city's process of industrialization and urbanization, challenging the dominant culture was as unimaginable as the act of cultural absorption was subconscious. The indisputably dominant Victorian culture, distinguished by an allegiance to the cult of respectability and traditionally associated with Broadway and Fifth Avenue, had effectively wiped out its working-class counterpart on the East Side.[1]

Late-nineteenth-century New York Bowery culture was also one obsessed with consumption. Ironically, this consumer culture, such as might be found in New York's theaters, dance halls, and museums, proved far more effective for bringing urban "low life" into the "respectable" fold than did the evangelical moral reform efforts of the 1860s, '70s, and '80s. It is within this atmosphere that *Maggie*'s tragic protagonists reside. But the cultural space *Maggie* occupies signals less a beginning than an ending; the richness of antebellum Bowery culture was stifled by its incorporation of Victorian codes of behavior, and Crane renders his characters prostrated by the contradictory effects. Though Crane does give lip service to the new consumer culture, he does not present it as a vehicle for personal individuation and cultural dissent. Those processes, on the Bowery at least, were vestiges of a former time. *Maggie*, in short, is not a story of rebellion but of conformity.

Victorian culture in New York was in its infancy when the Bowery's cultural and physical boundaries began to define themselves. The tensions that emerged were clearly contingent upon a mutual exigency of identity as related to cultural politics. Richard Butsch, in his "Bowery B'hoys and Matinee Ladies," acknowledges that "middle- and upper-middle class Americans wished to distinguish themselves from the uncultivated working class at the very time when the working class was politically ascendant, at least rhetorically" (385). As a result, a Gramscian "war of position" clearly took place, a conflict for cultural hegemony rather than state power, in which codes of behavior were the primary mechanisms of attrition. Proper social markers for Americans with "respectability" included certain clothes, levels of education, and speech patterns, along with many other codified social graces. These were all learned behaviors, however, and adoptable by the "vulgar" masses. The codes then became increasingly rarified and more difficult to interpret and adopt. Once firmly established, middle-class New Yorkers became obsessed with protecting the status of Victorian respectability, at the expense of the indecorous rabble. To ensure social order, however, they eventually condoned the proliferation of respectable morals and manners in order to regulate satisfactorily the behavior of the working class. By the 1890s, the Victorian ideology had become so entrenched in New York's social consciousness that the notion of respectability would have a sizable effect on the actions and value structure of the very working-class culture that initially despised it.

One of the finest commentaries on the cultural transformation of the Bowery in this context has been furnished by, of all people, Henry James. While slumming in the neighborhood of the Bowery at the age of sixty, following his return to the United States in 1904, James attended a theater performance that closely resembled the fictional space constructed by Stephen Crane a decade earlier. James observed there a "vertiginous bridge of American confectionery," which he identified as a bridge that transverses the gap between the Victorian codes being enacted on the stage and the level of the audience's assent. He speculated that these "almost 'high class' luxuries, circulating in such a company, were a sort of supreme symbol of the promoted state of the aspirant to American conditions" (196). The most fascinating dramatic action for James was not what was taking place on the stage but rather the unwritten dialogue between the audience and the notions of respectability the theater and, more importantly, the society at large was selling: "Nothing (in the texture of the occasion) could have had a sharper interest than this demonstration that, since what we pretend to do with them is thoroughly to school them, the schooling, by our system, cannot begin too soon or pervade their experience too much. Were they going to rise to it, or rather fall from it—to our instinct, as distinguished from their own, for picturing life?" (199). James observed a new social lesson, one diametrically opposed to what Walt Whitman had referred to in *Democratic Vistas* (1871) as "great lessons of nature," lessons of unique culture expression. "Were they to take our lesson submissively," James asks, "in order to get with it our smarter traps and tricks, our superior Yankee machinery?" (199). Venues of popular entertainment such as the one James described, ones boldly sworn to elevating Bowery life, did not answer Whitman's call in *Democratic Vistas* for "variety and freedom" but enforced, as James attested, "blank conformity to convention" (198).

If one takes into account this transformation of Bowery culture over the nineteenth century, Stephen Crane's central characters in *Maggie*—Jimmie, Maggie, and Pete—can be viewed as fragmented relics of a culture drowned out by rampant urban American growth and its effects on New York culture in the form of middle-class Victorianism. This essay addresses the place of Crane's writings in the cultural history of the Bowery, then, rather than their place in literary history. It has been argued that Crane's knowledge of New York and the Bowery culture he represents is secondhand, taken from Jacob Riis and the mass of Methodist moral reform tracts that abounded during that period (Benfey 63). Crane scholars find it difficult, however, to nail down precisely how well Crane may or may not have known the district. Regardless, Crane's novella is charged with a social energy that corresponds significantly with the Bowery and its past. Though Crane may have begun to conceptualize *Maggie* in Syracuse, before he had experienced Manhattan life to any substantial degree, in every chapter there exist salient references to the city's signature "respectable" culture and how it was both loathed and emulated by many of the Bowery's inhabitants.

Victorians themselves are not meant to be portrayed here as hobgoblins or bugaboos. Crane himself certainly points to no group or individual as inherently evil; his characters are products of a naturalistic environment that is beyond rational action. As a likable character from Crane's sketch "An Experiment in Luxury" wisecracks, "Nobody is responsible for anything. I wish to heaven somebody was, and then we could all jump on him" (*Crane* 550). Though there was no doubt a very real cultural conflict between vying groups, there is an aura of inevitability in the effect of urbanization on the Bowery, whether it be at the hands of Victorianism or some other cultural force. What immediately follows is a brief narrative account of the development of the historically resonant subculture from which Crane and others have drawn for their portraits of New York life, the Bowery B'hoys and G'hals. Following that, I will demonstrate how the novella *Maggie*, along with some of his other New York writing, illustrates the means by which that singular culture was suppressed.

While still a teenager, actor Frank Chanfrau ate regularly at the Broadway House, a small eatery on Grand Street in the middle of Manhattan's Lower East Side. At lunch one afternoon, Chanfrau overheard a boisterous young man howl to the waiter, "*Look a heah! Gimme a sixpenny plate ev pork and beans, and don't stop to count dem beans ...!*" This was Mose Humphreys, a printer at the *New York Sun* and one of the "fire boys" of the mid-1830s. Over a decade later, the playwright Benjamin A. Baker would catch wind of Chanfrau's comical mimicking of the then famous Bowery B'hoy's style of speech. Baker promptly composed a dramatic sketch for Chanfrau to perform on the popular stage. They showed it to William Mitchell, the proprietor of a Lower East Side venue, Mitchell's Olympic Theater. Mitchell criticized the play or, more specifically, Baker's writing, remarking that "the characters are good, but what a bad piece!" Months later, coming up short for a new idea, he consented to let Chanfrau give Baker's play, then entitled "New York As It Is," a trial performance (Brown 284).

When Chanfrau first strolled onto the stage with a swagger and a sneer, the clamorous audience plunked into a hushed silence. This might have been discomfiting for Chanfrau since they generally greeted their favorite actor with lusty applause, but the fact is, as drama historian Allston T. Brown notes, the audience "didn't recognize Chanfrau. He stood there in his red shirt, with his fire coat thrown over one arm, the stovepipe hat ... drawn over one eye, his trousers tucked into his boots, a stump of cigar pointing up from his lips to his eye, the soap locks plastered flat on his temples, and his jaw protruded into a half-beastly, half-human expression of contemptuous ferocity" (284). Chanfrau ripped the cigar from his mouth, spat on the stage, and bellowed, "*I ain't a goin' to run wid dat mercheen no more!*"[2] The audience was no longer silent. As reported in the *New York Herald* the next day (April 18, 1848), the crowd "climbed up to the stage boxes, and all seemed bent on genuine frolic. The police and officers connected with the theater were rendered powerless...." A mob of people pushed in from the street, but at length the police got it under control. They "hereupon commenced to clear the front of the stage amid the most deafening cheers," the *Herald* continues, "and some of the B'hoys were to be seen springing forward on the heads of their different groups of friends, from the stage, whom they joined in the pit, amid continued laughter" (qtd. in Buckley 392).[3]

Under its new name, "A Glance At New York In 1848," the play was performed for forty-eight consecutive nights, selling over forty thousand tickets, making it, up to that point, the most popular play in American history (Buckley 392–93). William Dean Howells later admitted to being wholly beguiled by its reception: "Some actor saw and heard things spoken with the peculiar swagger and whopperjaw utterance of the B'hoy of those dreadful old days ... and he put them on stage and spread the poison of them all over the land, so that there was hardly anywhere a little blackguard boy who did not wish to act and talk like Mose" (*Criticism* 271). Though this response appears to be criticism by a hopeless traditionalist, Howells appreciated the impact the play had on his own consciousness: "Other things have come and gone," he grants, "things of Shakespeare, of Alfieri, of Cervantes, but those golden works of a forgotten dramatist poet remain with me" (*Criticism* 271). The Baker sketch was, in short, an unintentional power play of cultural credibility. The Mose character empowered the "lower million" with both a defiant attitude and a comic voice. The B'hoy thereafter became a widely known dramatic presence on the American stage, and the stage was one of the most influential cultural vehicles of the time.

William Dean Howells rightly observes that Jimmie Johnson, Maggie's younger brother, was "an Ishmaelite from the cradle, who, with his warlike instincts beaten back into cunning, is what the B'hoy of former times has become in our more strenuously policed days" ("New York" 154). Indeed, there are numerous traits shared by Crane's characters and the B'hoys and G'hals of the old Bowery. Pete, for example, is described as having " an enticing nonchalance," with his hair "curled down over his forehead in an oiled bang" and a red scarf tied around his throat (25), while Maggie, like her G'hal counterparts, is a seamstress infatuated with the theater.[3] If we recall Chanfrau's performance while reading the following scene from Maggie— Crane's dramatic introduction of the character Pete—the comparability between stage and fictional characters is even more vivid: "Down the avenue came boastfully sauntering a lad of sixteen years, although the chronic sneer of an ideal manhood already sat on his lips. His hat was tipped with an air of challenge over his eye. Between his teeth, a cigar stump was tilted at the angle of defiance" (8). The analogy Howells proffers likening Crane's Jimmie to the B'hoys is, then, perhaps even more applicable to Pete, who will ultimately contribute to Maggie's metamorphosis from seamstress to street walker. At the same time, Crane makes Jimmie an admirer of fire engines, which seems to testify to the author's intent to evoke Bowery history, as the B'hoys were extreme in their fascination with fire fighting. "A fire engine," Crane remarks, "was enshrined in [Jimmie's] heart as an appalling thing that he loved with a distant dog-like devotion. They had been known to overturn street-cars" (23). To the B'hoys, fighting fires was a contact sport. Any activity, including socializing with their female counterparts, the G'hals, was immediately broken off by the sound of a distant fire signal. Those familiar with the Lower East Side would know at that point to keep their heads about them.

The B'hoy became recognizable as a distinct type in the popular consciousness of mid-nineteenth-century New York at a time when the establishment of urban "types" was vital to the evolution of the city's identity (Buckley 359). But much like the case with the rich and visible New York gay culture in the 1920s (Chauncey 335), the famed Bowery B'hoys of the 1840s attracted too much press in the eyes of the dominant culture and faced a subsequent backlash.

For instance, reporting on May 12, 1849, directly after the Astor Place Riots for *The Home Journal*, journalist N.P. Willis complains of the personal affronts men of "good society" had to endure at their hands: "If the English tragedian wishes to see the company that he offends, he has only to follow the well-dressed idler down the Bowery and observe the looks he gets from Mose and the soap-lockery as he goes along.... Let but the passive aristocratic party select a favorite, and let there be but a symptom of a handle for the B'hoys to express their dissent and the undercurrent breaks forth like an uncapped hydrant" (qtd. in Buckley 296). Not surprisingly, the negative feeling was mutual. A B'hoy character in popular novelist Ned Buntline's *The G'hals of New York* (1850) is seen railing in disgust against the Victorian lack of respect for his position in society. Complaining to his sister about their bad financial luck, their father having lost a substantial fortune, he is dumbfounded by the general lack of compassion they confront each day on the street: "Gas!" Will our rich 'quaintances recognize us in our rags as they used to do when we were proud and dressed like them? Will they even speak to us? No! They turn from us as though they thought we were going to rob 'em; and if you meet 'em in the street, they turn their eyes another way and hurry past you as if you had the small pox, and they were afraid o' ketchin' it!" (16). Parodying the B'hoys irreverence in *The B'hoys of New York* (1848), one of Buntline's characters, a newspaper editor self-styled as "THE B'hoy of New York," decides to change the title of a proposed article on lewd female exhibitionism from "SHAMEFUL" to "Chaste And Beautiful Representations Of Ancient Statuary" in order to, he vociferates, "Give the Puritans a dash!" (11–15).

Invoking these antebellum subalterns allows us to bring Crane's cryptically impressionistic images of Bowery culture into focus. American authors had certainly appropriated the characteristics of the B'hoys well before Crane. Both Melville and Whitman, for instance, discovered in the B'hoy a refreshingly American articulation. Indeed the character Henry Jackson in Melville's *Redburn* is described as dressing like a Bowery B'hoy (Reynolds, *Beneath* 285), and Whitman biographers Gay Wilson Allen and David S. Reynolds have attributed many of the characteristics of Whitman's "I" in *Leaves of Grass* to the B'hoy. "[Whitman's] whole persona," Reynolds argues, "wicked rather than conventionally virtuous, free, smart, prone to slang and vigorous outbursts—reflects the B'hoy culture" (*Walt* 155). Nineteenth-century reviewers labeled Whitman as the "Bowery B'hoy of Literature," and Whitman used "Mose Velsor," the name most commonly associated with the B'hoys in the popular press, as a pseudonym for many of his newspaper articles (Reynolds, *Walt* 105, 103). Whitman's choices characteristically disregarded the period's increasingly virulent modes of cultural discrimination.

As a protective rather than a purely egotistical measure on the part of the Victorian middle class, the dissemination of Victorian culture was enforced in all conceivable media. The most powerful aspect of Crane's Bowery writing in general, and *Maggie* in particular, is his ability to recognize this phenomenon in urban American culture. The results of a half-century's worth of cultural incorporation are transparent in Crane's characters and prose. Crane's fragmented style simulates the fragmented consciousness of Bowery dwellers at this point in the district's history. Though Crane's Jimmie is delivered to the audience as an urban Huckleberry Finn, if more violent in nature, his self-esteem is far less developed than it at first appears. His B'hoy-like mannerisms are heightened by his overcompensation in the face of cultural defeat. And the social arenas in which the characters interact demonstrate to what extent the culture at large is responsible.

In his sketch "An Experiment In Luxury" (1894), Crane cogently provides us with his take on cultural dissemination. While dining at his wealthy young friend's house, his narrator reflects on the derisive view of the very rich by the Christian middle class and their complementary condescension toward the very poor:

> Indicated in this light chatter about the dinner table there was an existence that was not at all what the youth had been taught to see. Theologians had for a long time told the poor man that riches did not bring happiness, and they had solemnly repeated this phrase until it had come to mean that misery was commensurate with dollars, that each wealthy man was inwardly a miserable wretch. And when a wail of despair or rage had come from the night of the slums *they had stuffed this epigram down the throat of he who cried out and told him that he was a lucky fellow. They did this because they feared.* (556, italics mine)

What is being taken to task here is the age-old custom of the church's designation of the poor as unfortunates and the rich as selfish, unhappy mongers. "'And, in the irritating, brutalizing, enslaving environment of their poverty,'" the narrator's friend insists, the poor "'are expected to solace themselves with these assurances ...'" (549). The "youth," as the focalizer of the story is called, is surprised by how functional and happy the wealthy family is. Further, there is no inherent love for the poor in the espoused vision, he learns; the espousers are simply terrified of the "other half" confronting their situation on their own terms.

This parable suggests the Victorian fear of a consumer class with access to and control over any and all consumable products. If the Bowery culture as epitomized in the antebellum years was being drummed out of existence because of what Victorians perceived as the threatening nature of subcultural activity, the culture of the Gilded Age's nouveau riche is equally condemned. The wealthy host in "An Experiment in Luxury" confidently sums up his position on the issue: "'it is impossible for me to believe that these things equalize themselves; that there are burrs under all rich cloaks and benefits in all ragged jackets, *and the preaching of it seems wicked to me*' " (549, italics mine). Both the B'hoys and the barons, in other words, were being demonized by the popular media of the time.

This cultural posturing and antagonism was a manifestation of the city's developing consumer culture, which Keith Gandal describes as providing "a sort of moral inspiration" (13) to slummers exploring the Bowery. For the Bowery population itself, however, acculturation served as a dampening force rather than a liberating one. In Pete's courtship of Maggie, for instance, he escorts her to a number of amusements that had burgeoned throughout the city to accommodate a growing body of consumers with increasingly standardized tastes. These include music halls, dance halls, theaters, dime museum freak shows, the Central Park Menagerie, and the Metropolitan Museum of Art. Crane's ironic observations of Victorian melodrama in particular, both toward the culture that creates it and the culture that buys into it, demonstrates that, in Miles Orvell's words, "if the stage is not 'realism' then by implication the novella *Maggie*, which tells these truths, is realism" (129). Crane portrays the theater as offering "an atmosphere of pleasure and prosperity," which "seemed to hang over the throng, born, perhaps, of good clothes and two hours in a place of forgetfulness" (70). As Maggie for the first time blissfully takes in the emollient scenes on stage, "no thoughts of the atmosphere of the collar and cuff factory came to her" (33). Happiness is thus equated with distractions and vicarious experience, a historical transformation that might be seen as the inception of the future culture of television, video games, and the Internet.

Throughout Crane presents Maggie's continual fall into the world of fantasy as a manifestation of cultural coercion. Maggie idealizes Pete, an actor in life who adheres to a bogus self-image of respectability. She is duped into trusting the facade. The fiction of the stage begins to distort the very reality it loosely represents, and the characters seem to comprehend each other only in melodramatic terms. When Maggie falls, her neighbors envision her as the Eve-like character that Crane designs her to be, and children "ogle her as if they formed the front row of a theatre" (65). Similarly, George Kelcey in Crane's second Bowery novella, *George's Mother* (1896), is overwhelmingly jealous of Maggie's attentions towards Pete, both of whom make appearances in the later novella. Like Pete, George aspires to be both Bowery tough and chivalric gentleman. And, like Maggie, George sees his beloved through the lens of popular drama. In his daydreams, George superimposes Maggie's form onto the mass-produced images of staged melodrama, and with a nod to the contributions of photography, he places the couple "in scenes which he took mainly from pictures[;] this vision conducted a courtship, strutting, posing, and lying through a drama which was magnificent from glow of purple" (236).

The standard venue for impressing young ladies on the Bowery was, indeed, the theater—and the paramount theatrical form in both *Maggie* and the New York it represents is the moral-reform drama. Initially developed by Moses Kimball and P. T. Barnum for museum theaters, moral-reform dramas were deliberately designed to address the needs of a middle class attentive to Protestant standards of decency (Butsch 383). If the theater had been a primarily working-class space in the opening decades of nineteenth-century New York, by the 1860s it drew a decidedly Victorian audience that determined its content and conduct. Middle-class values, as a result, were simultaneously acted out on the stage and absorbed by the audience. The consequent metamorphosis of theatrical space seems paradoxical in that consumption and respectability, previously oppositional paradigms (Butsch 375), were now inextricably intertwined. It is by showing how these oppositions play off of one another that Crane's work and its sociological contribution is brought into crystalline clarity. The mimetic nature of the exchange between buyer and seller, for instance, is made remarkably comprehensible. The central thematic irony of *Maggie* has been identified as "the self-righteous condemnation of a woman who is good by the very society responsible for her downfall" (Brennan 64), but there remains some question why this would be true historically. It is important to expose the origins and nature of this type of cultural dialectic, not just its manifestations, especially since foolish inconsistency seems to be the central aspect of Crane's *Maggie*.

Maggie Johnson is, among other things, used as a control in the Zolaesque experiment of looking at the New York popular theater as a means of understanding both the issue of class cultural consciousness and the popularized understanding of womanhood. For instance, each time Maggie exits the theater, she

> departed with raised spirits from the showing places of the melodrama. She rejoiced at the way in which the poor and virtuous eventually surmounted the wealthy and wicked. The theater made her think. She wondered if the culture and refinement she had seen imitated, perhaps grotesquely, by the heroine on the stage, could be acquired by a girl who lived in a tenement house and worked in a shirt factory. (37)

Crane is being ironic, perhaps even cruel here, in describing the exaltations of his heroine in this way, but his analysis of class aspiration nevertheless rings true. Most New Yorkers were complicit in this culture of conformity;

they had been nurtured to accept "refinement" as the ultimate state of being. Contemplating her suitor, rendered pretentious by the narration, Maggie observes instead that he "was extremely gracious and attentive. He displayed the consideration of a cultured gentleman who knew what was due." In addition, she "perceived that Pete brought forth all his elegance and all his knowledge of high-class customs for her benefit. Her heart warmed as she reflected upon his condescension" (31). While she is dreamily imaging a fantasy constructed by a culture at odds with her own, Pete is, in one of the few truly funny scenes of the book, chivalrously badgering the wait staff: "'Say, what deh hell? Bring deh lady a big glass! What deh hell use is dat pony?'" (31).

The theater scenes in *Maggie* demonstrate with subtle accuracy the trend towards what Richard Butsch calls the "taming" of the Bowery theatergoer. In contrast to Whitman's lusty descriptions of early Bowery dramatic performances in which the audience and the players interacted to create one large performance that transcended the limits of the play itself, the theatergoers of Maggie's world give themselves fully to one-way, passive entertainment. Refinement in late Victorian New York had become the status quo in the theater, if it had not yet completely taken hold of the music hall. The mores imposed on Victorian women in the streets of New York—to avoid eye contact, to dress down so as not to attract attention, to maintain emotional self-control, and so on—were swiftly transferred to the theater. Emotive expressions such as anger and laughter were no longer tolerated. Often dress codes were established, and hissing, drinking, eating, arriving late, and leaving early were forbidden at most venues.

In short, the proliferation of middle-class etiquette effectively "feminized" the theater, concurrently making it a feminine space while rejecting the fervent audience participation that had attracted its original audience. Proprietors increasingly changed the atmosphere of their venues to accommodate this new cult of middle-class female respectability, and they quickly came to understand that women, as Ann Douglas has argued, had gained supremacy over consumer culture (7). In 1866, for example, *The Spirit Of The Times*, a gentleman's magazine, complained that many men succumbed to the "bore of attending dull or even good performances for the sole purpose of escorting their Mary Janes" (qtd. in Butsch 392–93). Walt Whitman, in his nostalgic essay "The Old Bowery," poetically, though perhaps too sentimentally, mourns this refinement of the theater experience: "So much for the Thespian temple of New York fifty years since [the 1830s and 1840s], where 'sceptered tragedy went trailing by' under the gaze of the Dry Dock youth, and both players and auditors were of a character and like we shall never see again" (1216).

In Pete and Maggie's music hall as well, the reader is brilliantly introduced to the penetration of Bowery tastes by Victorian culture in the later decades of the nineteenth century. The crowd contains, Crane writes, all of "the nationalities of the Bowery," who "beamed upon the stage from all directions" (30). In the spirit of radical democracy, a singer appeals to the Irish workers in attendance by describing in one of her songs "a vision of Britain annihilated by America, and Ireland bursting her bonds." The climax of the performance is "The Star-Spangled Banner"; when the song begins, "instantly a great cheer swelled from the throats of this assemblage of the masses. There was a heavy rumble of booted feet thumping the floor. Eyes gleamed with sudden fire, and calloused hands waved frantically in the air" (32). Crane calls attention to this display of old Bowery behavior by smartly commencing with a dancer "attired in some half-dozen skirts," causing Maggie to wonder "at the splendor of the costume" and to lose herself "in calculations of the cost of the silks and laces" (31). For the finale of that part of the show, the dancer "fell into some of those grotesque attitudes which were at the time popular among the dancers in the theatres up-town, giving to the Bowery public the phantasies of the aristocratic theatre-going public, at reduced rates" (31–32). During all this, the audience is being attended to by little boys with "costumes of French chefs" selling "fancy cakes"[4] under gilded chandeliers, a spectacle substantiating the "vertiginous bridge of American confectionery" Henry James reports (30). Among the performers, a pair of girls listed as sisters—for rather obvious reasons of propriety—sing a duet "that," Crane ironically puts in, "is heard occasionally at concerts given under church auspices" while dancing in a way "which of course can never be seen at concerts given under church auspices" (32). The continuous and telling juxtapositions of old Bowery and new Victorian culture are thus served up to his readers just as Crane's boys in French chef hats serve up sweets to the fictional laborers.

Material consumption is not the only proselytizing mode we see in *Maggie*. In one scene involving a Protestant missionary, Crane brings the proverbial horse out from under the blanket. Jimmie Johnson is strolling past a mission church on the Bowery when he has an epiphany that calls to mind Stephen Dedalus on The Strand. The revelation is one that allows him to "clad his soul in armor." Inside the mission an evangelical preacher is sermonizing to a Bowery audience. In his sermon condemning sin, he addresses the crowd in "yous." It simply never occurs to him to use the first person plural. His grammar is, of course, restricted by the boundaries of permissible discourse. The sermonizer is a saved man and the audience damned because they have not yet been fully acculturated into what is perceived as the only tolerable cultural paradigm—the Victorian, the Christian, the respectable.

The philosopher animadverts a system that has no viable alternative. Jimmie, however, feels that he personifies an alternative culture inconceivable to this minister and his flock. The dialectical nature of the episode is clear to Crane: "A reader of words of wind-demons might have been able to see the portions of a dialogue pass to and fro between the exhorter and the hearers" (20). Jimmie stands alone in this crowd, a minority oppositional voice.

Maggie Johnson, in turn, somewhat dislocated in the Bowery world, is a figure under the gaze of her tenement's "philosophers," characters Crane assigns to deliberate over the nature of their condition. The young Maggie's initial deferment of Bowery behavior stumps them: "none of the dirt of Rum Alley seemed to be in her veins. The philosophers, up-stairs, down-stairs, and on the same floor, puzzled over it" (24). How is it, they ask themselves, that a girl born and raised on the Bowery could have escaped the then perceived stigma of Bowery existence? In many ways, this is the most self-reflexive point in the book. Crane himself is directly questioning his own motives for making Maggie such an anomaly. The novella, though singled out by many critics as the most artfully constructed Bowery tale ever written because of its combined expressionistic and realistic aspects, provides an acceptable heroine for mass consumption. Had the heroine been the more G'hal-like Nell, the street-smart but ultimately loathsome friend of Pete's, no one would have read her death as tragic; in fact, few middle-class readers would have bought the book at all.

Crane makes the final scene of Maggie's degradation palatable to his audience—the middle-class reader—by recycling the tragic circumstances of a girl who blossoms in a mud puddle, then meets a fateful death. In the 1893 edition, Maggie is killed by her client, a "huge fat man in torn and greasy garments" who "laughed, his brown, disordered teeth gleaming under a grey, grizzled mustache from which beer-drops dripped" (72). The grotesque man follows her until they stand together: "At their feet the river appeared a deathly black hue" (72). In the D. Appleton edition, which appeared three years later, Crane suggests that Maggie commits suicide, a trope of the Victorian melodrama: "She went into the blackness of the final block.... At the feet of the tall buildings appeared the deathly black hue of the river" (144). He made these changes to appease his more respectable readership, to expose the hypocrisy of the Bowery characters, and because he himself was equivocating. By having Maggie commit suicide, Crane could both punish her as a fallen woman and allow her to achieve redemption by contrition, thereby allowing the book to end on a sentimental note. Additionally, because Richard Watson Gilder, the editor of *Century Magazine*, was appalled by the dialogue in Crane's first *Maggie*, for the 1896 edition, D. Appleton and Company subsequently forced Crane to edit out all of its unseemly language before they would agree

to publish it (Wertheim iv). Crane submitted to constant concessions of this
kind throughout his career, as did many writers defer to the moral standard of
the Victorian world of publishing. The book market was not dissimilar, then,
to the theater in regard to censorship and gentrification.[5]

The son of a Methodist minister, Crane himself held contradictory
views on the dogma of "respectability." He was especially ambivalent about
prostitution: he had not, for instance, pressed charges on Doris Watts, a
prostitute who tried to blackmail him; he testified in court on behalf of Dora
Clark, a prostitute who was arrested in his company; and he probably married
Cora Stewart, a seasoned madam. But, as Laura Hapke asserts, "Crane never
resolved his ambivalence about the unchaste woman, a tension between
idealization and condemnation which his work on prostitution embodies"
(67). Crane could not fully accept, or fully deny, that a prostitute could
survive society's imposed and enforced judgments. Nevertheless, he himself
propagated the cultural construct that he openly rejected.

The overwhelming force of the sentimental and the respectable
unleashed in the novella are not only the product of determining institutions—
the church, the family, and the community—but the grotesque imposition of
middle-class mores onto the slum's inhabitants. No other aspect of the novella
is as much a testament to Crane's genius. Each of the primary characters in the
novella contributes to Maggie's fall. Each takes the side of popular morality
over familial and neighborhood ties. In one scene, even Jimmie consciously
broods over whether or not to forsake his sister in favor of his position in
society:

> Of course [he] publicly damned his sister that he might appear on
> a higher social plane. But, arguing with himself, stumbling about
> in ways that he knew not, he, once, almost came to a conclusion
> that his sister would have been more firmly good *had she better
> known why*. However, he felt that he could not hold such a view.
> He threw it hastily aside. (57, italics mine)

In a similarly self-reflexive moment, it "occurred to him to vaguely wonder,
for an instant, if some of the women of his acquaintance had brothers" (43).
Jimmie does not forgive or help his sister when she turns to prostitution, but
he is incapable of explaining to himself why. Indeed, his actions run counter
to his own constructed identity. His Bowery self is clearly weaker than the
identity that has been constructed for him by the "well-dressed men ... of
untarnished clothes" he so ardently deplores (21).

A brief glance at *George's Mother* provides us with another telling
example of this process of cultural discrimination and assent. The book, a

kind of chronologically contiguous sequel to *Maggie*, is a study of a young man from the country who is caught between three major cultural strains on the boulevard. One is his mother's moralistic devotion to the church and her constant appeals to him to attend mass with her; another is the alluring but violent and drunken life of the street and the friendships he rapidly acquires there; the last is a group of older drinkers who have Victorian aspirations but are far too dissipated to achieve respectability. All are essentially conformist alternatives. No one social group satisfies George, who longs to fit in but despairs when the options are presented to him. Crane explicitly reveals George's reluctance to join his mother at the local church: "In his ears was the sound of a hymn, made by people who tilted their heads at a prescribed angle of devotion. It would be too apparent that they were all better than he. When he entered they would turn their heads and regard him with suspicion. This would be an enormous aggravation, since he was certain that he was as good as they" (224). His actual uncertainty on this point is made clear in the unconscious slip in the second sentence. That is, he is unconvinced of his own equal standing with those he criticizes. Maggie faces a similar dilemma when she attends the theater. In fact, virtually all of Crane's major characters question their personal standing when they enter the various theaters of social construction.

Maggie's almost last word in the novella is the enigmatic utterance "Who?," a question that remains, at least superficially, unanswered in the text. To address that question, I will again draw from T. J. Jackson Lears who writes as follows:

> To resort to the concept of cultural hegemony is to take a banal question—"who has power?"—and deepen it at both ends. The "who" includes parents, preachers, teachers, journalists, literati, "experts" of all sorts, as well as advertising executives, entertainment promoters, popular musicians, sports figures, and "celebrities"—all of whom are involved (albeit often unwillingly) in shaping the values and attitudes of society. (572)

For Henry James, this exchange was realized in the popular theater he visited but not limited to it. James thinks of the "odd scene [at the theater] as still enacted in many places and many ways, the inevitable rough union in discord of the two groups of instincts, the fusion of the two camps by a queer, clumsy, wasteful social chemistry" (199).

This "wasteful social chemistry" brewed in New York as a result of the governing society's desire to bridle the effects of rampageous urban expansion. Unlike many European cities, New York in the nineteenth century promoted itself as a city free from economic class distinctions. In some ways I believe this was true and that the actual conflict was fought over cultural legitimacy and representation. Though Victorian and Bowery culture may have coexisted for a time in New York, Victorianism rapidly came to determine the values, sentiments, and prejudices of civil society on the Bowery, as well as throughout the city. If we accept Alfred Kazin's assertion that "the surest thing one can say about Crane is that he cared not a jot which way the world went" (68), it is equally true, as Hamlin Garland acknowledges, that Crane's *Maggie* "grew out of intimate association with the poor" (2). Describing Jimmie Johnson, Crane cuts a figure not unlike his own: "On the corners he was in life and of life. The world was going on and he was there to perceive it" (20). The Bowery which Crane presents so powerfully in *Maggie* is one that draws from a very real historical process: the modernization of slum dwellers whose cultural consciousnesses—specifically in regard to Bowery culture as it survived over the decades—conflicted with and were ultimately determined by nineteenth-century American Victorianism.

NOTES

1. I admit that "Victorian" is a highly unstable category, but I do not want the argument here to be obfuscated by semantics. I am using the term "Victorian" to identify the culture of middle- to upper-middle-class American Protestant moralism that manifested itself in a cult of "respectability" in the middle of the late nineteenth century.

2. "Mercheen" is Bowery dialect for a fire engine.

3. All references to Crane's work refer to the Library of America edition, unless otherwise noted in the citation. The "oiled bang" and "red scarf" constituted a fashion statement remarkably similar to the B'hoys' "soaplocks," long locks of hair that hung in front of their ears and were slicked down with bear grease or soap, and their penchant for wearing red shirts and scarves.

4. Butsch reports that "the indulgent nature of matinees and 'cream cakes' distinguished it from the museum theater as a 'woman's place' and indicated that it was an early facet of the culture of consumption" (390).

5. Significantly, the graphically violent, sexual, politically dissident, and wildly popular novels of the so-called "city mysteries" group of the 1840s and 1850s, led by George Lippard, Ned Buntline, John Vose, and George Thompson, among many others, have no substantial corollaries in the 1890s.

WORKS CITED

Benfey, Christopher. *The Double Life of Stephen Crane: A Biography*. New York: Alfred A. Knopf, 1992.

Brennan, Joseph X. "Ironic and Symbolic Structure in Crane's *Maggie*." *Maggie: A Girl of the Streets*. By Stephen Crane. Ed. Thomas A. Gullason. New York: Norton, 1979. 173–84.

Brown, Allston T. *A History of the New York Stage: From the First Performance in 1732 to 1901.* 1903. Vol. 1. New York: Benjamin Blom, 1964.

Buckley, Peter George. "To the Opera House: Culture and Society in New York City, 1820–1860." Diss. SUNY–Stony Brook, 1984.

Buntline, Ned. *The B'hoys of New York.* New York: Dick and Fitzgerald, 1848.

———. *The G'hals of New York.* New York: Dewitt and Davenport, 1850.

Butsch, Richard. "Bowery B'hoys and Matinee Ladies: The Re-Gendering of Nineteenth-Century American Theater Audiences." *American Quarterly* 46.3 (Sept. 1994): 374–405.

Chauncey, George. *Gay New York: Gender, Urban Culture, and the Making of the Gay Male World, 1890–1940.* New York: Basic Books, 1994.

Crane, Stephen. *Crane: Prose and Poetry.* Ed. J. C. Levenson. New York: Library of America, 1984.

———. "An Experiment in Luxury." 1894. Crane, *Crane: Prose and Poetry* 549–57.

———. *George's Mother.* 1896. Crane, *Crane: Prose and Poetry* 213–77.

———. *Maggie: A Girl of the Streets.* 1893. Crane, *Crane: Prose and Poetry* 5–78.

———. *Maggie: A Girl of the Streets.* New York: D. Appleton, 1896.

Douglas, Ann. *The Feminization of American Culture.* 1977. New York: Avon, 1978.

Gandal, Keith. *The Virtues of the Vicious: Jacob Riis, Stephen Crane, and the Spectacle of the Slum.* New York: Oxford UP, 1997.

Garland, Hamlin. Manuscript note concerning Stephen Crane's *Maggie.* Signed and undated. Two pages. Berg Collection of English and American Literature. New York Public Library. Astor, Lennox, and Tilden Foundation.

Hapke, Laura. *Girls Who Went Wrong: Prostitutes in American Fiction, 1885–1917.* Bowling Green: Bowling Green State U Popular P, 1989.

Howells, W. D. *Criticism and Fiction and Other Essays.* New York: New York UP, 1959.

———. "New York Low Life in Fiction." 1896. Rpt. in *Maggie: A Girl of the Streets,* by Stephen Crane. Ed. Thomas A. Gullason. New York: Norton, 1979. 154–55.

James, Henry. *The American Scene.* 1907. Bloomington: Indiana UP, 1968.

Kazin, Alfred. *On Native Grounds: An Interpretation of Modern American Prose Literature.* 1942. New York: Harcourt Brace, 1995.

Lears, T. J. Jackson. "The Concept of Cultural Hegemony: Problems and Possibilities." *American Historical Review* 90 (June 1985): 567–93.

Orvell, Miles. *The Real Thing: Imitation and Authenticity in American Culture, 1880–1940.* Chapel Hill: U of North Carolina P, 1989.

Reynolds, David S. *Beneath the American Renaissance: The Subversive Imagination in the Age of Emerson and Melville.* 1988. Cambridge: Harvard UP, 1995.

———. *Walt Whitman's America: A Cultural Biography.* 1995. New York: Vintage, 1996.

Wertheim, Stanley, ed. *The Merrill Studies in* Maggie *and* George's Mother. Columbus: Charles E. Merrill, 1970.

Whitman, Walt. *Poetry and Prose.* Ed. Justin Kaplan. New York: Library of America, 1996.

JUAN ALONZO

From Derision to Desire:
The "Greaser" in Stephen Crane's Mexican Stories and D. W. Griffith's Early Westerns

INTRODUCTION

During perhaps the most climactic and disturbing moment in D. W. Griffith's *The Greaser's Gauntlet* (1908), the narrative presents the lynching of the central character, the "greaser" in the film's title. A member of the lynch party ties a noose around the Mexican's neck and another secures the rope to the branch of a tree. In the next horrific instant, the mob raises the Mexican, and he is left hanging from the tree. Because of its verisimilitude, the scene is shocking, even to modern-day viewers. Fortunately for the Mexican, a woman intervenes on his behalf, and he is saved from a fate that befell many innocent real-life Mexicans on the western frontier.[1] The lynching scene in *The Greaser's Gauntlet* seemingly confirms Arthur Pettit's analysis of the Mexican's representation in early American film: that the Mexican, like his nineteenth-century dime novel predecessors, "remains a subject—someone to be killed or mocked, seduced or redeemed by Saxon protagonists" (132). Pettit's critique of Mexican stereotypes contains a binary quality—an understanding that sees stereotypes as only positive or negative—that persists in contemporary film scholarship on ethnic identity.[2] The conclusion of *The Greaser's Gauntlet*, however, challenges the binary critique of the stereotype in an important way. The greaser is not vanquished; instead, he goes on to perform the story's most heroic deed. Thus, Pettit's argument fails to explain the contradictory

From *Western American Literature* (Winter 2004), pp. 374–401. © 2004 by the Western Literature Association.

moments in film when the Mexican is spared total denigration, when film narrative simultaneously expresses repulsion for and attraction toward the Mexican subject. Such an argument does not account for what Homi Bhabha calls the ambivalence of stereotypical representation.

In this essay, I draw upon Bhabha's analysis of ambivalence for my reading of Mexican identity representation in two short stories by Stephen Crane and in several early films by D. W. Griffith at the turn of the twentieth century. Rather than contending that representations of the Mexican in Crane and Griffith are merely stereotypical and derogatory, I read in their depictions a wavering—sometimes derisive, sometimes admiring—attitude toward the Mexican subject. Crane's stories demonstrate an indirect regard for the Mexican in their refusal to make the Anglo-American the definitive victor over his Mexican rival. Crane reveals a sense of equality between Anglo and Mexican combatants at odds with the dime novel tradition. I read Crane's evenhanded treatment of the Mexican and Anglo as expressing ambivalence toward the Anglo-American, specifically, in myths about the western hero. Thus, Crane engages the positive figuration—the positive stereotype—of the Anglo male and subverts it. In the second half of the essay, I focus on the emergence of the "greaser" film stereotype in the films of D. W. Griffith from 1907 to 1910 and argue that the greaser constitutes not the reproduction of dime novel stereotypes but an ambivalent form of racial discourse. Griffith's often inconsistent appraisal of the Mexican suggests that Anglo-America's relation to ethnic minorities in general and Mexicans in particular encompasses contradictory feelings of derision and desire.

Because the film medium relied heavily upon popular literature for its narrative and stereotypical tropes at the turn of the century, an assessment of early film calls for a comparison with its literary precursors. Juxtaposing Griffith with Crane in particular makes sense because they were nearly contemporaries: Crane wrote his Mexican stories at the end of the nineteenth century, at a moment when writers were beginning to question the heroic themes of the western adventure story; Griffith, for his part, began his career at the beginning of the twentieth century, and among his earliest movies are precursors to film Westerns. Each, therefore, engages the Western adventure story at a pivotal moment in its development. Furthermore, Crane and Griffith take up the representation of the Mexican in idiosyncratic fashion, breaking with the expectations of the Western genre: Crane departs from an established tradition while Griffith confounds an emerging one before its conventions are established. Although they maintain canonical status within their respective art forms, each has also been criticized for his depiction of ethnic identities. In Crane's case, such critiques not only lack nuance but also misread his evaluation of the heroic codes of conduct practiced by Anglos and

Mexicans alike. In Griffith's instance, critiques of his racist cinematic practices are well founded but do not account for the contradictory moments when he admits the Mexican's humanity. I place Crane's stories and Griffith's films in comparative tension to show that negative stereotypes of Mexican identity are seldom strictly negative. The ambivalent re-articulation of the Anglo in Crane and the wavering representation of the Mexican in Griffith reveal that these subjects are constructed using similar stereotypical operations, that the derogation of one subject often requires the exaltation of the other.

In his chapter "The Other Question," Bhabha's analysis of the stereotype in the colonial context undermines the now conventional view of the stereotype as it has been conceptualized since Gordon Allport in *The Nature of Prejudice* (1954). Allport holds that stereotypes "are primarily images within a category invoked by the individual to justify either love-prejudice or hate-prejudice" (189). This either/or construction depends on the concept of "fixity" in order to sustain the stereotype's "ideological construction of otherness" (Bhabha 66). Fixity is a form of representation that permits the Manichaean oppositions between self and other: one is awarded qualities of good and the other qualities of degeneracy and evil. While fixity implies rigidity and static qualities, it also implies a fix-ation or fear that must be repeated in order to reassure itself, and it is in its repetition that fixity marks its impossibility. Bhabha draws a homology between fixity and the stereotype: both concepts move between "what is always 'in place,' already known, and something that must be anxiously repeated" (66). In its impossible fixity, the stereotype expresses an ambivalent and vacillating discourse. Most useful for my critical concerns is a reading of the possibility of a "*productive* ambivalence" in "that 'otherness' which is at once an object of desire and derision" (67). For Bhabha, ambivalence operates in two ways. Initially, it "is the force of ambivalence that gives the colonial stereotype its currency: ensures its repeatability in changing historical and discursive conjunctures; informs its strategies of individuation and marginalization"; and thus makes possible the subjectification of the other (66). In its ambi-valence, ambivalence produces continuously changing representations of a supposedly unchanging, fixed other. Yet the stereotype's ambivalence also signals uncertainty, an oscillation between desire and derision for the object of representation. Therefore, a reading of ambivalence "reveals ... the boundaries of colonial discourse and it enables a transgression of these limits from the space of that otherness" (67). In the analysis that follows, Crane's critique of dime novel conventions delineates the "boundaries" of Anglo-American self-representation, while Griffith's wavering engagement with the "greaser" provides access to the earliest formation of film stereotypes before their full development in later Westerns.

I have made reference to Arthur Pettit as an early critic of Mexican characterization in both literature and film. Pettit documents the genesis of literary stereotypes and their subsequent transformation into the film medium, and Crane is among the writers he alleges participate in the denigration of the Mexican. Pettit notes that in conquest fiction, "the concept of Anglo-Saxon superiority and Mexican inferiority ... is sustained by constant repetition of tried and tested positive American projections of themselves juxtaposed to negative projections of the Mexican as opposition" (xx). This cultural antagonism determines the criteria for the " 'Tex-Mex' formula scoundrel" in the dime novel, which includes "the fictional need for villains who offer maximum contrast to the heroes; the actual presence of some difference in skin color between the two ethnic groups; and the unabashed racial bigotry that characterized the United States between the first years of manifest destiny and the outbreak of the Civil War" (23). As a subset of racial bigotry, we add a sense of cultural superiority, which assumes that Anglo-American cultural institutions are inherently superior to the institutions of other peoples. The dime novels of the era contain Mexican characters such as "arrogant hidalgos, lazy peons, evil bandidos, sexy señoritas, and loose-principled priests, all of whom offer unfavorable contrast to the chaste and enterprising Protestants" (26). Among these characters, the most prevalent are the greaser *bandidos*, who, Pettit notes, "are burdened with a formidable set of easily identified, ethnic, stereotyped features," including "long, greasy hair coiled under huge sombreros, scraggly *mustachios* ..., tobacco-stained fingers and teeth, and grotesque dialect and curses. Above all, the Beadle [publishing house] bandidos are characterized by complexions shading from pitch black through dark brown to orange, yellow, olive, and gray" (39–40). By 1859, these negative characterizations are fully established and incorporated by the writers of the Beadle and Adams publishing house, widely recognized for introducing the dime novel (Robinson 27).

The most often used descriptive words for the Mexican in dime novels are "coward" and "greaser." In *Bernard Lile* (1856), Jeremiah Clemens repeatedly employs the word "greaser" to describe Mexicans: "The people look greasy, their clothes are greasy, their dogs are greasy, their houses are greasy—everywhere grease and filth hold divided dominion" (214). Raymund Paredes argues that "if one surveys the dime novels of the last third of the nineteenth century, it becomes clear that the Mexican—and not the Indian—is the most contemptible figure in western popular fiction" ("Image" 171). By 1885, "the dark-complected Mexican *mestizo* had become a stock figure in western paperback fiction," according to Paredes. "He functioned as the ultimate villain, leering out from behind his grimy *serape* and invariably clutching his deadly *cuchillo*" (180). Both the year and the image of the serape upon which Paredes focuses are significant, for Stephen Crane would transform the image of the serape into something other than the expected stereotype to which Paredes alludes.

STEPHEN CRANE AND THE MEXICAN

I have thus far presented a doleful picture of the Anglo's estimate of the Mexican in nineteenth-century dime novels and adventure fiction, and critics contend that this denigration continues into the twentieth century. In his analysis of turn-of-the-century western fiction, Pettit contends, "Unlike the Beadles and Buntlines, whose Saxon heroes again and again imposed North American order on Mexican chaos, the twentieth-century pulp tales have their pecking order established not only from their first page, but even earlier—in the minds and emotions of their readers" (111). He argues, in other words, that twentieth-century pulp tales cater to the racial biases of their readers. More recently, in a discussion about the representation of Mexican sexuality in western fiction, José Limón observes that if "the Mexican woman in her full eroticization has critical meanings and possibilities beyond the mere stereotype," the Mexican male, with "none of the exotic sexuality, the freer play of the erotic given the figure of the Mexican woman ... is a rhetorical construction that exemplifies the term 'stereotype' in its most negative sense" (136). He concludes that in the "rhetorical construction of Mexican men, there is no ambivalence, no rhetorical quarter given; nor ... has this unambivalence attenuated in our own time" (137).

To a significant degree, these analyses correctly assess the nineteenth- and twentieth-century literary landscape. Clemens's *Bernard Lile*, for instance, refers to one of the Mexican deck-hands on his steamer as a born thief who " 'would murder his brother for a *peso*, and betray any thing but his priest for half the money' " (215). Yet we must also recognize that some degree of affinity exists between Anglo and Mexican combatants. Limón writes that "in the context of the Anglo male's symbolic desire for the Mexican woman, we can now see between these two men a psychological relationship of difference but also of identity, aggression, and mutual narcissism" (136). I would add that identity occurs not only in the Anglos's desire for the Mexican woman, but also in his recognition and grudging admiration—narcissistic or otherwise—of something of himself in the Mexican. We see this vacillation between recognition and negation—this ambivalence—in even the most dyspeptic representations of the Mexican, even in *Bernard Lile*, when the narrator acknowledges that in the battle of Palo Alto, "[t]he Mexicans are said to have fought bravely and well" (213).

Stephen Crane's short stories about the West and Mexico recognize the Mexican's equality with his Anglo-American rival. Yet if we are to accept Raymund Paredes's arguments, Crane's western stories enact a Darwinian struggle between Anglo and Mexican and express a familiar contempt for the doomed Mexican. In "Stephen Crane and the Mexican," he writes that "[t]his scenario is common in Crane's western stories; the relationship between Mexican and Anglo must inevitably disintegrate into violence," and it is usually "the Mexican who starts the trouble. He is a meddler, a persistent agitator. He reeks of violence and brutality—qualities which are very much a part of his way of life" (32). According to Paredes, "[t]he surest proof of how cheaply Crane values the Mexican is that in his stories, the Mexican never 'holds steady,' but collapses and disintegrates, his doom assured" (37). Paredes's essay, published in 1971, established the critical consensus on Crane, that he reinforces the negative stereotype of the Mexican as villain. My own reading of Crane's work fundamentally disagrees with Paredes's assessment. Crane is less concerned with deriding the Mexican than with deflating the myth of the Western hero, which he achieves through an unprejudiced depiction of Mexican characters.

Unlike Paredes, I read a greater degree of play, discrepancy, and respect for the Mexican in Crane's stories, particularly in "One Dash—Horses" (1896) and "The Three White Mice" (1896), in which Crane questions the dime novel's vision of the cowardly and villainous Mexican in contrast to the heroic Anglo. In his critique, Paredes concentrates on moments when the Anglo's life is threatened by Mexican adversaries. He measures Crane's regard for the Mexican by the way the Anglo and Mexican cope with their fears as they face each other. The "crucial difference between Crane's Mexican and Anglo" is that "the Anglo responds to a challenge or threat with courage, reacting coolly and weighing his options, working quickly to stay alive" (34). The Mexican, on the other hand, typically recoils in fear.

"One Dash—Horses" recounts the near-death experience of Richardson and his servant, José, during their travels in Mexico. The two men encounter trouble one night at a lodging house, when Mexican bandits enter Richardson's sleeping quarters and threaten to steal his gun and saddle. Richardson, though, faces the Mexicans in seemingly stoic manner. A closer examination of this story, however, reveals that Richardson does not act heroically; rather, he seems catatonic with terror. Additionally, it is not Richardson's cool response to danger but José's efficiency and watchfulness that saves Richardson from certain death. In the initial encounter between Richardson and the Mexican bandits, Richardson is woken by a guitar and hears a Mexican gruffly telling his companions that if the American does not hand over his pistol, saddle, and money, "I will kill him! ... [I]f he will not give them, you will see!" (15). Unlike the hero of *Bernard Lile*, Tom Simpson, who unflinchingly confronts numerous greasers, "Richardson felt the skin draw tight around his mouth, and his knee-joints turned to bread. He slowly came to a sitting posture.... This stiff and mechanical movement ... must have looked like the rising of a corpse in the wan moonlight" (15). As he responds to the threat, "[t]he tumultuous emotions of Richardson's terror" render him incapable of understanding Spanish and demonstrate the extent of his fear (16).

Crane's first visual depiction of the Mexican seems to follow the stereotypical tropes of the dime novel, and its visceral impact gives the reader pause: "the red fight of a torch flared into the room. It was held high by a fat, round-faced Mexican, whose little snake-like mustache was as black as his eyes, and whose eyes were black as jet. He was insane with the wild rage of a man whose liquor is dully burning at his brain. Five or six of his fellows crowded after him" (16). This description of the Mexican, undoubtedly stereotypical, helps us understand why critics of racial representation have responded so strongly to Crane. We have before us the Mexican *bandido* in all his unambivalence. But for all the negativity that we may read in the Mexican's portrayal, we should not lose sight of Crane's representation of the Anglo "hero" as well.

As the Mexican enters, Richardson sits "very straight and still, his right hand lost in the folds of his blanket" (16). The reader knows that within the folds of the blanket lies the pistol to which he clings. The bandit does not see the pistol, but he suspects it is nearby, since this is the object he covets. Although the Mexican threatens and curses, Richardson remains still, "staring at the fat Mexican with a strange fixedness of gaze, not fearful, not dauntless, not anything that could be interpreted. He simply stared" (16). Richardson is, in other words, frozen beyond fear by the situation. Crane infuses the narrative with humor in showing the Mexicans confused by Richardson's response.

> Ah, well, sirs, here was a mystery. At the approach of their menacing company, why did not this American cry out and turn pale, or run, or pray them mercy? The animal merely sat still, and stared, and waited for them to begin. Well, evidently he was a great fighter; or perhaps he was an idiot. Indeed, this was an embarrassing situation, for who was going forward to discover whether he was a great fighter or an idiot? (16)

Some critics read the Mexicans' indecisiveness as a sign of their fear before the brave American. Cecil Robinson, for instance, claims that the Mexicans back down as Richardson holds the revolver in front of them: "for all their drunken rage, as the American held a gun on them and stared coldly in their direction, they kept back. Not one of them was quite drunk enough to want to be the sacrificial victim that would be required if the American was to be overpowered. The deadlock was finally broken with the sound of giggling girls" (192). Robinson assumes that Richardson "stare[s] coldly" at the Mexicans, but the American is in fact immobilized by sheer terror. As the lead Mexican delays pouncing on him, "this pause was a long horror [for Richardson]; and for these men who could so frighten him there began to swell in him a fierce hatred." Though he feels hatred, he does not act but only longs "to be capable of fighting all of them" (17). Additionally, it is not that the Mexicans are not "quite drunk enough"—they are thoroughly inebriated—as much as they are calculating and waiting for Richardson's response. Finally, the Mexicans are not deterred by the gun pointed at them, since they cannot in fact see it—because it lies under the folds of a blanket. It is the gun they have come to steal, so the reader must assume they know it is at hand.

A classic interpretation of the Mexicans' depiction following the positive/negative binary would see their actions as simply negative. A reading of the stereotype's ambivalence, on the other hand, examines the specific deployments of the Mexicans' characterization in relation to the supposedly superior Anglo-American. In the agonizingly long moment when Richardson awaits the Mexicans' attack, José stirs, and the bandits begin beating and berating him. As they bully Richardson's servant, they "continually ... turned their eyes to see if they were to succeed in causing the initial demonstration by the American." Clearly, they are testing Richardson to determine if he is brave enough to come to José's defense. Though he holds the gun under his blanket, Richardson merely "look[s] on impassively" (17). Thus, Crane's Mexicans are not simply bullies, but experts in the arts of provocation and intimidation. The Anglo is not stoic but incapable of mastering his fear. This reversal is clearly at odds with critical expectations and assumptions.

The stereotypical inversion extends yet further. While the Mexicans return to their drinking and carousing, the Anglo hero experiences the unlikely emotion of longing "to run" (18). At dawn, Richardson and José finally manage their escape. Both men exhibit nervousness and fear, but it is José who keeps his wits. We learn, for instance, that while Richardson makes all kinds of loud noises with his clanging spurs, José capably "had his own saddle girth and both bridles buckled in a moment. He curled the picket ropes with a few sweeps of his arm." Richardson, on the other hand, is still too shaken for quick and effective action. His fingers "were shaking so that he could hardly buckle the girth. His hands were in invisible mittens" (20). This unexpected characterization is at variance with Paredes's claim that Crane's Yankee, "under the threat of death operates with a detached efficiency; the Mexican, his mind turned to mud, becomes a pathetic fool. Through his bravery, the Anglo achieves nobility; the Mexican, in his shameful cowardice, falls into contempt" (34). This particular scene suggests the opposite, as the Mexican moves with an "efficiency" and a "nobility" that eludes the Anglo.

In his treatment of Richardson's false courage and lack of judgment, Crane again uses humor and adds irony to undercut the efficacy of the Anglo hero as Richardson and José flee from their attackers. For instance, when Richardson looks upon José, he sees a weaker man:

> Riding with José was like riding with a corpse. His face resembled a cast in lead. Sometimes he swung forward and almost pitched from his seat. Richardson was too frightened himself to do anything but hate this man for his fear. Finally, he issued a mandate which nearly caused José's eyes to slide out of his head and fall to the ground like two coins. "Ride behind me—about fifty paces." (21)

Richardson's want of judgment lies in his assumption that he is riding with an inferior. Thus, although José appears to be a coward in Richardson's eyes, Crane uses José's forced position in the rear guard to show Richardson's feigned bravery and his need of the Mexican's protection. "Richardson had resolved in his rage that at any rate he was going to use the eyes and ears of extreme fear to detect the approach of danger; and so he established his servant as a sort of an outpost" (22). Richardson, of course, could have served as outpost just as well, since he has embodied "extreme fear" from the beginning of the story. Crane, therefore, refuses to idealize the Anglo at the expense of the Mexican in his depiction of the relationship between the two cultures. Jamie Robertson has more generally observed that in the myth of Western heroism, Crane "never succumbed to the dream world of the dime novelist.... His ... heroes participate in the convention of popular Western fiction that individual courage gives meaning to life, but that convention is always ironic" (243–44). As Robertson recognizes, "the clichés of the Western are here, including the inferior Mexican, but they are Richardson's clichés, not Stephen Crane's" (248). Applied to this story, Crane's deflation of the western myth means that the Anglo is not so easily the Mexican's superior. At story's end, José once again proves to be the more capable of the two men when Richardson loses the trail and is "recalled to it by the loud sobs of his servant" (22). As the Mexican bandits catch up and give final chase, it is José, "terror-stricken, who at last discover[s] safety" when he spots the

Mexican rural police force just over a ridge, rides to them, and saves his and Richardson's life (23).

Although an initial reading of "One Dash—Horses" may lead a reader to believe that Crane's characterization of the Anglo-American is far more favorable than that of the Mexican, further analysis reveals that Crane felt empathy and respect for the Mexican. Although narrative space concentrates on the figure of the Anglo, we see small instances of admiration for the Mexican, as when José prepares for a night of rest.

> José threw two gigantic wings of shadow as he flapped his blanket about him—first across his chest under his arms, and then around his neck and across his chest again—this time over his arms, with the end tossed on his right shoulder. A Mexican thus snugly enveloped can nevertheless free his fighting arm in a beautifully brisk way, merely shrugging his shoulder as he grabs for the weapon at his belt. (14)

The narrative viewpoint is objective here. We do not see José from Richardson's perspective but from the perspective of the narrative voice. The movement of the Mexican in this description connotes a speed and finesse, an efficiency and grace, that recalls nothing of the slovenly greaser.

Stephen Crane's travels in the West and Mexico during the period in which he wrote his western stories allowed him to glimpse how Mexican people of all classes lived on a daily basis. He could have come away with an impression of Mexico like that found in *Bernard Lile*, where "[a]n American whose ill fortune has made him for any number of days, a sojourner in the city of Metamoras, can have no difficulty in tracing the origin of the term 'greaser'" (214). Crane, however, sees the intercultural assessment of a different people as part of the ill-informed "arrogance of the man who has not yet solved himself and discovered his own actual futility" ("The Mexican Lower Classes" 435). Forewarning future readers of his western fiction—and readers of dime novels and adventure fiction—Crane determines in his western sketches (written as dispatches for American newspapers) "that the most worthless literature of the world has been that which has been written by the men of one nation concerning the men of another" (436). Thus, Crane exhibits an awareness of the myopic perspective of Anglo-American cultural imperialism.

We may take Crane's precautionary statement as a guide for reading "The Five White Mice," which treats the encounter of the New York Kid, the San Francisco Kid, and their friend, Benson, with three Mexican men in a dark Mexico City street. The crucial moment in the story picks up the three men on their way home. Benson and the San Francisco Kid are inebriated, and the sober New York Kid acts as their escort. As they make their way along the street, they come upon three men, and Benson bumps into one. The Mexican is offended by the American's carelessness and tempers rise, but the tension is broken when the New York Kid brandishes a pistol, and the Mexicans are sent on their way. Because the story ends with the Mexicans' defeat, critics have read "The Five White Mice" as yet another instance of Mexican denigration.[3] The story, however, demonstrates Crane's attraction to the codes of honor and ritualistic behavior which he sees in the Mexican's masculinity. In one of his dispatches from Mexico City, for example, Crane comments upon the city's bullfighters, who "are a most impressive type to be seen upon the streets.... They are always clean-shaven and the set of the lips wherein lies the revelation of character, can easily be studied. They move confidently, proudly, with a magnificent self-possession. People turn to stare after them" ("The City of Mexico" 431). In this dispatch, Crane joins Ernest Hemingway in his fascination for the figure of a heroic Mexican masculinity, which also appears in the Mexicans of "The Five White Mice."

The story's tension lies in the disturbance of masculine codes of honor when the Mexican's grievances are not acknowledged by Benson, the drunk American. "The Mexican wheeled upon the instant. His hand flashed to his hip. There was a moment of silence during which Benson's voice was not heard raised in apology. Then an indescribable comment, one burning word, came from between the Mexican's teeth" (46–47). Benson's failure to provide an apology insults the Mexican's code of honor. With his hand on the pummel of his knife, the Mexican asks, "Does the señor want fight?" (47). The New York Kid immediately tries to move his friends away, but the San Francisco Kid, himself very drunk, affirmatively answers the Mexican's challenge. Subverting the stereotypical conventions of the drunk Mexican, Crane presents the Americans' drunkenness as leading them to act recklessly. The New York Kid reluctantly joins the fray, and he too stands with his hand at his hip, but his coat conceals a revolver. Crane freezes this moment in the narrative to provide an intimate glimpse of the New York Kid's admiration for and fear of the Mexican.

> This opponent of the New York Kid was a tall man and quite stout. His sombrero was drawn low over his eyes. His serape was flung on his left shoulder. His back was bended in the supposed manner of a Spanish grandee. This concave gentleman cut a fine and terrible figure. The lad, moved by the spirits of his modest and perpendicular ancestors, had time to feel his blood roar at [the] sight of the pose. (48)

Despite knowing he is better armed than the men he faces, "[t]he Eastern lad suddenly decided that he was going to be killed" (48).

The reader would expect the Anglo to act bravely and without hesitation at such a decisive moment, but instead the New York Kid's finger is only "tremoring on the trigger" (50). Realizing that they are outmatched, the knife-carrying Mexicans finally show their own fear. "The fulsome grandee sprang backward with a low cry. The man who had been facing the 'Frisco Kid took a quick step away. The beautiful array of Mexicans was suddenly disorganized" (50). Paredes sees this as a moment in which Crane shows the Anglo's contempt for the Mexican's "cowardice because it is hidden behind a colossal pretentiousness" (34). More accurately, however, Crane demonstrates that the Anglo and the Mexican stand as equals in their capacities to experience fear and in their attempts to hide it with feigned courage:

> The cry and the backward steps revealed something of great importance to the New York Kid. He had never dreamed that he did not have a complete monopoly of all possible trepidations. The cry of the grandee was that of a man who suddenly sees a poisonous snake. Thus the Kid was able to understand swiftly that *they* were *all* human beings. *They* were unanimous in not wishing for too bloody combat. There was a sudden expression of *equality*. (50, emphasis added)

While some readers may understand Crane's use of "they" as applying only to the Mexicans, the addition of "equality" implies that all the men present are equal in their experience of fear.

Finally seeing that he has the upper hand. the New York Kid "pounced forward and began to swear.... He was bursting with rage because these men had not previously confided to him that they were vulnerable.... And after all there had been an equality of emotion, an equality: he was furious" (51). The way in which Crane frames the New York Kid's thoughts suggests that one man's bravery increases in direct proportion to the other's fear. Crane shows that Anglos and Mexicans alike struggle with controlling these impulses. In the story's ending, there is little to suggest the Mexican's lack of bravery and nothing that implies the Anglo's contempt. The New York Kid is furious, but he is furious because the Mexicans "had not previously confided to him that they were vulnerable"—that is, they had not previously evinced that they were as emotionally vulnerable as the New York Kid. Thus, he is angry that he lacked an understanding of the "equality of emotion" all the men feel.

In a typical dime novel, when the Mexican greaser sees the Anglo draw his weapon, he runs. In "The Five White Mice," the Mexicans and

Anglos act according to the rituals of a duel. Realizing that they are literally outgunned, the Mexicans step backward, but they do not turn their backs on the Americans. Their leader acknowledges defeat, but he does not lose his dignity. He speaks to the New York Kid "in a tone of cynical bravado" and asks, " 'Well, señor, it is finished?' " To this the New York Kid responds, " 'I am willing' " (51). And most significant of all, they bid each other good night as each group of men disappears into the streets of Mexico City. This final exchange implies, once again, that Crane places these men shoulder to shoulder, thus subverting the dime novel convention of heroic Anglos and cowardly Mexicans.

Crane's Mexican fiction enables a different reading of the Mexican and Anglo than the conventional dime novel. His critique of the inflated myth of the Western hero, along with his treatment of the Mexican as the Anglo's equal, permits a questioning of the stereotypes that sustained the relation of dominance between Anglo and Mexican during the nineteenth century. Significantly, Crane's ironic reversal of these stereotypes provides us the critical lens with which to examine the American cinema, which was just emerging as Crane's stories were being published. If Crane's stories demonstrate a manifest subversion of Mexican stereotypes in critical opposition to dime novel conventions, then D. W. Griffith's early Western movies stand somewhere in between, evidencing a latent desire for the Mexican, even as these films deride the Mexican "greaser."

FROM DIME NOVELS TO EARLY WESTERNS:
THE GREASER IN D. W. GRIFFITH'S FILMS, 1907–1910

Thus far, I have argued that Stephen Crane presents a Mexican subject who stands his ground against the Anglo-American dime novel hero, contrary to ethnocritical interpretations of the 1970s and '80s. In American film, D. W. Griffith is regarded as one of the utmost practitioners of racist cinematic practices, and this identification is well deserved. Notwithstanding this incontrovertible assessment—especially with respect to Griffith's treatment of African Americans—Griffith may be positioned beyond the either/or binary of the conventional critique of the stereotype. Mexicans appear in several of Griffith's early films set in the West, and in the title of one film, Mexican identity is explicitly and derogatorily foregrounded. In spite of the use of the word "greaser" to identify Mexican characters, the presence of *Mexicanidad* in Griffith's early Westerns encompasses contradictory points of attraction and repulsion.

Griffith started making Westerns for the Biograph Company in 1907, and Mexican characters appeared in his films only a year later. Because copies of Griffith's early movies are extremely rare—prints are currently housed at the Library of Congress, where I first saw the films I discuss in this essay—critics have only a tenuous understanding of these films' racial politics.[4] Raymund Paredes and Arthur Pettit, for instance, have pointed to the long tradition of denigrating representations in dime novels, followed by the uncritical adaptation of these depictions into a cinematic language.[5] While their claims correctly assess much of the literary and cinematic production at the turn of the twentieth century, they inadvertently participate in an either/or binary that declares representations may only be positive or negative. Their critiques do not account for the complexity of ethnic representation, the moments in which literary and cinematic texts express ambivalence toward the ethnic subject.

Derision and desire coexist in the emergence of the "greaser" stereotype in Griffith's work from 1907 to 1910. During this period, Griffith directed at least seven films whose Mexican content oscillates between sympathetic and hostile representations, depending on a particular film's narrative imperatives. Such films include *The Fight for Freedom, The Tavern-Keeper's Daughter, The Greaser's Gauntlet, The Red Girl*, and *The Vaquero's Vow*, all from 1908, and *The Thread of Destiny* and *Ramona*, both from 1910. The ultimate fate of Mexican characters in most of these films is deleterious; characters either die or vacate the narrative space to make way for the Anglo-American hero. Nevertheless, the greaser stereotype constitutes not merely the reproduction of dime novel stereotypes; it is an ambivalent racial discourse. Griffith's films place the Mexican subject in multiple representational postures and allow us to see the stereotype's "*effectivity*," its "repertoire of positions of power and resistance, domination and dependence," according to Bhabha (67). A reading of Mexican identity representation in terms of the analytic of ambivalence exposes the limits of stereotypical discourse and the complex relation of attraction and repulsion between the Anglo subject and the Mexican who is the object of stereotypical fixation. This relation reveals the impossibility of simplifying any culture to the imperatives of the stereotype and demonstrates the limitations of the positive/negative critique which has traditionally responded to stereotypical production.

It is difficult to imagine that the director who created *The Birth of a Nation* (1915) may be read "ambivalently," as I have proposed. One of *Birth*'s commentators, Clyde Taylor, notes that the film constitutes "an incomparable racial assault," one of those "national allegories in which the definition of national character simultaneously involves a co-defining anti-type" (15). We could assume that the Mexican fares no better in Griffith's representational universe, and if we were to read the July 24, 1908, issue of the *Biograph Bulletin*—a promotional play-bill—our assumptions would seem to be borne out. The *Bulletin* introduces the main character in *The Tavern-Keeper's Daughter* (1908) as "the fairest flower that e'er blossomed in the land of the golden sun." Then, it ominously introduces her antagonist as "one of those proletarian half breed Mexicans, whose acidulate countenance was most odious to all, particularly the girl" (qtd. in *Griffith Project*, vol. 1, 71). Yet despite all indications to the contrary, the Mexican constitutes not a "co-defining anti-type," but a far more complicated and ambivalent figure. Several of Griffith's early Westerns suggest a strong fascination with Mexican character that goes beyond the simple race hatred which critics ascribe to Griffith in the case of African American characterization.

The discussion that follows focuses on *The Tavern-Keeper's Daughter* and *The Greaser's Gauntlet*, which inaugurate the thematic of the bad Mexican redeemed. *The Tavern-Keeper's Daughter* takes place in California and treats the plight of a tavern owner and his daughter. As I have noted, the *Biograph Bulletin* sensationally describes the Mexican as "one of those proletarian half breed Mexicans, whose acidulate countenance was most odious to all, particularly the girl." In this typical fear-of-miscegenation plot, the Mexican makes unwanted advances, is rejected, and subsequently returns with rapacious intentions. He reveals his "cruel, black nature" and behaves like an "infuriated beast." But at the moment when this "brute" is poised to commit the awful act, "he is attracted by the childish prattle" of a baby. "His heart is softened by the pure, innocent chatter of the child, and he drops on his knees before the crib and prays to God to help him resist his brutal inclinations" (71). I have quoted from the *Biograph Bulletin* extensively because in the silent era before the introduction of intertitles, such a promotional publication strongly shaped an audience's understanding and interpretation of a film's narrative and ideological structure. For instance, without the aid of this publication, the audience might not have interpreted that the villain is a "half breed Mexican," since his costume is more western than ethnic—although a kerchief on his head marks his Mexicanness.

The language of the *Biograph Bulletin* synopsis naturalizes the Mexican's psychology. An insatiable desire for the white woman is part of his "cruel, dark nature," and he must beg God to deliver him from his "brutal inclinations." Although the *Bulletin*'s titillating language is reprehensible, the film stops short of having the greaser commit an act that would be unacceptable to its emerging middle-class audience. *The Tavern-Keeper's Daughter*, then, reveals several ambivalent aspects of early film. First, the film displaces a prurient, pornographic desire to witness the spectacle of rape. This displacement occurs through the convenient location of such desire in an ethnic other, as well as in the final and safe prevention of that same act. Second, this film reveals Anglo-America's ambivalent relation to those ethnic subjects it came to dominate.

The film is most probably set in post-1848 California, and although the Mexican is dangerous, he has already been defeated, his lands taken. What remains is for Anglo-American values to take hold, and the paternalistic, almost revival-tent denouement produces the salvation the Mexican requires. Third, it is crucial that the Mexican contain within himself the possibility of Christian salvation. This means that, even as we consider the Protestant aversion to Catholicism, the film implicitly recognizes the commonality of the Anglo's and Mexican's Christian faith.

The plot structure of *The Greaser's Gauntlet* follows a similar pattern as *The Tavern-Keeper's Daughter*, but with significant additions. Initially the title character of The *Greaser's Gauntlet* is not a despicable personage; according to the *Biograph Bulletin*, Jose is a "handsome young Mexican" who "leaves his home in the Sierra Medra [*sic*] Mountains to seek his fortune in the States" (qtd. in *Griffith Project*, vol. 1, 75).[6] He travels to a border town where a new railroad line is being built. In the convoluted story, Jose is accused of stealing from another man and is subsequently saved from hanging by Mildred, who discovers that a Chinese servant has taken the money. Mildred saves Jose a moment before he is to be hanged, and Jose expresses his gratitude by presenting her with the embroidered wrist of a gauntlet. The embroidery is of a cross sewn onto the gauntlet by Jose's mother, who gave it to him as a reminder of his Catholic values and heritage. Jose "swears that if she ever needs his help he will come to her," with the gauntlet symbolizing "a token of his pledge" (76).

Working against the interdiction of romance between an ethnic male and a white female, *The Greaser's Gauntlet* requires the attraction between Mildred and Jose for its narrative coherence. From their earliest encounter, when Mildred walks into a saloon with her fiancé, Mildred and Jose are immediately attracted to each other, of which the *Bulletin* makes no note. Facing Mildred, Jose removes his hat in salutation, and she simply keeps her eyes level with his and smiles. As she leaves, she turns to look at Jose one last time. It is through this short encounter that Mildred intuits Jose's "goodness" and innocence, even before she discovers the Chinese servant's guilt. Thus, although the couple exchanges neither romantic words nor overt gestures, the *Biograph Bulletin* describes Mildred as "pleading" his innocence because she "really believes him" (76). Later in the narrative, when she has just saved Jose from hanging, Mildred and Jose stand alone, as Jose offers her the glove. The moment is charged with their unspoken fascination for each other. Jose gives Mildred the glove, and "as she takes it[,] her eyes sink deep into his heart, enkindling a hopeless passion for her," while she "promises to always keep his token with her" (76). That *The Greaser's Gauntlet* should use the attraction between a white woman and a "greaser" to maintain narrative tension goes against the conventions that the film Western would establish only a few years later. In *Broncho Billy and the Greaser* (1914) and *An Arizona Wooing* (1915), for example, the Mexican makes unwanted advances upon the white female, only to be repulsed by the Anglo hero.

Although Mildred and Jose demonstrate mutual attraction, Mildred is engaged to another man, the head engineer, Tom Berkeley. The main villain of this story, as it turns out, is not Jose, but Bill Gates, the assistant engineer who also has an intense desire for Mildred. Time passes, Mildred and Tom marry, and Jose, for his part, "takes to drinking and goes to the depths of degradation" because he "cannot obliterate the sweet face of the girl" (76). One day, Bill encounters Mildred and insults her, but Tom arrives in time to thwart him. Bill becomes infuriated, "swears vengeance and going to a low tavern for help comes upon Jose, drunk of course, and with him and another greaser, they waylay Tom's carriage" (76). The men kidnap Mildred and take her back to the tavern. Jose, who is now Bill's lackey, initially does not recognize Mildred because he is too inebriated. It is at this point in the story that the gauntlet reappears and makes possible Jose's redemption.

> There upon the floor is the cross embroidered wrist of the gauntlet, which Mildred has dropped.... Jose seizes it and the truth at once dawns upon him.... So with the ferociousness of a wolf he leaps at the throat of Gates and after a terrific battle, drops him lifeless to the floor, as the husband and friends burst into the room. The tables are now turned and Mildred has a chance to thank him for his deliverance. Jose at the sight of the cross, makes a solemn resolution, which he immediately fulfills— to return to his dear old mother in the mountains in whose arms we leave him. (76)

In the film, Jose does not send Bill "lifeless to the floor" but spares the man's life at Mildred's behest. Thus, Jose is twice redeemed, first by his mother's cross, then by Mildred's intervention.

Jose undergoes a spectacular redemption in *The Greaser's Gauntlet*, one that reveals the conflicted relationship between Anglo-Americans and Mexicans in particular, and between Anglo-Americans and other ethnic subjects in general. On the surface, Griffith's vision of the Mexican in this film seems paternalistic: the Mexican is presented as essentially good but in need of strong moral guidance. He cannot act from his own volition; instead, he is led astray by the evil Bill Gates and later redeemed by the saintly Mildred. A more nuanced reading, however, uncovers the latent meaning of the Mexican's redemption. Jose is clearly Catholic, and the gauntlet signifies his adherence to his faith. Contemporarily, we can read Jose's redemption as evidence of the strength of his religious values. Therefore, he does not require a paternalistic guidance but can draw upon his own Catholic resources. Whether or not Griffith intended such an implication, there is an embedded recognition of the Mexican's Christian faith and recognition, on a perhaps deeper level, of common values between the Anglo-American and the Mexican.

Consistent with the film's paternalism is its refusal to accept the Mexican on American land. By making Jose an immigrant, *The Greaser's Gauntlet* elides the history of Spanish and Mexican settlement in the southwestern United States before the Anglo-American's arrival. Jose is thus made alien in a land that fellow Mexicans had long inhabited. At the end of the film, he must return to Mexico to his mother, for there is ultimately no room for his cultural values in the American West. The film positions Jose's chivalry and faith above the amoral drunkenness that pervades the lower sectors of this western town, but it is ultimately the moral strength of people like Mildred's husband, Tom Berkeley—a strength symbolized by his role as an engineer and builder of the railroad—that will claim the West for the Anglo-American nation.

The film is more problematic with respect to other ethnicities, specifically Chinese Americans. If we recall, Mildred saves Jose from lynching when she discovers that a Chinese waiter is responsible for the theft. Thus, it is only by replacing one despised ethnic subject with another that the film is able to deliver the Mexican from harm. In this way, *The Greaser's Gauntlet* reenacts the historical machinations of Anglo-American railroad companies during the construction of railroad lines in the Southwest. With the availability of cheap Mexican labor along border towns, the preferred labor pool consisted of Mexicans rather than Chinese, and the film expresses this change by placing the Chinese waiter below the Mexican in its racial hierarchy. Notwithstanding the film's seemingly stereotypical complicity with U.S. dominance, I would still maintain that ultimately the film's ambivalence subverts this complicity.

One source of the film's more ambivalent representation is its merging of technical achievement with ethnic representation: *The Greaser's Gauntlet* is the first American film to employ the cut-in within a narrative framework, and it does so in the lynching scene in which Mildred saves Jose. As a camera technique, a "cut-in" produces "an instantaneous shift from a distant framing to a closer view of some portion of the same space" (Bordwell and Thompson 478). A cut-in has the effect of enlarging—in either medium or close-up shot—an important detail within the frame. In this scene, Griffith uses the cut-in to more closely frame the emotive exchange between Jose and Mildred. Although, as Tom Gunning notes, the cut-in is "not a Griffith invention," this film marks the first use of a cut-in to present "a detail essential to the story" (78).

I call attention to Griffith's use of the cut-in in *The Greaser's Gauntlet* because, as in his use of the close-up in *Ramona* (1910), this is an instance in which "technical 'innovations' are a means of ideological encoding that have been used in highly precise ways," as Chon Noriega has argued with regard to the latter film (217–18). Additionally, the cut-in in *The Greaser's Gauntlet* produces a racial encoding of startling dimensions. Griffith's use of the cut-in confounds critical expectations because one would assume that Griffith, infamous for his racist attack upon African Americans in *The Birth of a Nation*, would employ this narrative technique to highlight the purported deviousness of the Mexican or to focus on the negatively valenced racial difference between these two figures. This is what I expected coming to the film when I read a short description of the cut-in. Instead, as Gunning elaborates, the "exchange between Mildred and Jose ... carries emotional overtones of gratitude, unspoken love, and devotion which effect later narrative development. The cut-in brings us closer to the human figures.... [I]t transforms the actors from distant figures to recognizable characters with visible faces and expressions" (80). Griffith's use of the cut-in is surprising because it does in fact bring the viewer closer to the racial difference between Jose and Mildred but not in a denigrating manner. The fullness of character the cut-in produces means that in this particular moment, Jose the greaser escapes the stereotypic one-dimensionality critics have come to expect. Despite Griffith's conflicted relationship with American ethnicity, the movie gives the Mexican a human complexity. Additionally, as Gunning hints, the detail shot of Jose bestowing the gauntlet upon Mildred adds a historical dimension to his character, since the presentation of the gauntlet forms a "narrative armature" linking Jose, his mother, and Mildred (80). The importance of this linkage in terms of ethnic analysis is that it gives Jose a history and a connection to an ethical universe that the typical film greaser does not enjoy. The effect is to further humanize the Mexican.

I have thus far argued for the ambivalent and contradictory relationship, particularly in Griffith's films, between early American film and ethnic representation. In *The Red Girl* (1908), Griffith again expresses paternalistic sympathy for an ethnic subject, the Native American Girl in the film's title. Not unlike *The Greaser's Gauntlet*, however, *The Red Girl*'s sympathy toward the Native American heroine requires that another ethnic subject be placed in the role of the villain. This time, Griffith chooses a Mexican woman as the scoundrel, and she is particularly evil. The unnamed Mexican sets the story in motion when she sneaks into the hotel room of a female miner, Kate, and steals her gold. In her escape, the Mexican woman convinces the Red Girl and her "half-breed" husband to hide her, but she then betrays the Red Girl by seducing her husband. The "Mexican Jezebel" convinces the half-breed to kill his wife. "To this end they plan a torture. Binding her hands and feet, they take her to a large trunk of a dead tree, which overhangs the river and here they hang her" (*Biograph Bulletin*, qtd. in *Griffith Project*, vol. 1, 94). Eventually, the Red Girl frees herself and helps Kate find the thief, leading to the Mexican woman's arrest. Like *The Greaser's Gauntlet*, in which the Chinese servant serves as a scapegoat for the tacit acceptance of the Mexican, *The Red Girl* places the Mexican woman in the role of scapegoat, and she makes possible a symbolic reconciliation between whites and Native Americans. In its depiction of the Mexican woman, the film veers toward titillation that is only explainable as an attempt to shock audiences into returning to theaters. In the film's most sensational scene, the Mexican woman ambushes a sheriff's deputy, shoots him, slaps him, and then kicks him, all the while laughing at her victim's fate.

In its antipathy and misogyny toward the Mexican woman, *The Red Girl* shows the uneven characterization of Mexican identity in Griffith's films. A short time later, in his production of *The Thread of Destiny* (1910), Griffith would return to a favorable presentation of Mexican identity. *The Thread of Destiny* is the most sympathetic of the early Griffith films which treat Mexican characters. The film is about a young couple, Frances Deland and Pedro Juan Moreno y Calderon, who meet and immediately fall in love. The intertitles describe Frances, played by Mary Pickford, as "a delightful bit of American girlhood." Curiously, the film demonstrates an awareness of the constructed nature of stereotypes, for it notes that Pedro is "a Spanish aristocrat to his countrymen—only 'another impudent greaser' to the white settlers." Between their affections stands Buck Larkin, who insults Frances and is then easily defeated by Pedro. Buck turns the townsmen against Pedro by accusing him of cheating at cards, but in the end Pedro and Frances escape and get married. *The Thread of Destiny* is worthy of note for several reasons. First, the narrative explicitly treats an intercultural, if not interracial, relationship. Second, Pedro is clearly the male protagonist of this movie, and he is shown as physically and ethically superior to Buck and the townsmen, who are depicted as rabble-rousing gamblers. Third, the film's antagonist is a white American. Finally, the Mexican survives through the last reel without meeting a violent end. Though I have called attention to *The Thread of Destiny*'s sympathetic portrayal of the Mexican, we see traces of its unease with race in its attempt to distinguish Pedro as a Spanish aristocrat. The film's intertitles emphasize his class position, and his costume is highly ornate. The film is thus pulled in several directions at once: it elevates the Mexican greaser to the status of upper-class Spaniard in order to make the bond between the Mexican and a white woman acceptable to its audience.

One question we may ask as we watch these movies is why does Griffith choose to populate his films with so many ethnic subjects, be they Native American, Chinese American, African American, or Mexican American? Part of the reason is that these figures represent otherness, and they thus provide the visual spectacle required to attract early filmgoers. Additionally, these ethnic subjects offer a titillating yet containable threat. Scott Simon comments that the "number of Mexicans populating Griffith's early work suggests they were more than an excuse for eye-catching set design and exotic costuming. Mexicans could be assumed to be hot-blooded and violent, never terribly far from crimes of passion" (*Griffith Project*, vol. 1, 114). These viewer assumptions notwithstanding, we cannot ignore the instances in which, for some Mexican subjects, Griffith gives ethnic representation a degree of complexity and stirs the viewer to identify with ethnic characters. These early films exemplify the ambivalent qualities of stereotypical representation. They demonstrate that we need to expand our vision beyond the positive/negative binary to understand that amidst and through even the worst stereotypes the American imagination expresses simultaneous derision and desire for the Mexican.

Yet questions remain in regards to the marked differences between Griffith's representations of Mexicans and Native Americans and his representations of African Americans. One possible reason for this difference is the racist political agenda Griffith pursues in *The Birth of a Nation*, which necessitates the completely dehumanized figures he produces. *Birth* instantiates white fear of an empowered African America, which was very palpable to conservative whites in the post-Reconstruction era. Recall, for instance, the scene in the statehouse, in which blacks are shown taking charge of state politics. Within the Western genre at this moment, on the other hand, ethnicity is less threatening, and at this time, the American West is the only setting in which a Mexican or Native American may be viewed. As Gregory Jay has noted, a "pervading myth about the final days of the Indian spread throughout U.S. culture" at the turn of the century (8). Perhaps the sense of guilt for an accomplished conquest also applied to the Mexican, who had lost his lands in the U.S.-Mexican War of 1848, although it appears that the eruption of the Mexican Revolution and the emergence of the Western hero reinstated the Mexican as a threat. A second and more plausible reason for the variety of representation with respect to Mexicans and Native Americans may have to do with the youth of the Western genre in the years between 1907 and 1910. Gunning observes, for instance, that "[t]he hallmarks of Griffith's early Westerns ... contrast a great deal with the genre as it developed later." One major difference is that "the emphasis on a masculine and ethical Western hero remains strikingly absent" in Griffith (in *Griffith Project*, vol. 1, 94). As the Western genre establishes itself in the second decade of the twentieth century, actors such as Broncho Billy Anderson, William S. Hart, and Tom Mix come to symbolize the white, masculine, and ethical hero to which Gunning refers. These heroes must define themselves—and by extension, the American character—against an antitype that came to be played by the Mexican villain.

Griffith and Crane stand at seemingly opposite ends of the trajectories of their respective art forms, yet they produce similarly ambivalent results. Griffith's inconsistent appraisal of the Mexican suggests a film genre in its early stages, yet to establish its conventions of greaser villains and Anglo heroes. Crane's ironic stance vis-à-vis the Western hero places him outside the dime novel tradition. Griffith's Mexican is alternately untrustworthy, rapacious, and cowardly, but also brave and noble. The Mexican's contradictory representation in Griffith enables us to see the limits of stereotypical discourse. Crane, on the other hand, consciously avoids depicting the Mexican as a stereotypical greaser or bandit, and he evinces deep unease for the transcendent Anglo hero. Critics who have concentrated exclusively on José's servility or the grandee's treachery have overlooked Crane's admiration for José's competence and his respect for the grandee's code of honor. The appearance of Mexican identity in Griffith and Crane confirms the strong fascination that the American imagination has held for Mexican culture and suggests that the unequal relation between the two cultures has provided the ground upon which the United States has defined itself.

My alternative and ambivalent reading of literature and film stereotypes suggests, more broadly, that ethnicity has always been a fundamental constituent of American identity. The presence of *Mexicanidad* in American culture has come into view not only in the oppositional and binary relationship between the Anglo and the other but also in the more complicated relation of attraction and repulsion between these two figures. Provocatively, because Anglo-America has dominated the production of the discourse on identity, various ethnic subjects have often been relegated to the "negative" position— the Chinese in *The Greaser's Gauntlet* or the Mexican woman in *The Red Girl*—depending on the ideological imperatives of the particular discourse. A reading of the stereotype based on Bhabha's notion of ambi-valence helps us see the very fluidity of the stereotype, the lack of fixity that permits the ethnic subject to subvert its negative determinations and uncover its constructed character. The stereotype's ambivalence suggests, finally, that ethnic subjects must affirm their undeniable presence in the American imaginary in a far greater range of texts than was previously understood. Examining these texts may prove very difficult—as the lynching scene in *The Greaser's Gauntlet* painfully demonstrates—but ultimately highly productive, for only a reevaluation of such texts will demonstrate the thorough imbrication of race and culture in America, as well as the hidden fissures of avowal/disavowal upon which Anglo-American cultural dominance has rested.

NOTES

1. In *Anglos and Mexicans in the Making of Texas, 1836–1986* (1987), David Montejano documents that between 1915 and 1917, as a consequence of the transformation of the Texas economy from one based on ranching to one based on farming, struggles over land led to an insurrection by Texas Mexicans. At the height of these tensions, the lynching of Mexicans rose markedly (122).

2. Ella Shohat and Robert Stam classify the view that stereotypes are either only positive or only negative as "'stereotypes and distortions' analyses." As they note, a great deal of "the work on ethnic/racial and colonial representation in the media has been 'corrective,' devoted to demonstrating that certain films ... 'got something wrong'" (178). The positive/negative critique was initially very important for cataloguing stereotypes of ethnic minorities. Examples of this style of critique include Pettit's *Images of the Mexican American in Fiction and Film* (1978), Raymund Paredes's "The Image of the Mexican in American Literature" (1973), and Blaine P. Lamb's "The Convenient Villain: The Early Cinema Views of the Mexican-American" (1975). Significantly, this type of analysis tends to take as given that early films *only* present stereotypes that negatively determine subjectivity.

3. In "Unraveling the Humanist," Stanley Wertheim criticizes Crane for depicting the Mexican "as degenerate, menacing, and violent, yet ultimately cowardly" (70).

4. I would like to thank Charles Ramírez Berg of the University of Texas at Austin for helping me acquire copies of these films.

5. Paredes writes that by 1910, "filmmakers had faithfully translated the literary formulations of Mexican villainy into a visual medium; significantly, the depiction of the 'bad Mexican' in American culture had been extended beyond literary boundaries" ("The Image" 207). Similarly, Pettit argues that at the beginning of the twentieth century, the U.S. cinema "simply follow[s] patterns established" by its fictional antecedents (132). We should note that neither Pettit nor Paredes had the opportunity to see many of these films firsthand, having to rely on descriptions.

6. Unlike the "José" of "One Dash—Horses," the "Jose" of *The Greaser's Gauntlet* carries no accent in his name. I have not explored to what extent Crane insisted on "José," but evidently the writers of the *Biograph Bulletin* saw no need to include the customary accent over the final syllable.

WORKS CITED

Allport, Gordon W. *The Nature of Prejudice.* Reading: Addison-Wesley, 1954.
Bhabha, Homi K. *The Location of Culture.* London: Routledge, 1994.
Bordwell, David, and Kristin Thompson. *Film Art: An Introduction.* 5th ed. New York: McGraw-Hill, 1997.

Clemens, Jeremiah. *Bernard Lile; an Historical Romance, Embracing the Periods of the Texas Revolution and the Mexican War*. Philadelphia: J. B. Lippincott, 1856.

Crane, Stephen. "The City of Mexico." *Tales, Sketches, and Reports*. Vol. 8 of *The University of Virginia Edition of the Works of Stephen Crane*. Charlottesville: University Press of Virginia, 1973. 429–32.

———. "The Five White Mice." *Tales of Adventure*. Vol. 5 of *The University of Virginia Edition of the Works of Stephen Crane*. Charlottesville: University Press of Virginia, 1970. 39–52.

———. "The Mexican Lower Classes." *Tales, Sketches, and Reports*. Vol. 8 of *The University of Virginia Edition of the Works of Stephen Crane*. Charlottesville: University Press of Virginia, 1973. 435–38.

———. "One Dash—Horses." *Tales of Adventure*. Vol. 5 of *The University of Virginia Edition of the Works of Stephen Crane*. Charlottesville: University Press of Virginia, 1970. 13–25.

Griffith, D. W. *The Birth of a Nation*. Biograph, 1915.

———. *The Fight for Freedom*. Biograph, 1908.

———. *The Greaser's Gauntlet*. Biograph, 1908.

———. *Ramona*. Biograph, 1910.

———. *The Red Girl*. Biograph, 1908.

———. *The Tavern-Keeper's Daughter*. Biograph, 1908.

———. *The Thread of Destiny*. Biograph, 1910.

———. *The Vaquero's Vow*. Biograph, 1908.

The Griffith Project. Gen. ed. Paolo Cherchi Usai. 5 vols. London: British Film Institute, 1999.

Gunning, Tom. *D. W. Griffith and the Origins of American Narrative Film*. Urbana: University of Illinois Press, 1991.

Jay, Gregory S. "'White Man's Book No Good': D. W. Griffith and the American Indian." *Cinema Journal* 39.4 (Summer 2000): 3–26.

Lamb, Blaine P. "The Convenient Villain: The Early Cinema Views of the Mexican-American." *Journal of the West* 14.4 (October 1975): 75–81.

Limón, José E. *American Encounters: Greater Mexico, the United States, and the Erotics of Culture*. Boston: Beacon, 1998.

Noriega, Chon A. "Birth of the Southwest: Social Protest, Tourism, and D. W. Griffith's *Ramona*." *The Birth of Whiteness: Race and the Emergence of U.S. Cinema*. Ed. Daniel Bernardi. New Brunswick, N.J.: Rutgers University Press, 1996. 203–26.

Paredes, Raymund A. "The Image of the Mexican in American Literature." Diss. University of Texas at Austin, 1973.

———. "Stephen Crane and the Mexican." *Western American Literature* 6.1 (Spring 1971): 31–38.

Pettit, Arthur G. *Images of the Mexican American in Fiction and Film*. College Station: Texas A&M University Press, 1980.

Robertson, Jamie. "Stephen Crane, Eastern Outsider in the West and Mexico." *Western American Literature* 13.3 (Fall 1978): 243–57.

Robinson, Cecil. *Mexico and the Hispanic Southwest in American Literature*. Rev. from *With the Ears of Strangers*. 1963. Tucson: University of Arizona Press, 1977.

Shohat, Ella, and Robert Stam. *Unthinking Eurocentrism: Multiculturalism and the Media*. London : Routledge, 1994.

Taylor, Clyde. "The Re-Birth of the Aesthetic in Cinema." *The Birth of Whiteness: Race and the Emergence of U.S. Cinema*. Ed. Daniel Bernardi. New Brunswick, N.J.: Rutgers University Press, 1996. 15–37.

Wertheim, Stanley. "Unraveling the Humanist: Stephen Crane and Ethnic Minorities." *American Literary Realism 1870–1910* 30.3 (Spring 1998): 65–75.

KEVIN J. HAYES

Image and Emblem in
The Red Badge of Courage

S urveying the prehistory of cinema, Brian Winston found that a recent study of the subject fell short of ideal because it failed to answer a fundamental question: 'Why 1895?'.[1] To paraphrase and, in so doing, expand Winston's question: What factors—social, cultural, technological, discursive—came together in the mid 1890s to create the conditions necessary for cinema to happen at that particular moment? This question assumes that important cultural developments occur when they do because they represent a simultaneous coming together of a variety of disparate factors. This question could also be levelled at *The Red Badge of Courage*, the first edition of which appeared in 1895. Not only can the same question be asked of both cinema and *Red Badge*, the answer in each case may be much the same, for Crane's Civil War novel—the finest war novel in the language, some say—embodies a visual sensibility not dissimilar to that of the cinema.

While using the cinema as a model to understand *Red Badge* may seem anachronistic, it is important to realize that by the time Crane was writing, moving images as entertainment had already become a part of the popular culture. For decades, panoramas had been attracting mass audiences. Long rolls of fabric onto which were painted scenes illustrating a variety of historical or geographical subjects, panoramas were stretched across a stage and unfurled as audiences witnessed the scenes they depicted. Great battles of

From *Stephen Crane*, pp. 36–44. © 2004 by Kevin J. Hayes.

the Civil War remained the most popular subjects for panoramas from the end of the war to the end of the century. The most ambitious ones attempted to depict thousands of soldiers. Though familiar with the panorama as popular entertainment, Crane did not take it as a model for his war novel. Whereas Civil War panoramas strived for epic effects, the *Red Badge* is deliberately narrow in scope.

A reference to panoramas in 'Killing His Bear', another of Crane's Sullivan County sketches, prefigures *Red Badge* in terms of the way contemporary visual culture could be subsumed within a personal vision, however. Describing how the little man of the story foresaw the results of his hunting experience, Crane wrote: 'Swift pictures of himself in a thousand attitudes under a thousand combinations of circumstances, killing a thousand bears, passed panoramically through him' (*W* viii. 250). Crane's little man anticipates the behaviour of his little soldier in *Red Badge*. The swiftness with which the images move through his mind anticipates motion pictures.

Before Thomas Edison began marketing his kinetoscope, people had other technical ways to view moving images; the camera obscura, marketed as a device for popular amusement, could be found at various resort locations in the United States including Ocean Grove, New Jersey, a vacation spot Crane described in his 1892 sketch 'Joys of Seaside Life'. Discussing the various amusements available there, he paid particular attention to the camera obscura: 'People enter a small wooden building and stand in a darkened room, gazing at the surface of a small round table, on which appear reflections made through a lens in the top of the tower of all that is happening in the vicinity at the time. One gets a miniature of everything that occurs in the streets, on the boardwalk or on the hotel-porches. One can watch the bathers gambolling in the surf or peer at the deck of a passing ship' (*W* viii. 512–13).

'Joys of Seaside Life' records the fascination with moving images that existed before motion pictures began being exhibited. While early motion pictures often gave audiences views of various faraway places and events, the popularity of the camera obscura as a sideshow indicates that moving images were fascinating in and of themselves. The images people saw reflected from the surface of the circular table, after all, came from their present surroundings. They easily could have walked outside the wooden building and witnessed the source of the moving images much more clearly than the images themselves. Instead they were intrigued to see how their world could be mediated, represented, and projected. Crane's gambolling bathers suggest that the camera obscura also sanctioned an otherwise unacceptable voyeurism. While staring at bathers was improper, staring at moving images of bathers within the confines of the camera obscura building was acceptable and even expected.

The visual culture significantly influenced the critical discourse in Crane's day, and some of his reviewers used critical terminology linking his work to the moving image. Harold Frederic, for one, found that *Red Badge* had the 'effect of a photographic revelation' and compared Crane's verbal imagery to that of a camera that could record movement in 'the same way battle painters depict horses in motion, not as they actually move, but as it has been agreed by numberless generations of draughtsmen to say that they move. At last, along comes a Muybridge, with his instantaneous camera, and shows that the real motion is entirely different' (*CH* 119). Eadweard Muybridge ingeniously proved, through a series of stop-motion photographs, that a galloping horse did indeed lift all four legs from the ground simultaneously. Much as Muybridge was able to capture motion using still images, Crane could capture moving images via the static medium of the printed word. The language of other reviewers confirms the affinity between Crane's novel and motion pictures. Another characterized *Red Badge* as a 'precipitate outpouring of lively pictures'. Writing two years later, that is, after motion pictures began being exhibited, a British reviewer offered a general observation on Crane's visual imagery. 'Lifelike as Mr. Crane's pictures are', he observed, 'they have something of the spasmodic jerkiness of the kinetoscope' (*CH* 200, 205).

The opening sentence of the novel has the quality of the opening scene of a motion picture: 'The cold passed reluctantly from the earth and the retiring fogs revealed an army stretched out on the hills, resting'. In a fond appreciation of *Red Badge*, Nigel Andrews, film critic for the *Financial Times*, likens this sentence to 'the opening scene of a good movie, only better'.[2] Andrews follows a number of earlier commentators who found in *Red Badge* an affinity with motion pictures. After quoting the novel's opening in his monograph *Stephen Crane*, Edwin Cady, who elsewhere emphasizes the montage-like quality of Crane's prose, asserts that Crane 'handles point of view more like a movie camera than perhaps any predecessor had done'.[3] Throughout the novel Crane's choice of words frequently conveys two qualities characteristic of motion-picture spectatorship, the projection and the visual perception of the moving image.

Henry Fleming or 'the youth', as Crane terms his soldier-protagonist, has a vivid imagination. Hearing stories from other soldiers and reading accounts of the war prior to enlisting in the Union army, Henry easily pictures what war must be like: 'His busy mind had drawn for him large pictures, extravagant in colour, lurid with breathless deeds' (*RB* 3). Not only does he imagine the broad sweep of battle, he also foresees much detail in close-up. The graphic stories of those who have seen action allow him to envision 'red, live bones sticking out through slits in the faded uniforms' (*RB* 7). Furthermore, Crane's narrative point of view reinforces Henry's viewpoint. Though told from the third person, *Red Badge* is usually focalized from Henry's perspective. In other words, a third-person narrator articulates Henry's thoughts and verbalizes his mental imagery.

Though Henry sees the war in his mind's eye before going into battle, he perceives it as a spectator, not a participant. He foresees battle scenes, yet he cannot see himself in them. After enlisting, yet before entering battle, Henry, along with the rest of his unit, must wait almost interminably before entering battle. During that time he tries hard to imagine how he will react yet still cannot do so. His inability to envision himself in battle makes him uneasy, so he resolves to observe everything closely in order to gather the information that will allow him to foresee his behaviour in battle. Generally speaking, Henry's process of information-gathering is non-verbal. His eyes function as his primary sense organs. He often fixes his gaze on the characteristic icons of battle and thus privileges the familiar and the recognizable. Upon seeing batteries being lead by their standard bearers in the distance, for example, Henry devotes his attention to their flags and, in so doing, feels 'the old thrill at the sight of the emblems' (*RB* 29). His attention to the flag in this case establishes a precedent for his subsequent behaviour. The emblems of battle become the visual signs by which he navigates himself through the ensuing conflict.

After surviving his first skirmish, Henry experiences tremendous relief. As a result, he no longer feels the need to envision how he will react in battle because he now concludes that he does indeed have the courage to face conflict. Self-satisfied, he can perceive himself from an external point of view and picture himself as a combat soldier: 'Standing as if apart from himself, he viewed that last scene. He perceived that the man who had fought thus was magnificent' (*RB* 30). His brief personal experience allows him to do something that his third-hand information gathering had not, to envision war as a participant and not merely as a spectator.

The pictures Henry can now see in his mind's eye are more recollections of recent events than projections of the future, however. They do not prepare him for further combat. Having mistaken the initial skirmish for the entire battle, he is unprepared for the following action. After assuming he has survived the battle without losing his nerve, he must now confront additional dangers. Neither his experience nor his imagination has prepared him for the new challenge. He loses courage and flees. After reaching a safe distance, however, he turns to witness the action he has fled: 'Then he began to run in the direction of the battle. He saw that it was an ironical thing for him to be running thus toward that which he had been at such pains to avoid. But he said, in substance, to himself that if the earth and the moon were about to clash, many persons would doubtless plan to get upon roofs to witness the collision' (*RB* 38). Those who have studied the prehistory of the cinema have identified the *badaud* or gawker as the nineteenth-century precursor of the cinema spectator, and this is the role Henry assumes upon fleeing the battle, as Crane's diction makes clear: 'He stood, regardant, for a moment. His eyes had an awe-struck expression. He gawked in the direction of the fight' (*RB* 39).

Henry continues to gawk as he wanders aimlessly behind the lines. His gawking does have a vague purpose, however: he seeks a way to reintegrate himself within the battle. Witnessing a line of wounded soldiers, Henry perceives them with a pang of envy: 'He conceived persons with torn bodies to be peculiarly happy. He wished that he, too, had a wound, a little red badge of courage' (*RB* 42). Callously, Henry perceives battle wounds not in terms of pain inflicted but in terms of symbolic value. Not even the sight of his mortally wounded friend Jim Conklin, whose side 'looked as if it had been chewed by wolves' (*RB* 45), dissuades Henry from his fascination with the emblematic value of battle scars.

The visible wound, an emblem of war rather than war itself, provides the key for Henry to imagine himself in battle. Understanding the results of battle abstractly, he can envision himself within the conflict:

> Swift pictures of himself, apart, yet in himself, came to him—a blue desperate figure leading lurid charges with one knee forward and a broken blade high—a blue, determined figure standing before a crimson and steel assault, getting calmly killed on a high place before the eyes of all. He thought of the magnificent pathos of his dead body.... He thought that he was about to start fleetly for the front. Indeed, he saw a picture of himself, dust-stained, haggard, panting, flying to the front at the proper moment to seize and throttle the dark, leering witch of calamity. (*RB* 51)

Seeing himself as a brave soldier, Henry creates an ideal image analogous to the emblems that so capture his attention. Like the emblems of war, Henry's pictures of himself are idealized abstractions. These personal images as a brave soldier become so obvious to him that, much like the cinema, they appear as moving pictures projected before a vast audience: 'He saw himself chasing a thought-phantom across the sky before the assembled eyes of mankind' (*RB* 56).

Though recovering the ability to envision himself in battle, Henry is still not ready to return to combat. Encountering a group of soldiers scattering from the front lines, he seeks answers to explain the confusion. He becomes so desperate for information that he clutches one of the soldiers and refuses to let go. Struggling to free himself, the other soldier swings his rifle, which hits Henry in the head with sufficient force to break the skin and cause some bleeding. Reuniting with his regiment late that evening, Henry tells a different story to explain the cause of his wound: 'I got shot' (*RB* 62). With these three words, Henry creates a narrative fiction to explain the cause of his wound and, in so doing, transforms an injury borne of confusion and panic into a red, yet surreptitious badge of courage.

As members of his regiment accept Henry's fiction as truth, he becomes quite self-satisfied, and his imagination lets him project himself as a hero to an audience of eager onlookers. He imagines himself 'in a room of warm tints telling tales to listeners' and foresees 'his gaping audience picturing him as the central figure in blazing scenes' (*RB* 73). Henry has transformed himself from a gawker to the object of gawkers. His wound lends credence to his lie, and Henry, now reunited with his unit, has successfully obscured his cowardly desertion.

Henry's behaviour beyond this point in the novel has been open to much critical debate. The controversy that has dogged *The Red Badge of Courage* over the course of its history involves the issue of Henry Fleming's maturity. Does Henry mature over the course of the novel, turning himself from frightened youth into courageous soldier? Or does he remain immature and self-centred even as he seems to enter combat? While the version of *Red Badge* edited by Henry Binder from Crane's original manuscript in the 1970s would seem to have answered the question once and for all, the controversy rages nonetheless.

Instead of asking whether Henry matures in battle, perhaps it would be more productive to ask how he copes with the dangers of battle. No longer fleeing from combat in a physical sense, Henry copes with danger through flights of fancy: he faces combat by enacting personal fantasies of bravery. Having formed mental images of battle, he now projects himself into those images.

The emblems of battle provide the connection between the real war and the combat Henry imagined. The flag becomes something he can cling to for its emblematic value. As Kermit Vanderbilt and Daniel Weiss have observed, the flag is Henry's fantasized charm against danger, and he endows it with extraordinary power.[4] Articulating what the flag means to Henry, Crane observes, 'It was a creation of beauty and invulnerability. It was a goddess, radiant, that bended its form with an imperious gesture to him. It was a woman, red and white, hating and loving, that called him with the voice of his hopes. Because no harm could come to it, he endowed it with power. He kept near as if it could be a saver of lives and an imploring cry went from his mind' (*RB* 88).

The flag has such power that it can animate the dead. Seeing the colour sergeant perish, Henry and a fellow soldier grab the flagstaff simultaneously: 'He made a spring and a clutch at the pole. At the same instant, his friend grabbed it from the other side. They jerked at it, stout and furious, but the colour-sergeant was dead and the corpse would not relinquish its trust. For a moment, there was a grim encounter. The dead man, swinging with bended back seemed to be obstinately tugging, in ludicrous and awful ways for the possession of the flag' (*RB* 88). Their struggle more closely resembles a boys' game than it does proper behaviour in battle. Henry finally captures the flag for himself by pushing his friend away.

The flag, combined with his surreptitious wound, combine to make Henry seem a ferocious soldier. Both flag and wound, after all, serve the same function in his mind. Both are emblems of war. Even as his emblems allow him to re-enter battle, Henry remains a spectator, however. Crane wrote, 'The youth, still the bearer of the colours, did not feel his idleness. He was deeply absorbed as a spectator. The crash and swing of the great drama made him lean forward—intent eyed, his face working in small contortions. Sometimes, he prattled, words coming unconsciously from him in grotesque exclamations. He did not know that he breathed; that the flag hung silently over him, so absorbed was he' (*RB* 99). Henry gawks in much the same way he had after running from battle. The difference is that, equipped with his emblems—red badge and red, white, and blue—he can imaginatively and actually project himself into battle.

Henry's seeming deeds of bravery become, for him, mental pictures to be viewed again and again:

> But the youth, regarding his procession of memory, felt gleeful and unregretting, for, in it, his public deeds were paraded in great and shining prominence. Those performances which had been witnessed by his fellows marched now in wide purple and gold, hiding various deflections. They went gaily, with music. It was pleasure to watch these things. He spent delightful minutes viewing the gilded images of memory. (*RB* 106)

What remains in his memory are not images of dead and dying, but images of himself. Henry has become the star of his own movie.

NOTES

1. Brian Winston, 'Fumbling in the Dark', *Sight and Sound*, February 2001, 11.
2. Nigel Andrews, 'Faced with the Horror of War: Rereadings', *Financial Times*, 6 September 1997.

3. Edwin H. Cady, *Stephen Crane* (New York: Twayne, 1962), 120.

4. Kermit Vanderbilt and Daniel Weiss, 'From Rifleman to Flagbearer: Henry Fleming's Separate Peace in *The Red Badge of Courage*', *Modern Fiction Studies*, 11 (Winter 1965/66), 378.

Chronology

1871	Stephen Crane is born in Newark, New Jersey, on November 1, to Jonathan Townley, a Methodist minister, and Mary Helen Crane. He is their fourteenth child.
1871–1872	The Crane family moves to Port Jervis, New York.
1880	Father, Jonathan Townley Crane, dies.
1883	Family relocates to Asbury Park, New Jersey, where Crane attends school.
1885	Writes first story "Uncle Jake and the Bell Handle;" enrolls at Pennington Seminary, Pennington, New Jersey.
1887	Withdraws from Pennington.
1888	Enrolls at Hudson River Institute (Claverack College), Claverack, New York; works for brother, Townley Crane, at his press bureau at Asbury Park in the summer.
1890	First sketch is published in Claverack College magazine *Vidette*; enters Lafayette College; fails classes and drops out at Christmas.
1891	Transfers to Syracuse University; plays on varsity baseball team; works as correspondent for the *New York Tribune*; first short story, "The King's Favor," appears in college magazine; writes early drafts of *Maggie*; quits school in June; his mother, Mary Helen Crane, dies in December.
1892	Publishes five "Sullivan County Sketches" in the *New York Tribune*; "Broken-Down Van" is published; Crane is

dismissed from the *Tribune*; moves to Manhattan.

1893   Privately prints *Maggie: A Girl of the Streets* under the pseudonym Johnston Smith; begins writing *The Red Badge of Courage*.

1894   Abridged version of *The Red Badge of Courage* is published in the *Philadelphia Press*; several stories are published in *The Arena* and *New York Press*.

1895   Writes articles for *Bachellor-Johnson Syndicate*; collection of poems *The Black Riders and Other Lines* is published; *The Red Badge of Courage* is published in full to enormous popularity, especially in England.

1896   Publishes *George's Mother* and *The Little Regiment*; travels to Florida to report on the Cuban insurrection.

1897   On a trip to Cuba, the ship sinks and Crane is adrift for fourteen days; "The Open Boat" is published; meets Cora Taylor; covers Greco-Turkish War from April to May reporting for *New York Journal* and *Westminster Gazette*; publishes *The Third Violet*.

1898   War correspondent during Spanish-American War for *New York World* and *New York Journal*; *The Open Boat and Other Tales of Adventure* are published; Stephen and Cora settle in Sussex, England; the stories "Death and the Child," "The Blue Hotel," and "The Bride Comes to Yellow Sky" are published.

1899   A book of poems, *War Is Kind*, is published; *The Monster and Other Stories*, and *Active Service* are published; Crane returns to England to reside at Brede Palace with Cora; begins writing *The O'Ruddy*, his last novel.

1900   *Whilomville Stories* and *Wounds in the Rain* are published. Stephen Crane dies of tuberculosis on June 5 at the age of 28 in a sanatorium in Badenweiler, Germany. He is buried in Hillside, New Jersey.

Contributors

HAROLD BLOOM is Sterling Professor of the Humanities at Yale University. He is the author of 30 books, including *Shelley's Mythmaking, The Visionary Company, Blake's Apocalypse, Yeats, A Map of Misreading, Kabbalah and Criticism, Agon: Toward a Theory of Revisionism, The American Religion, The Western Canon,* and *Omens of Millennium: The Gnosis of Angels, Dreams, and Resurrection. The Anxiety of Influence* sets forth Professor Bloom's provocative theory of the literary relationships between the great writers and their predecessors. His most recent books include *Shakespeare: The Invention of the Human,* a 1998 National Book Award finalist, *How to Read and Why, Genius: A Mosaic of One Hundred Exemplary Creative Minds, Hamlet: Poem Unlimited, Where Shall Wisdom Be Found?,* and *Jesus and Yahweh: The Names Divine.* In 1999, Professor Bloom received the prestigious American Academy of Arts and Letters Gold Medal for Criticism. He has also received the International Prize of Catalonia, the Alfonso Reyes Prize of Mexico, and the Hans Christian Andersen Bicentennial Prize of Denmark.

JOHN BERRYMAN was a major figure in American poetry and often considered one of the founders of the Confessional school of poetry. He authored many books, including *Dream Songs,* his most well-known.

ERIC SOLOMON is Professor of English at San Francisco State University. He is the author of *Stephen Crane: From Parody to Realism*.

DANIEL WEISS is the President of Lafayette College.

CHESTER L. WOLFORD is Professor of Business and English at the Pennsylvania State University, where he has taught for twenty years. He is the author of *The Anger of Stephen Crane*.

AMY KAPLAN is Professor of English at University of Pennsylvania. She is the author of *The Social Construction of American Realism* and coeditor of *Cultures of U.S. Imperialism* with Donald Pease. Her most recent book is *The Anarchy of Empire in the Making of U.S. Culture*.

CHRISTOPHER BENFEY is Mellon Professor of English at Mount Holyoke College. He is the author of *Degas in New Orleans*, *The Double Life of Stephen Crane*, and *Emily Dickinson and the Problem of Others*. His most recent book is *The Great Wave: Gilded Age Misfits, Japanese Eccentrics, and the Opening of Old Japan*.

PAUL SORRENTINO, Professor of English at Virginia Tech, is the editor of *Stephen Crane Studies*. He is also the coauthor of *The Crane Log: A Documentary Life of Stephen Crane, 1871–1900*, with Stanley Wertheim, and the editor of the book *Stephen Crane Remembered*.

GEORGE MONTEIRO, Professor of Portuguese Literature and American Literature at Brown University, is the author of *Stephen Crane's Blue Badge of Courage*.

ROBERT M. DOWLING received his Ph.D. in English and American studies from the Graduate Center of the City University of New York. He is currently a Lecturer in English at the U.S. Coast Guard Academy.

JUAN ALONZO is an Assistant Professor in the Department of English at Texas A&M University. He specializes in Mexican American literature and ethnic representation in American film.

KEVIN J. HAYES is the author of many books, including *Stephen Crane*, *Poe: The Printed Word*, and *The Critical Response to Herman Melville's Moby-Dick* (editor).

Bibliography

Alonzo, Juan. "From Derision to Desire: The 'Greaser' in Stephen Crane's Mexican Stories and D. W. Griffith's Early Westerns." *Western American Literature* 38, no. 4 (2004): 374–401.

Bassan, Maurice, Ed. *Stephen Crane: A Collection of Critical Essays*. Englewood Cliffs, NJ: Prentice-Hall, 1967.

Beer, Thomas. *Stephen Crane: A Study in American Letters*. Introduction by Joseph Conrad. New York: A. A. Knopf, 1923.

Benfey, Christopher. *The Double Life of Stephen Crane*. NY: Knopf, 1992.

Bergon, Frank. *Stephen Crane's Artistry*. New York: Columbia University Press, 1975.

Berryman, John. *Stephen Crane: A Critical Biography*. New York: Sloane, 1950.

Brown, Bill. *The Material Unconscious: American Amusement, Stephen Crane, and the Economies of Play*. Cambridge, MA: Harvard UP, 1996.

Cady, Edwin H. *Stephen Crane*. Boston: Twayne Publishers, 1980.

Colvert, James B. "Unreal War in *The Red Badge of Courage*." in "Stephen Crane in War and Peace," a special issue of *War, Literature, and the Arts: An International Journal of the Humanities* (1999): 35–47.

Crisman, William. " 'Distributing the News': War Journalism as Metaphor for Language in Stephen Crane's Fiction." *Studies in American Fiction* 30, no. 2 (2002): 207–227.

Davis, Linda H. *Badge of Courage: The Life of Stephen Crane*. NY: Houghton Mifflin, 1998.

DeBona, Guerric. "Masculinity on the Front: John Huston's *The Red Badge of Courage* (1951) Revisited." *Cinema Journal* 42, no. 2 (2003): 57–80.

Dowling, Robert M. "Stephen Crane and the Transformation of the Bowery." In *Twisted from the Ordinary: Essays on American Literary Naturalism*. Ed. Mary E. Papke. Tennessee Studies in Literature, Number 40. Knoxville: University of Tennessee Press, 2003. 45–62.

Fraser, John. "Crime and Forgiveness: *The Red Badge* in Time of War." *Criticism* 9 (Summer, 1967): 243–256.

Gandal, Keith. *The Virtues of the Vicious: Jacob Riis, Stephen Crane, and the Spectacle of the Slum*. Oxford, England: Oxford University Press, 1997.

Gibson, Donald B. *The Fiction of Stephen Crane*. Carbondale: Southern Illinois UP 1968.

———. *The Red Badge of Courage: Redefining the Hero*. Boston: Twayne Publishers, 1988.

Giles, Ronald. "Responding to Crane's 'The Monster'." *South Atlantic Review* 57, no. 2 (1992): 45–55.

Gullason, Thomas A., ed. *Stephen Crane's Literary Family: A Garland of Writings*. Syracuse, N.Y.: Syracuse University Press, 2002.

Habegger, Alfred. "Fighting Words: The Talk of Men at War in *The Red Badge of Courage*." In *Fictions of Masculinity: Crossing Culture, Crossing Sexualities*. Ed. Peter F. Murphy. New York: New York University Press, 1994. 185–203

Hayes, Kevin J. *Maggie: A Girl of the Streets (A Story of New York)*. Boston, MA: Bedford, 1999.

———. "How G. I. Joe Read Stephen Crane." *Stephen Crane Studies* 9, no. 1 (2000): 9–14.

———. *Stephen Crane*. Tavistock, Northumberland: Northcote House in association with the British Council, 2004.

Hoffman, Daniel. *The Poetry of Stephen Crane*. New York: Columbia UP, 1957.

Katz, Joseph, ed. *Stephen Crane in Transition: Centenary Essays*. DeKalb: Northern Illinois UP, 1972.

———. "The Maggie Nobody Knows." *Modern Fiction Studies* 12 (1966): 200–212.

Kelly, Richard J. and Alan K. Lathrop, eds. *Recovering Crane: Essays on a Poet*. Ann Arbor: University of Michigan Press, 1993.

Kuga, Shunji. "Feminine Domesticity and the Feral City: Stephen Crane's *George's Mother, Maggie*, and 'A Detail.'" *Stephen Crane Studies* 13, no. 2 (2004): 21–31.

Lolordo, Nick. "Possessed by the Gothic: Stephen Crane's 'The Monster'." *Arizona Quarterly* 57, no. 2 (2001): 33–56.

Marshall, Elaine. "Crane's 'The Monster' Seen in the Light of Robert Lewis's Lynching" *Nineteenth Century Literature* 51, no. 2 (Sept 1996): 205–224.

Mitchell, Lee Clark, ed. *New Essays on* The Red Badge of Courage. Cambridge, Cambridge University Press, 1986.

Mitchell, Verner D. "Reading 'Race' and 'Gender' in Crane's *The Red Badge of Courage*." *College Language Association Journal* 40, no. 1 (Sept 1996): 60–71.

Monteiro, George. *Stephen Crane's Blue Badge of Courage*. Baton Rouge: Louisiana State University Press, 2000.

Morgan, William M. "Between Conquest and Care: Masculinity and Community in Stephen Crane's *The Monster*." *Arizona Quarterly* 56, no.3 (2000): 63–92.

Nagel, James. *Stephen Crane and Literary Impressionism*. University Park, PA: Pennsylvania State University Press, 1980.

———. "The American Short-Story Cycle and Stephen Crane's *Tales of Whilomville*." *American Literary Realism* 32, no. 1 (Fall 1999): 35–43.

Pizer, Donald, ed. *Critical Essays on Stephen Crane's* The Red Badge of Courage. Boston: G.K. Hall, 1990.

Richardson, Mark. "Stephen Crane's *The Red Badge of Courage*." *American Writers Classics, I.* Ed. Jay Parini. New York: Thomson Gale, 2003. 237–255.

Robertson, Michael. *Stephen Crane, Journalism, and the Making of American Literature*. New York, NY: Columbia University Press, 1997.

Schaefer, Michael W. *A Reader's Guide to the Short Stories of Stephen Crane*. A Reference Publication in Literature. New York: G.K. Hall; Prentice Hall International, 1996.

———. "Stephen Crane in the Time of Shock and Awe: Teaching *The Red Badge of Courage* During the Iraq War." *Stephen Crane Studies* 13, no. 2 (2004): 2–9.

Solomon, Eric. *Stephen Crane: From Parody to Realism*. Cambridge: Harvard University Press, 1966.

Sorrentino, Paul. *Stephen Crane Remembered*. Tuscaloosa: University of Alabama Press, 2006.

———. "Stephen Crane's Struggle with Romance in *The Third Violet*." *American Literature* 70, no. 2 (June 1998): 265–291.

Stevenson, James A. "Beyond Stephen Crane: Full Metal Jacket." *Literature/ Film Quarterly* 16, no. 4 (1988): 238–243.

Szumski, Bonnie, ed. *Readings on Stephen Crane*. Greenhaven Press Literary Companion to American Authors. San Diego, CA: Greenhaven, 1998.

Wertheim, Stanley. *The Crane Log: A Documentary Life of Stephen Crane 1871–1900*. New York: G.K. Hall, 1994.

———. *A Stephen Crane Encyclopedia*. NY: Greenwood, 1997.

Wolford, Chester L. *The Anger of Stephen Crane: Fiction and the Epic Tradition*. Lincoln: University of Nebraska Press, 1983.

———. *Stephen Crane: A Study of the Short Fiction*. Boston: Twayne Publishers, 1989.

Acknowledgments

"Crane's Art" by John Berryman. From *Stephen Crane*, pp. 263–293. © 1950 by William Sloane Associates. Reprinted by permission.

"Love and Death in the Slums" reprinted by permission of the publisher from *Stephen Crane: From Parody to Realism*, by Eric Soloman, pp. 19–44, Cambridge, Mass.: Harvard University Press, Copyright © 1966 by the President and Fellows of Harvard College.

" 'The Blue Hotel': A Psychoanalytic Study" by Daniel Weiss. From *Stephen Crane: A Collection of Critical Essays*, edited by Maurice Bassan, pp. 154–164. © 1967 by Prentice-Hall, Inc. Reprinted by permission.

"This Booming Chaos: Crane's Search for Transcendence" by Chester L. Wolford. Reprinted from *The Anger of Stephen Crane: Fiction and the Epic Tradition* by permission of the University of Nebraska Press. Copyright © 1983 by the University of Nebraska Press.

"The Spectacle of War in Crane's Revision of History" by Amy Kaplan. From *New Essays on* The Red Badge of Courage, edited by Lee Clark Mitchell, pp. 77–108. © 1986 by Cambridge University Press. Reprinted by permission of Cambridge University Press.

"Introduction" by Christopher Benfey. From *The Double Life of Stephen Crane*, pp. 3–12. Copyright © 1992 by Christopher Benfey. Reprinted with permission by Melanie Jackson Agency, LLC.

Paul Sorrentino, "Stephen Crane's Struggle with Romance in *The Third Violet*," in *American Literature*, Vol. 70, No. 2 (June, 1998), pp. 265–291. Copyright © 1998 by Duke University Press. All rights reserved. Used by permission of the publisher.

"The Drunkard's Progress" by George Monteiro. From *Stephen Crane's Blue Badge of Courage*, pp. 48–59. © 2000 by Louisiana State University Press. Reprinted by permission.

"Stephen Crane and the Transformation of the Bowery" by Robert M. Dowling. From *Twisted from the Ordinary: Essays on American Literary Naturalism*, edited by Mary E. Papke, pp. 45–62. © 2003 The University of Tennessee Press. Reprinted by permission.

"From Derision to Desire: The "Greaser" in Stephen Crane's Mexican Stories and D. W. Griffith's Early Westerns" by Juan Alonzo. From *Western American Literature* (Winter 2004), pp. 374–401. © 2004 by the Western Literature Association. Reprinted by permission.

"Image and Emblem in *The Red Badge of Courage*" by Kevin J. Hayes. From *Stephen Crane*, pp. 36–44. © 2004 by Kevin J. Hayes. Reprinted by permission of Northcote House.

Every effort has been made to contact the owners of copyrighted material and secure copyright permission. Articles appearing in this volume generally appear much as they did in their original publication with few or no editorial changes. In some cases foreign language text has been removed from the original essay. Those interested in locating the original source will find bibliographic information in the bibliography and acknowledgments sections of this volume.

Index

Characters in literary works are indexed by first name (if any), followed by the name of the work in parentheses

Adventures of Huckleberry Finn
  (Twain), 125
Algren, Nelson, 33
Allport, Gordon
  The Nature of Prejudice, 169
Alonzo, Juan, 204
  on Crane's Mexican stories
    compared to Griffith's stories,
    167–91
Alter, Robert, 120
Ambassadors, The (James), 24, 108
American literature
  humorists, 23
  idealism, 7, 26
  impressionism, 9–12, 25–26, 67,
    69–70
  naturalists, 79
  poets, 11–15, 21–23
  writers, 1–2, 5, 7–8, 21, 23–25,
    28, 30–32, 47, 57–58, 67, 69,
    77, 100, 103, 108, 111, 151–53,
    160
Anderson, Sherwood, 8
Andrews, Nigel, 195
Arizona Wooing, An (film), 183
Arts of Intoxication (Crane, J.), 135
Austen, Jane, 22

"Backward Glance o'er Travel'd
  Roads, A" (Whitman), 57
Baker, Benjamin A., 152
  "A Glance At New York In
    1848," 153–54
Barnum, P.T., 158
Battles and Leaders of the Civil War,
  77, 83
Bear, The (Faulkner), 31
Beaver, Harold, 2
Beer, Thomas
  on Crane, 17, 106–7
Beggar's Opera, The (Gay), 41
Bellamy, Edward
  Looking Backward, 85
Benfey, Christopher, 204
  on Crane's lifetime, 103–11
Benjamin, Walter, 87–88
Bernard Lile (Clemens)
  Mexican representation in, 170–
    71, 173, 176
Berryman, John, 203
  on Crane's work, 7–28, 56, 105,
    111
Birth of a Nation, The (film)
  racism in, 180, 185, 187
Blackmur, R.P., 12

Black Riders and Other Lines, 29
  anarchy of, 68
  criticism, 14, 16
  fear in, 107–8
  publication, 113
  writing of, 10
Blood Meridian (McCarthy), 2
Bloom, Harold, 203
  introduction, 1–6
  on *The Red Badge of Courage*, 1–6
"Blue Badge of Cowardice, The"
  (short story), 63
"Blue Hotel, The" (short story), 8
  card game in, 52–53, 55
  Crane's travels to the west in,
   5–6
  fantasy in, 28
  irony of, 6, 19–20
  Johnnie Scully in, 51, 53, 55
  language in, 23
  linked to *The Red Badge of
   Courage*, 1, 5–6
  narrative, 6, 105
  Pat Scully in, 6, 51, 54–55
  psychoanalytic interpretation of,
   47–56
  structure of, 51
  study of fear, 47
  Swede in, 18–20, 26, 47, 51–55,
   70, 105
  Swede's corpse in, 6
  terror and violence in, 47, 50–51
Borges, Jorge Luis, 123
"Bowery B'hoys and Matinee
  Ladies" (Butsch), 150
Boyesen, H.H., 32
"Bride Comes to Yellow Sky, The"
  (short story)
  Crane's travels to the west in, 5
  happiness in, 8
  Jack Potter in, 5–6
  language in, 23

  linked to *The Red Badge of
   Courage*, 1, 5–6
  Scratchy Wilson in, 5–6
  society in, 27
Broncho Billy and the Greaser (film),
  183
Brontë, Emily
  Wuthering Heights, 9
Brown, Allston T., 153
Bunner, H.C., 32
Buntline, Ned
  The G'hals of New York, 155
Butsch, Richard
  "Bowery B'hoys and Matinee
   Ladies," 150

Cady, Edwin H.
  on Crane, 111–12, 195
Cather, Willa, 106
  Crane's influence on, 8
Chanfrau, Frank, 152–54
Chekhov, Anton
  work of, 24, 27
"Clan of No Name, The" (short
  story), 8
  language in, 23
Clemens, Jeremiah
  Bernard Lile, 170–71, 173, 176
Cocteau, Jean, 38
"Concept of Cultural Hegemony,
  The" (Lears), 150
Conrad, Joseph
  Crane's influence on, 2, 4–5, 25,
   60, 104
Crane, Hart
  Voyages, 17
Crane, Jonathan Townley (father)
  Arts of Intoxication, 135
  death, 106
  evangelical Methodist, 1, 106,
   112–13, 162
Crane, Mary Helen (mother) 105–6

Crane, Stephen
  animism, 11
  birth, 103, 105–6, 149
  criticism, 19
  death, 1–2, 4–5, 7, 9, 17, 61, 104,
    109, 130
  education, 107
  illnesses, 1, 5, 23, 67, 104, 108
  influences of, 1–2, 5, 8, 60
  influences on, 1, 4, 8, 34
  and journalism, 1–2, 103–5
  letters, 16, 29, 107–8, 115,
    128–30
  and religion, 1, 15, 57–73, 105,
    107–8
  and war, 1–2, 4–5, 8, 27, 47, 49,
    67, 70, 70, 72, 75–101, 103
Crane, Townley (brother), 126
Crawford, F. Marion
  Saracinesca, 79
Crouse, Nellie
  Crane's relationship with,
    128–30
Cuban War, 47
Cummins, Maria, 32

Dante, 71
"Dark Brown Dog, A" (short story)
  humor in, 8
Daughter of the Tenements, A
  (Townsend), 33, 37
Davis, Richard Harding, 32
  The Princess Aline, 79
"Death and the Child" (short
  story), 8
  art of denial in, 66, 68
  consciousness in, 62
  correspondent in, 98–99
  overinsistence in, 9
  Peza in, 64–66
  publication, 58
Defoe, Daniel, 23

Democratic Vistas (Whitman), 151
Development of the American Short
  Story (Pattee), 23
Dickens, Charles
  work of, 21, 23
Dickinson, Emily
  poetry, 11–12, 15, 104
Dime novels
  Crane's objection to, 170–73,
    178–79
Dodd, Seymour
  The Song of the Rappahannock, 81
Dooley, Patrick, 120
Dostoevsky, Fyodor, 28
Douglas, Ann, 159
Dowling, Robert M., 204
  on Crane's life in the Bowery,
    149–65
Dreams (Schreiner), 15
Dreiser, Theodore, 33, 106
  Crane's influence on, 8, 25, 38
  Sister Carrie, 37
Dryden, John, 23
  Essay of Dramatic Poesy, 22

Edison, Thomas, 194
Eliot, George, 21
Eliot, T.S., 16
Emerson, Ralph Waldo, 27
  influence on Crane, 8, 10
"End of the Battle, The" (short
  story), 8
"Episode of War, An" (short story),
  8
Essay of Dramatic Poesy (Dryden), 22
Evil That Men Do, The (Fawcett), 33
"Experiment in Luxury, An" (short
  story), 8
  criticism of society in, 34, 156
"Experiment in Misery, An" (short
  story), 8
  criticism of society in, 34, 65

Farrell, James, 33
Faulkner, William, 2
  The Bear, 31
Fawcett, Edgar
  The Evil That Men Do, 33
Fight for Freedom, The (film), 180
Fitzgerald, F. Scott
  Crane's influence on, 8
"Five White Mice, The" (short
  story)
  Benson in, 176–77
  fraternal competition, 49
  Frisco Kid in, 49, 176–79
  language in, 22
  matched game imagery in, 52
  Mexican in, 49–50, 52, 176–79
  Mexican representation in,
    176–79
  New York Kid in, 47, 50, 52, 56,
    176–79
Ford, Ford Madox, 104, 111
Fowles, John
  The French Lieutenant's Woman, 120
"Fragment of Velestino, A" (short
  story), 63–64
Frederic, Harold, 23, 195
French Lieutenant's Woman, The
  (Fowles), 120
Freud, Sigmund
  "rescue of fantasies" theory, 2
Frost, Robert
  poetry, 11, 106

Gandal, Keith, 157
Garland, Hamlin, 10
  friendship with Crane, 29, 164
Garnett, Edward
  on Crane, 9–10, 18, 25, 137
Gay, John
  The Beggar's Opera, 41
Geismar, Maxwell
  on *George's Mother*, 137

George's Mother, 9
  Bleeker in, 142–45
  Blue Billie in, 145
  Charley Jones in, 139–40,
    142–43
  dreams in, 27, 31, 157
  Fidsey Corcoran in, 144–45
  George Kelcey's rise and fall
    as a drinker in, 136, 138–40,
    142–46, 157, 163
  irony in, 138, 142
  moral balance in, 137, 162
  mother's death in, 138, 145
  Mrs. Kelcey's hymn, 141–42
  Mrs. Kelcey and the WCTU,
    136, 140, 142, 145–46, 163
  reviews of, 137–38, 142
Gerard, Louise, 126
G'hals of New York, The (Buntline),
  155
"Ghost, The" (play), 126
Gilder, Richard Watson, 161
Gilman, Charlotte Perkins
  In This Our World, 126
"Glance At New York In 1848, A"
  (Baker), 153–54
Goethe, Johann Wolfgang
  influence on Crane, 8, 26
Grant, Ulysses S., 80
Graves, Robert
  on poetry, 14, 16
Greaser's Gauntlet, The (film)
  Mexican representation in, 167,
    180–86, 188–89
"Grey Sleeve, A" (short story), 129
Griffith, D.W.
  An Arizona Wooing, 183
  The Birth of a Nation, 180, 185, 187
  Broncho Billy and the Greaser, 183
  The Fight for Freedom, 180
  The Greaser's Gauntlet, 167,
    180–86, 188–89

Mexican characterization in
   films, 167–91
The Red Girl, 180, 185–86, 188
The Tavern-Keeper's Daughter,
   180–83
*The Thread of Destiny and
   Ramona*, 180, 185–86
The Vaquero's Vow, 180

Hapke, Laura, 162
Hardy, Thomas
   Tess, 24
   work of, 21
Hawthorne, Nathaniel
   work of, 23, 28, 104
Hayes, Kevin J., 204
   on *The Red Badge of Courage*,
      193–200
Hemingway, Ernest, 177
   Crane's influence on, 8, 10
   "The Killers," 55
   and war writing, 2, 5, 100
Henley, W.E., 15
Henry Fleming (*The Red Badge of
   Courage*), 18
   actions, 50–51, 53, 91–93
   analytic mind of, 47, 49, 70–71
   career, 48, 92–94
   counterphobic techniques, 48,
      54, 88, 90, 198
   doom, 56
   flight, 2–3, 48–50, 64–65, 92, 95,
      197–99
   heroism, 25, 66–67, 69, 86–88,
      94–95, 97, 105, 195–99
   impersonal, 26
   irony of, 19
   memories, 94, 99, 196, 199
   pride, 27
   recreation of self, 193–200
   romantic dreams of, 31, 82–84
Higham, John, 79

Hobson, J.A., 96
Holmes, Oliver Wendell, 95
   Memorial Day Address, 78
Homer, 2, 58, 70
   The Odyssey, 59
Hope, Anthony
   Prisoner of Zenda, 79
"Horses—One Dash" (short story)
   language in, 22
Howells, William Dean
   Crane's interview with, 112–15,
      126, 130
   criticism, 15, 32, 80, 108, 114,
      119–21, 145, 153–54
How the Other Half Lives (Riis), 32, 34
Hubbard, Elbert, 115–16
Humphreys, Mose, 152

"Illusion in Red and White, An"
   (short story), 8
Il Trovatore (Verdi), 126–27
"In the Tenderloin" (short story)
   girl in, 30–31
   social implications in, 30–31
   Swift Doyer in, 29–31
In This Our World (Gilman), 126

James, Henry, 2, 104
   The Ambassadors, 24, 108
   friendship with Crane, 4
   work of, 23, 28, 151, 160, 163
James, William, 107
Johnson, Samuel, 7
   work of, 22–23
Joyce, James, 24
   Ulysses, 120
"Joyside of Seaside Life" (short
   story)
   voyeurism in, 194
"Judgment of the Sage, The" (short
   story)
   message of fiction in, 35–36

Jungle, The (Sinclair), 38
Jungle Book, The (Kipling), 2

Kaplan, Amy, 120, 204
  on Crane and war, 75–101
Kazin, Alfred, 164
Keats, John
  work of, 21–22
Kermode, Frank, 32
"Kicking Twelfth, The" (short
  story)
    language in, 23
"Killers, The" (Hemingway)
  Ole Anderson in, 55
"Killing His Bear" (short story),
  194
    transcendence in, 57, 70
Kimball, Moses, 158
"King's Favor, The" (short story)
  Gerard's career in, 126
  old chieftain in, 69
Kipling, Rudyard
  The Jungle Book, 2
  The Light that Failed, 79
  work of, 23–24, 79, 113

L'Assommoir (Zola), 34
La Traviata (Verdi)
  allusions to in *The Third Violet*,
    126–30
Lawrence, T.E.
  Crane's influence on, 8
Lears, Jackson, 80, 163
  "The Concept of Cultural
    Hegemony," 150
Leaves of Grass (Whitman), 155
Leslie, Amy, 130
Levenson, J.C., 61
Lewis, Sinclair
  Crane's influence on, 8
Light that Failed, The (Kipling), 79
Limón, José, 171

Lincoln, Abraham, 80
"Little Regiment, The" (short
  story), 9
London, Jack, 23, 79
Looking Backward (Bellamy), 85

Maggie (*Maggie: A Girl of the
  Streets*), 67, 152
  death, 4, 20, 32, 43–44, 161
  dreams, 69, 105, 157
  fall of, 37, 39, 41–43, 157,
    161–62
  family and lover of, 4, 19, 27, 32,
    36–44, 157–61
  fear, 40
  infatuation with theater, 154,
    158–60, 163
  irony and realism in, 4
  sweatshop job, 37–38
Maggie: A Girl of the Streets
  the Bowery in, 4, 31, 33, 41,
    150–52, 154–62, 164
  ironic sympathy in, 29–46, 62,
    159
  jealousy theme in, 19
  Jimmie in, 32, 36–37, 39–44,
    152, 154, 156, 160–62, 164
  language in, 22, 24, 34, 40, 161
  narrative, 4, 44, 105, 152, 159
  Nellie in, 42, 44
  Pete in, 19–20, 26–27, 32, 36–
    43, 152, 157, 159–60
  poverty in, 4, 32–34, 36, 38–39,
    41
  publication, 43, 113, 149–50
  rejection of Christianity in,
    68–69
  satire, 36, 44
  society in, 8, 27, 34, 36–38, 41,
    44, 58, 65, 150–51, 162
  structure of, 39
  suffering in, 20, 32, 137

Tommie in, 38, 40
  water imagery in,
  writing of, 104
Mailer, Norman
  and war writing, 2, 100
Major, Charles
  When Knighthood Was in Flower, 79
"Man Adrift on a Slim Spar, A"
  (poem), 1, 8
  dream in, 17
Maupassant, Guy de
  work of, 24, 27
McCarthy, Cormac
  Blood Meridian, 2
McClure, S.S., 113, 115
Melville, Herman, 2, 5
  Redburn, 155
  work of, 23, 54
Memorial Day Address (Holmes), 78
Mencken, Henry Louis
  work of, 23–24
Mexican characterization
  in literature and film, 167–91
Mitchell, William, 153
Monster and Other Stories
  language in, 23
  rejection of culture in, 68
  society in, 8, 27
Monteiro, George, 204
  on *George's Mother*, 135–47
Murphy, Brenda
  on *George's Mother*, 138
Muybridge, Eadweard, 195
"Mystery of Heroism, A" (short
  story), 8
  Collins in, 20

Naturalism, 4, 25
Nature of Prejudice, The (Allport),
  169
Norris, Frank, 25
  work of, 79–80

"Notes toward a Supreme Fiction"
  (Stevens), 57

Odyssey, The (Homer), 59
"Old Bowery, The" (Whitman), 159
"Once I Saw Mountains Angry"
  (poem), 8
"One Dash-Horses" (short story)
  José in, 172–76
  Mexican representation in,
  172–76
  narrative, 176
  Richardson in, 172–76
"Open Boat, The" (short story), 8
  art of denial in, 66, 68
  Billy Higgins in, 20, 26
  Christian epic in, 60–62
  correspondent in, 99
  Crane's own experiences in, 5,
  31
  fate in, 27
  irony in, 62, 64
  language in, 22–23, 59
  linked to *The Red Badge of
    Courage*, 1, 5–6
  man against nature in, 31
  narrative, 31, 67
  restraint off, 9
  survivors in, 5–6, 20–21, 28,
  58–60
O'Ruddy, The
  writing, 130
Orvell, Miles, 157

"Pace of Youth, The" (short story)
  happiness in, 8
Paredes, Raymund
  on Mexican characterization,
  170–72, 174, 180
Pattee, Fred Lewis
  *Development of the American Short
    Story*, 23

Pearce, Roy Harvey, 69
Pease, Donald, 87
Pettit, Arthur
  on Mexican representation in
    literature and film, 167, 170–
    71, 180
Poe, Edgar Allan
  work of, 16, 23–24, 27–28
Pollard, Josephine
  "Stolen; or, the Mother's
    Lament," 136
Pound, Ezra
  poetry of, 11, 15–16
"Price of the Harness, The" (short
  story), 8
  Jim Conklin in, 49
  matched game imagery in, 52
  Nolan in, 47, 49–50, 52
Prince Otto (Stevenson), 79
Princess Aline, The (Davis), 79
Prisoner of Zenda (Hope), 79
Pulitzer, Joseph, 75, 97

Realism, 4
  and Crane, 25, 31, 38, 111–13,
    116, 120, 130, 157
  transcendental, 38, 58, 61, 65
Red Badge of Courage, The, 8, 16, 28
  the Civil War in, 1–2, 4–5, 9, 31,
    47–49, 51, 65–66, 75–88, 90,
    92–100, 103–5, 115, 193–94,
    196–99
  color sergeant's death in, 3–4,
    21, 49, 92, 199
  dance of death in, 21, 27, 54, 61, 70
  domestic images, 83
  emotion in, 47, 51
  expressionism in, 2
  the flag in, 3–4, 51, 91–94, 196,
    199
  irony in, 19, 49, 60, 62–63, 196
  Jim Conklin in, 88, 93, 197

language in, 22, 24–25, 34, 54,
    84, 87, 94, 193
  linked to Crane's short stories,
    1–6
  matched game imagery in, 52
  memory in, 94
  narrative, 82–84, 86–87, 89,
    91–92, 94, 96, 100, 105, 107,
    195, 198
  publication, 75, 78, 104, 113–15,
    128, 130, 193
  reinterpreting the past in, 81–82
  rejection of literature and
    history in, 68–69
  reviews of, 87, 95, 99, 104, 195
  source for, 77
  Wilson in, 48
  writing of, 58, 104, 108, 113,
    193
Redburn (Melville), 155
Red Girl, The (film)
  Mexican representation in, 180,
    185–86, 188
Reed, Kenneth, 60
"Reluctant Voyagers, The" (short
  story)
  humor in, 8
  protagonists in, 58
Remington, Fredric, 97, 107–8
Riis, Jacob
  How the Other Half Lives, 32, 34
Robertson, Jamie, 175
Robinson, Cecil
  on Mexican representation,
    173–74
Robinson, Edwin Arlington, 11
Roe, E.P., 32
Romanticism, 31
Roosevelt, Theodore, 107–8
  on the Civil War, 78, 80–81, 95
Runyon, Damon, 33
Ryder, Albert Pinkham, 106–7

Sandburg, Carl
  Crane's influence on, 8, 15
Saracinesca (Crawford), 79
Schreiner, Olive
  Dreams, 15
  influence on Crane, 8, 15
Scott, Walter
  work of, 79, 91
Sevastopol (Tolstoy), 26, 28
Shakespeare, William, 2
  work of, 21, 23, 28, 153
"Shame" (short story), 8
Sinclair, Upton
  The Jungle, 38
Sister Carrie (Dreiser), 37
Solomon, Eric, 81, 116, 203
  on *George's Mother*, 137–38
  on *Maggie: A Girl of the Streets*,
    29–46
Song of the Rappahannock, The
  (Dodd), 81
Sorrentino, Paul, 106, 204
  on *The Third Violet*, 111–33
Southworth, E.D.E.N., 32
Spanish-American War
  correspondent, 2, 49, 66, 76,
    80–81, 96–99, 103–4
Spofford, William, 63
Stein, Gertrude, 106–7
Stevens, Wallace
  "Notes toward a Supreme
    Fiction," 57
  work of, 69, 71, 104
Stevenson, Robert Louis, 107
  Prince Otto, 79
"Stolen; or, the Mother's Lament"
  (Pollard)
  mother's defeat in, 136, 138–39
Strong, Josiah, 85
"Sullivan County Sketches"
  five stories, 194
  language in, 22

Swift, Jonathan
  work of, 21, 31

Tavern-Keeper's Daughter, The
  (film)
  Mexican representation in,
    180–83
Taylor, Bayard, 32
Taylor, Cora (common-law wife)
  affair with Crane, 2, 4, 103, 108
  madam, 2, 103
Tess (Hardy), 24
Thackeray, William Makepeace
  work of, 21
Thiess, Albert, 126
Third Violet, The
  allusions to Verdi's operas in,
    126–30
  artistic battles in, 114–15, 121,
    123–24, 128
  Billie Hawker in, 114–19,
    121–30
  Florinda O'Connor in, 114, 119,
    125, 127
  George Hollanden in, 114–15,
    121–22, 124–25, 129
  Grace Fanhall in, 114, 116–19,
    121–25, 127–29
  "Hearts at War" in, 116–17, 129
  irony, 119
  Jem Oglethorpe in, 114, 122
  language, 118, 124–25, 128
  Lucian Pontiac in, 124
  narrative, 121–22, 124
  Pennoyer in, 123
  Purple Sanderson in, 115
  realism, 112–13, 116, 120, 130
  reviews of, 111
  romance of, 111–33
  word play in, 121, 123–26
  writing of, 115, 120, 130
Thomson, J.A.K., 18

Thread of Destiny and Ramona, The
  (film)
  Mexican representation in, 180,
    185–86
"Three Miraculous Soldiers" (short
  story), 9
"Three White Mice, The" (short
  story)
  Mexican representation in, 172
Tolstoy, Leo
  influence on Crane, 2, 8, 26
  Sevastopol, 26, 28
Townsend, Edward
  A Daughter of the Tenements, 33,
    37
Turner, Frederick Jackson, 58
Twain, Mark
  Adventures of Huckleberry Finn, 125
  influence on Crane, 8, 23

Ulysses (Joyce), 120
"Upturned Face, The" (short
  story), 8

Valéry, Paul, 16
Vanderbilt, Kermit, 198
Vaquero's Vow, The (film), 180
Verdi
  Il Trovatore, 126–27
  La Traviata, 126–30
"Veteran, The" (short story), 8
  irony in, 62
Virgil, 2
Virginian, The (Wister), 107
"Virtue in War" (short story), 8
Voyages (Crane, H.), 17

War Is Kind, 1
  cruelty and pity in, 14–15, 17
  poetry in, 8, 12–14
"War Memories" (short story), 9
  fear and ineffectiveness in, 68, 99

narrative, 99
  tone of, 66–68
Warner, Susan, 32
Webster, John
  The White Devil, 17
Weiss, Daniel, 198, 203
  on "The Blue Hotel," 47–56
Wells, H.G.
  on Crane, 9, 26, 104
Wertheim, Stanley, 106
When Knighthood Was in Flower
  (Major), 79
Whilomville Stories, 71
White Devil, The (Webster), 17
Whitman, Walt, 69
  "A Backward Glance o'er
    Travel'd Roads," 57
  Democratic Vistas, 151
  influence on Crane, 8, 11–12, 15
  Leaves of Grass, 155
  "The Old Bowery," 159
Willard, Frances E.
  WCTU documents, 136–37,
    139–41, 145
Willis, N.P., 154
Winston, Brian, 193
Wister, Owen, 108
  The Virginian, 107
Wolford, Chester, L., 204
  on Crane and religion, 57–73
Woman's Christian Temperance
  Union
  documents, 135–37, 139–40,
    143–45
Wordsworth, William, 18
Wuthering Heights (Brontë, E.)
Wyndham, George, 26

Zola, Émile
  influence on Crane, 4
  L'Assommoir, 34